Diese Publikation wurde als 152. Katalog von der Alfried Krupp von Bohlen und Halbach-Stiftung im Rahmen des Förderpreises „Kataloge für junge Künstler“ gefördert.

This publication was supported as Catalogue No. 152 by the Alfried Krupp von Bohlen und Halbach-Stiftung under its support prize “Catalogues for Young Artists.”

The miniaturist's hands were cramped. "I need a vacation from my vacation," he mumbled to no one. He didn't have a bonebook yet, so he ripped a page from his most beloved *gâvur*[1] masters: then off he went to the far corners of the map, depending on what you consider to be the centre.

He set up his gay little pink easel near the border. Queer green lights danced aggressively in the sky. They reminded him of the towering monsters he created and abandoned during the last plague, rusting somewhere in storage. Rust never sleeps and so neither would he. Paralyzed with terror (dramatic), he cleaned his tiny brushes until dawn broke. In this biz an air of sangfroid was paramount.

Clouds shapeshifted to form sigils up above. An "N" materialised, followed by an "O". Eventually a letter with a tail, found only in his mother tongue; the sweetest relief. He painted, if you could call it that. Everything is incorporated and nothing is discarded. Ever. Like an honest meal. With insatiable hunger, paisley *buta*[2] sprouted out of literally everywhere in the form of sweat, blood, or tears. Good thing he was fond of paisley. For what felt like centuries it went on.

And then one day, shameless and spent but with a pocketful of coins, he returned home. Sweetmeats coiled with *tahin* and *pekmez*[3] spiraled joy across his table. Tendonitis soothed and all dead canaries revived. He could finally tear at the bread again.

He no longer worshipped God; he had found somebody new.

1 Christian, Ottoman slur/pejorative.
2 An almond-shaped ornament derivative of the cypress tree: بته.
3 Tahini & molasses.

Table of contents

Tidbits for Diminutive Materialism

The Snack, the Artist, and the Outlier (As They're Eating Through Elif Saydam's Miniatures and The World)

Maxi Wallenhorst

1. The Snack (She/Her)

First, you find the snack hanging out in the realm of the Späti. *Späti* is the diminutive of Spätkauf, a Berlin corner store; although, taken on the level of the snack, it seems to hint at a world in which everything is a little bit diminutive and yet, not at all harmless. Its smallness is not a register of diminishment, but of the too-much that's too in-your-face, or in-your-mouth. Right at the heart of commodification propped up by urges—"whether they arise, for example, from the stomach or in the imagination"[1]—that's where the snack lives.

You begin to perceive the snack by perceiving her environment. In Elif Saydam's *Zu spät (I)*, one of several Späti-themed paintings, the environment of the snack looks like this: a labyrinth is layered on top of a shop sign printed onto a canvas in grayscale. Like in real life, the Späti marks a zone of light inconsistency where different backgrounds bleed into one another. The labyrinth is literally made of gold, leaf gold, its outer rings of copper and silver. The symbolism gently caricatures its own obviousness, while still being a bit symbolic. The pathways of the labyrinth are adorned with lemons—it's unclear whether you could eat them—and cartoonish little hearts on the verge of turning into emojis in messages. Some of the hearts are broken! The snack, sandwiched in-between elaborate intimate style and low-fi commodity aesthetics, cannot but take its surroundings personally.

The snack is defined, according to the Cambridge Dictionary, as a "small amount of food that is eaten between meals, or a very small meal." Here, you could imagine the snack as a person, too, or as an allegorization of a certain set of techniques of moving through the world. At the same time, sometimes, a snack is just a snack, or a cigar. The snack is a person in the sense of being interpellated by, e.g. a gay person who would say: "They're such a snack!" when they find someone so hot they have to belittle them a bit, just into consumability. From appetite to desire, the problem of the snack is figuring out what to embody and what to objectify in a world that burns you out like a simple carb.

Operating from the smallness that the Späti offers, the snack moves through the world by attempting to orient and pace everyday life—which is intense. The snack goes against and within the rhythm of this everyday life and the tact that contemporary excesses of a workday impose on it. The snack hopes to find both caloric energy and hot pockets of her own time *on* her own time. She does her thing, not unrelated to the intuition of hunger but with counterintuitive temporality: the sugar high of a Snickers bar, or even a Snickers ice cream bar, might adorn one's break from work, or heartbreak, so that it expands, or conflates, as the mood demands. Snacking can include not-eating, too: in anticipation of even a heterosexual date, opening up an entire day to the possibility of being touched on the bench in front of a Späti, a city, a world, thereby avoiding full meals.

One of the material conditions that two of the most popular modern allegories, the flaneur and worker, share is the snack, however figuratively. The snack herself, however, is a bad flaneur. Partly because she's not granted the same invisibility, and partly because to her, the uncertainty of her neighbourhood is not nonthreatening. The appetite for something highly unspecific is also a tool for navigating a precarious environment, and includes dreaming of a different one, while not thinking about it at all. Lauren Berlant describes the snack "as a technique for pulling the world in

1 Karl Marx, *Capital, Vol.I: Critique of Political Economy,* translated by Ben Fowkes, Penguin Books, 1976, p. 125.

and pushing it away according to [one's] own terms and sense of pacing."[2] The snack is good at being too literal, in this sense. She eats up the street. Which Späti is open at different points in your workday and/or nightlife? Which one carries your favourite brand of Yum Yum, or is gentrified enough to have oat milk? Intimate study of a place's snacks pulls and stretches one's attempts to internalize calculated routes, turns it flexible in some places, inert in others.

When some speak of this as *Späti culture,* they easily mistake it for a treat of urban modernity that holds up the persistence of individual agency in the face of abjection—the snack, despite everything, makes it work, fails better. (Berlin is such an intense projection surface for this fantasy that years ago, the city even integrated this into its own marketing phrases: *arm aber sexy*, poor but hot.) On the other hand, the cartographic skill of the snack is also one of the conditions under which capitalist appropriation has made her a compass of gentrification. A snack that is rich in *one*, often white, way, prefigured by the aesthetics of Instagram food photography, becomes a sign of increasing development value. Rich, here, just means rich. Both accounts mistake the snack for a cute endpoint of infrastructure. But the snack is messier than that. The snack *is* cute. As Sianne Ngai has famously put it, however, the evaluation of the cute is a mixed vibe. At its heart, she rediscovers "ugly or aggressive feelings, as well as the expected tender or maternal ones."[3] You could eat it or suck it up, before the snack does that to you. Along with the food items that are rolling through Ngai's essay, Gertrude Stein's roastbeef and Francis Ponge's orange, the snack further spells out the diminutive as an intimate space in the middle of everyday life. The snack doesn't imagine that variety of intimacy, which others would perhaps call "embodiment" or "desire," as something delineated on micro- and macro-levels by anemic ideas of pronouns, ready-made trauma, and abstract borders. The snack is a bit of a joke, in that sense. She renders the problem of having a body as something that intrinsically has to do with obscure details, with a stale iced tea called Durstlöscher that is popular with skateboarders. "[A]mong other things," Berlant writes, "the practice of eating provides a way to negotiate one's incoherence while not organizing a personality to compensate for it."[4] The snack constantly devours traces of life, sandwiched between affect and its commodification. As one allegory from biology has it, the intestines don't really count as *inside*. The snack insists that there's more to gut feeling than bourgeois inwardness. Or, more precisely, that there's less.

2. The Artist (He/Him)

Then, you meet the artist in the realm of Kotti. You could think of Kotti as a constellation of snacks abstracted into development value. *Kotti* is the diminutive of Kottbusser Tor, a Kreuzberg spot that supposedly encapsulates a distinct Berlin feeling—the artist *does* love working there—although to call it a "Berlin feeling" romanticizes the conflict that is also always going on in Kotti: always a cop car exerting pressure from one side, always gentrification exerting pressure from the other, levitating invisibly above the neon signs. In the middle of this is the space the artist inhabits: partly instrumentalized, partly withdrawn into an observer position that's just barely observant: that's the space the artist inhabits.

2 Lauren Berlant, *Cruel Optimism*, Duke University Press, 2011, p. 135.
3 Sianne Ngai "The Cuteness of the Avantgarde," *Critical Inquiry*, Vol. 31, No. 4 (Summer 2005), p. 816.
4 Berlant, *Cruel Optimism*, p. 135.

You begin to perceive the artist by perceiving his environment. In Saydam's miniature *Artists (Kotti)*, it's made of cute little details but these cute little details are not merely a place to get lost and nostalgic in—they also nudge their surroundings towards a scale the artist thinks of as the world. This world is a place in which the rent is too high. The background is stressed. "Die Miete ist zu hoch!!!" it says, on a medievally long banner unrolled from a window. The exclamation marks, intimately swung, suggest a personal space as if exploding onto the street. The window—trompe-l'oeil, elaborately fake, and as such supposed to offer depth to an interior—here faces the street. Anchoring it, at the center of the constellation, in a zone that is seemingly street-level, shimmers something uncannily homely: an ornament, plucked and personalized from a sixteenth-century Ottoman miniature. Everything looks like a street scene if you think of the "street" as something in which interior and exterior are constantly rearranged by the abstractions of life under racial capitalism. As such, the street is not a merely interesting panorama but a scene that vibrates with the class politics of taste and the histories of migration that any notion of the street, the neighbourhood, the city as one with itself, does.

The ornament is adorned with lemons, flowers and grapes, some of which look dangerously pale. In the realm of Kotti, the artist often encounters strange fruit, some seemingly made of plastic, some gone: where the snackable tilts into the decorative, only barely aestheticized, you find the world of the artist. The artist is good at figuring out what to eat and what would just look good, and especially good at knowing what would look even better. The artist is stuck half-way on the road between what Adorno despised as "cuisine and pornographic" and autonomous art. The artist is very midbrow.

In this world where everything is still a little bit diminutive, the artist is a person, an allegorization of a set of techniques to move through the world, and sometimes the artist is just a stand-in for a painting, something within a painting, tiny. In some depictions, he is carrying a suitcase that says "Strike!" and the exclamation mark is almost exploding its contours. What's inside! Whether the strike is a rent strike or an artistic blow, he's still in the picture, occupying space. This performative contradiction, in which they're refusing the conditions under which they're also selling out, is cute. It's the artist's starting point for figuring out what to do. The artist is a bad flaneur because the street isn't his living room, it's his workplace. And he wants to shine.

One of the ways to move through the world of Kotti, for the artist, is to refine a cranky and all the more precise organizing principle for figuring out how a set of mixed feelings, crisp abstractions, sparkling stickers and formal ideas relate. (That is not a bro-y conceptual approach: it's a run-off-the-mill strategy for trying to figure out the inconsistencies in an environment.) How they do not relate. In experimenting with different kinds of proximities, the artist susses out the hot spots of interiorization and exteriorization that hold his surroundings together. There is material value: literal gold. There is sentimental value: roses, intended for someone who actually exists. The artist has developed this method that he's half-jokingly called "diminutive materialism:" you take value, then scale it down until it deflates, until you're able to approach it from the side of real life, including the actually existing fantasies within. This requires virtuosic irony because you can't just "take" value: the objectivity that it exudes is a bad special effect, spectral. On the contrary, the artist renders value, from abstract to aesthetic, as tangled up within social relations and, right there, a little bit silly, life-defining, cruel. Interior, and the interiority within, glow up as mediated by property, value, labor—and simultaneously as a product of how actual people make their surroundings their own. How pretty that looks.

Take the trans flag that someone is letting down for us from the other side of another trompe-l'oeil window: it is in itself diminutive, based, as creator Monica Helms has confirmed, on the colors that are assigned to the genders of babies. It could either be a commodified reference to sentimental righteousness, the palette of which fits nicely, but, even if it effectively belittles the processes of embodiment and exclusion it refers to, it also works as a casual symbol by which people are able to recognize each other. Or misrecognize each other in a way that they can bear. Sometimes it is when it is diminished, scaled down to its environment, that a demand can become meaningful, carefully planted into a facade. Trans liberation doesn't mean anything until it does, for you. Thus, it is at the risk of being cringe that the artist knows: the diminutive matters. It churns out space that feels more like our own, down to the level of a face in the middle of a busy street. Aesthetics are not a luxury commodity, although they can be. Kay Gabriel writes: "[A] desire that mediates between the drives and actuality [. . .] discloses an aesthetic orientation towards the world that on the scale of political struggle helps to determine *some* of the coordinates for liberation."[5] Everyone deserves a transformation of how value mediates the ins and outs of ordinary life. Everyone deserves a body that feels better and personal space that extends beyond the bourgeois interior.

3. The Outlier (They/Them)

At last, you meet the Outlier in the realm of the field? The field is a constellation of Kottis minus coherence. The Outlier, you read in a pamphlet, "watches it all unfold from the fields, a scene to which they are bound to, outside of / forevermore." Attached to a metal structure with cable tie, and yet also somewhere else entirely: that's where the Outlier nests.

In Saydam's *The Outlier*, they take shape right in the middle of what could be a Constructivist costume design or flayed skin, in a zone where the still-conceptual and the already-lived are presented in pink. Their quilt-structured surface is littered with elements of an unknown symbolic order: sandy prints of discounter honey, fake dollar bills, Keine Werbung stickers just like those people put on their Berlin letterboxes in an attempt to hold the flood of ads at bay. Darker smudges in the background suggest organic activity. Red ribbons are a sign of their dedication. The Outlier says: "It's only poetry if it's against the law." They also say "OPEN!," incorporating a shop sign right where their back would be, and also where their crotch would be. "If it's not against the law, it's not poetry," the Outlier says, quoting Robert Ashley there.

The Outlier is a person, an allegorization of a certain set of techniques to move through the world, and sometimes the Outlier is just a dream. The Outlier obviously is the most abstract, simultaneously the most annoying of the three, and yet their style of abstraction is just a middle of the road way of staying in an ordinarily stressful situation while also dropping out of it. The Outlier is a bad flaneur because their insistence that everything has

5 Kay Gabriel, "Gender as Accumulation Strategy," *Invert Journal*, Issue 1 (online).

to change is too much. They want it all. They walk into glass doors sometimes. The Outlier moves through the world by dreaming of a different one while not mistaking this different world for a world entirely separated from the one they are moving through. In order to do that, the Outlier breaks down the world until it's small enough to leave space for fantasies pop up. The diminutive, for the Outlier, means: "Oh, my dear little state of the world. It truly doesn't have to be like this."

At the very end of an exposé of *The Arcades Project*, Walter Benjamin famously wrote, "In the convulsion of the commodity economy, we begin to recognize the monuments of the bourgeoisie as ruins even before they have crumbled."[6] Always still half asleep, the Outlier *does* begin to recognize that. The Outlier is not just good at imagining an *otherwise* of things but also good at organizing what it takes to get better at imagining an otherwise of things. In the end, the Outlier knows, we'll have to build barricades. We'll also have to build spas for everyone, even though, counterintuitively, they might be entangled with a kind of openness that has little to do with the pastel-coloured idea of sustainability that mindfulness apps promise. "For most," Berlant writes, "potentiality within the overwhelming present is less well symbolized by energizing images of sustainable life […] than it is expressed in regimes of exhausted practical sovereignty, lateral agency, and, sometimes, counterabsorption in episodic refreshment, for example in sex, or spacing out, or food that is not for thought."[7] The diminutive openness of a Späti, in this sense, as it's incorporated by the Outlier, might *also* hint at the fact the relationship of need and satisfaction could be transformed. *Eat the rich!* is a cute slogan until, dear reader, we actually start to eat, with the appetite of whatever literalism we can stomach that day.

6 Walter Benjamin, *The Arcades Project*, translated by Howard Eiland and Kevin McLaughlin, Harvard University Press, 1999, p. 13.

7 Berlant, *Cruel Optimism*, p. 119.

Ufacık Materyalizme dair Serpintiler
Lokma, Sanatçı, ve Öteki
(Elif Saydam'ın minyatürlerini ve dünyayı çiğnerlerken)

Maxi Wallenhorst

Lokma (abla)

İlk önce Lokma, Späti çevresinde oyalanırken bulunur. *Späti,* Spätkauf diye bir Berlin bakkalının küçültme ismidir. Lokma'ya göre düşünülürse ama, Späti her şeyin biraz ufacıksa da hiç masum olmadığı bir dünyayı ima etmiş gibi görünür. Ufacıklığı, azaltıcılık anlamına değil, yüze veya ağza vurumcu bir fazlalık anlamına gelir. "[M]ideden veya hayalden mesela kaynaklanmasından bağımsız olarak"[1] ihtiyaç üstüne bastırılan nesneleştirmenin özünde: işte tam orada yaşar Lokma.

1 Karl Marx, *Capital, Vol.I: Critique of Political Economy*, çv. Ben Fowkes, Penguin Kitapları 1976, s.125.

Lokma'yı algılamaya başlamak, çevresini algılamaktadır. Elif Saydam'ın Späti konulu birkaç resminden "Zu Spät (I)" adlı birindeki Lokma'nın çevresi böyle görünür: tuval üzerine gri tonla basılan bir dükkan tabelasının üzerine katman katman yayılmış bir labirent. Gerçek hayatta olduğu gibi, Späti değişken ışıklı ve çeşitli arka fonların birbirine karıştığı bir alan belirtir. Labirent gerçekten altındır, altın yaprağı yani, ve dış geçitleri bakır ve gümüştür. Biraz sembolik duran sembolizmi kendi besbelliliğini nazikçe karikatürleştirir. Labirentin geçitleri, yenip yenemeyeceği belli olmayan limonlarla ve karikatür gibi emojiye dönmek üzere olan ufacık gönüllerle süslenir. Gönüllerin bir kısmı kırıktır! Lo-fi meta estetiğiyle ayrıntılı samimi bir tarzın arasında sandviç gibi sıkışmışken Lokma'nın çevresini üzerine alınmaması mümkün değildir.

Lokma, Cambridge Sözlüğüne göre, "öğünler arasında yenen az miktarda yiyecek veya çok küçük bir öğün" diye tanımlanır.

O anlamda Lokma ya bir insan, ya dünyayı dolaşmak için bir dizi tekniğin alegorisi, ya sadece bir lokma olarak da hayal edilebilir. Bazen Lokma sadece bir lokma, bir sigaradır. Onu biraz küçük görmek zorunda olduğu kadar seksi bir kişiyle karşılaşınca "but şugar" diyecek bir lubunya tarafından mesela kimliğini verildiği anlamında yani, Lokma bir insandır. İştahtan isteğe kadar, Lokma bizi tüketecek bir dünyada neleri bedenselleştireceğimizi ve neleri nesneleştireceğimizi bulma sorunudur.

Späti'nin sunduğu küçüklükten çalışarak, Lokma yoğun bir günlük hayatı doğrultup düzenlemeyi deneyerek dünyayı dolaşır. Lokma, ritmine ve iş gününün modern ifratın yüklediği inceliğine hem göre hem de karşı gider. Lokma, kaloriye ek olarak kendi zamanını kendi zamanında azar azar bulmak ister. Kendi işlerini açlığın sezgisinden bağımsız olarak yapmaz, ama zamansallığını sezgilere aykırıdır. Bir Snickersın ya da bir Snickers çubuk dondurmanın verdiği şeker sarhoşluğu kişinin iş molasını veya gönül yarasını yayılsın veya birleşsin diye süsleyebilir. Lokmalamak yemek yememeyi de dahil edebilir: heteroseksüel bir randevu bile beklenirken mesela, bir Späti'nin, bir şehrin, bir dünyanın önünde ellenme ihtimaline bütün bir gün açılması için.

Modern alegorilerin en popülerlerinden olan Flanör ve İşçi'nin birbiriyle paylaştıkları materyal durumların biri Lokma'dır, ama sadece mecazen paylaşırlar. Lokma'nın kendisi kötü bir flanördür ama. Kısmen aynı görünmezliğe sahip olmadığı için, kısmen de mahallesinin güvenilmezliği ona tehditsiz olmadığı için. Belirsiz bir şeye duyulan iştah aynı zamanda güvencesiz bir çevreyi gezmek için bir araçtır, başka bir çevreyi hayal ederek veya çevreyi hiç düşünmeyerek gezmek de dahil. Lauren Berlant, Lokma'yı "dünyayı [kişinin] kendi şartlarına ve hız anlayışına göre çekmek ve iterek uzaklaştırmak için bir teknik"[2] olarak tanımlar. Lokma, kelime

2 Lauren Berlant, *Cruel Optimism*, Duke Üniversite Basını 2011, s.135.

kelime anlama konusunda fazla iyidir bu anlamda. Sokakları yiyip bitirir. İş gününüzün ve/veya eğlence hayatınızın çeşitli noktalarında hangi Späti açıktır diye sorar. Hangisinde en sevdiğiniz Yum Yum markası satılır, hangisi yulaf sütünün satıldığı kadar soylulaştırılmıştır? Bir mekanın lokmalarını yakından incelemek, kişinin hesaplanmış rotaları içselleştirme girişimlerini çekeleyip uzatarak, bazen esnek bazen de atıl hallere getirir.

Bunlar *späti kültürü* olarak bahsedildiğinde, kolaylıkla bireysel failliğin kalıcılığını gösteren kentsel modernitenin bir keyfiyle karıştırılır: Lokma her şeye rağmen her şeyi yoluna koyabilir, daha iyi kaybedebilir. (Berlin, bu fantezi için o kadar kuvvetli bir projeksiyon yüzeyidir ki, yıllar önce şehir bunu kendi pazarlama sloganlarına bile *arm aber seksi*, fakir ama seksi, diye ilave etti.) Öte yandan, Lokma'nın kartoğrafik becerisi, kapitalist ödeneğin onu soylulaştırmaya yönelik bir pusulaya döndürdüğü koşullardan da biridir. Instagram'daki yemek fotoğrafçılığının estetiği tarafından önceden delalet edilmiş ve genellikle beyaz bir şekilde bereketli bir Lokma, artan geliştirme değerinin işaretine dönüşür. Bereketli, burada sadece zengin demektir. Her iki hesap, Lokma'yı enfrastrüktür için cici bir bitiş noktası olarak görür. Fakat Lokma bundan daha dağınıktır.

Ama gerçekten cicidir Lokma. Bununla birlikte, Sianne Ngai'nin ünlü bir şekilde belirttiğine göre, cici olanın değerlendirilmesi ağızda karışık bir tat bırakır. Özünde, "beklenen şefkatli ya da annelik hislerinin yanı sıra çirkin ya da agresif hislerini"[3]

3 Sianne Ngai, "The Cuteness of the Avantgarde": *Critical Inquiry*, cilt 31, sayı 4 (Yaz 2005), s. 816.

yeniden keşfeder. Lokma karşılık vermeden önce, yenip bitirilmelidir. Ngai'nin makalesinden yuvarlanan gıda maddeleriyle birlikte, Gertrude Stein'ın rostosu ve Francis Ponge'nin portakalı mesela, Lokma, ufacık olanı günlük yaşamın ortasında samimi bir mekan olarak daha açıklar. Lokma, kişinin, cansız zamir, kullanışlı travma, ve soyut sınır kavramları tarafından mikro ve makro düzeylerde tanımlanan bir şey olduğu için, "bedenselleştirme" veya "arzu" diyebileceği samimiyet tarzını hayal etmezdir. Lokma biraz şaka gibidir o anlamda. Bir vücuda sahip olma sorununu, kaykaycılar arasında popüler olan Durstlöscher adlı bayat bir buzlu çayla, belirsiz ayrıntılarla içsel olarak ilgili bir şey haline getirir. Lauren Berlant, "bu arada, yemek yeme pratiği, kişinin tutarsızlığını tazmin edici bir kişilik düzenlemeden, tutarsızlığını idare etmenin bir yolunu sağlamaktadır"[4] diye yazar. Lokma, duygulanım ve duygulanımın nesneleştirmenin arasında sandviç gibi sıkışmış bir yaşamın izlerini sürekli yutar. Biyolojiye ait bir alegorinin anlattığı gibi, bağırsaklar gerçekten iç olarak sayılmazdır. Lokma, içgüdüsel duygunun burjuva içselliğinden daha fazla olmasında ısrar eder. Ya da daha doğrusu, daha az olmasında.

4 Berlant, *Cruel Optimism*, s.135.

Sanatçı (abi)

Sonra Sanatçı, Kotti çevresinde tanıştırılır. Kotti, soyutlaştırılıp geliştirme değerine dönüşen bir Lokma'lar birleşmesi olarak düşünülebilir. Kotti, Kottbusser Tor diye bir Kreuzberg noktasının küçültme ismidir. Sözde özel bir Berlin tadını açıklarmış (Sanatçı orada çalışmayı çok sever), ama buna özel bir Berlin tadı demek, içindeki sürmekte olan çatışmayı romantikleştirmektedir: Kotti'ye bir tarafından baskı uygulayan bir polis arabası her zaman vardır, diğer tarafından neon tabelaların üzerinde görünmez bir şekilde havada kalıp baskı uygulayan soylulaştırma her zaman vardır. Kısmen araçsallaştırılmış kısmen de zar zor gözlemleyen bir konuma çekilmiş, bunların tam ortasında: işte tam orada yaşar Sanatçı.

Sanatçı'yı algılamaya başlamak, çevresini algılamaktadır. Elif Saydam'ın "Artists (Kotti)" adlı minyatürünün gösterdiği Kotti cici ve ufak ayrıntılardan yapılmış, ama bu cici ve ufak ayrıntılar sadece kişinin kaybolup nostaljik kalabileceği bir yer değildir. Bu dünya, rantın çok yüksek olduğu bir yerdir. Arka fon stres olmuştur. Bir pencereden açılan, sanki ortaçağ dönemine aitmiş gibi görünen bir bayrak üzerinde "Die Miete ist zu hoch!!!" (Kiralar çok yüksek!!!) der. Samimi bir şekilde sallanan ünlem işaretleri, sokağa patlıyormuş gibi bir kişisel alana ima eder. Pencere *trompe-l'oeil*, göz yanılmasıdır yani, ve ayrıntılı bir sahte olduğu için bir iç manzarasına açması beklenebilse de burada sokağa bakar. Bu birleşmenin ortasında, görünüşte sokak düzeyinde, esrarengiz bir şekilde çirkin bir şey parlar: 16. yüzyıl Osmanlı minyatüründen koparılıp kişiselleştirilmiş bir süs. *Sokak*, iç ve dışın ırksal kapitalizm altındaki yaşamın soyutlamaları tarafından sürekli yeniden düzenlediği bir mekan olarak düşünülürse, her şey bir sokak sahnesi gibi görünür. Bu haliyle, sokak sadece ilginç bir panorama değildir, aynı zamanda bir sokak, mahalle, veya şehrin kendisiyle bütünlüğünün herhangi kavramının yaptığı gibi sınıfsal zevk siyasetiyle ve göç tarihleriyle titreşen bir sahnedir.

Süs, bazıları tehlikeli bir dereceye kadar solgun görünen limonlar, çiçekler ve üzümlerle süslenmiştir. Kotti'nin çevresinde, Sanatçı sıkça garip meyvelerle karşılaşır, bazıları görünüşte plastikten yapılmış, bazıları gitmiş: lokmalananın dekoratif hale zar zor geldiği, zar zor estetikleştirildiği yerde, Sanatçı'nın dünyası bulunur. Sanatçı, hangisini yiyeceğini ve hangisinin sadece iyi görüneceğini bulma konusunda iyidir ve özellikle hangisinin daha iyi görüneceğini bilme konusunda iyidir. Sanatçı, Adorno'nun "mutfak ve pornografik" diyerek hor gördüğü şeyden özerk sanata giden yolun yarısında sıkışmıştır. Sanatçı orta derece kültürlüymüştür.

Her şeyin hala biraz ufacık kaldığı bu dünyada, Sanatçı bir insan, dünyayı dolaşmak için bir dizi tekniğin alegorisi, ve bazen sanatçı sadece bir resmin vekili, resimde bir ayrıntı, ufak bir şeydir. Bazı tasvirlerde "Strike!" (Grev!) yazılı bir bavul taşır, ve ünlem işareti neredeyse konturlarını patlamak üzeredir. İçinde neyi varmış! İster kira grevi ister sanatsal bir grev olsun, Sanatçı yerini kaplayarak resimde kalır. Kendisini sattığı koşulları da reddettiği bu performatif çelişkisi cicidir. Bu, sanatçının ne yapacağını bulmak için başlangıç noktasıdır. Sanatçı kötü bir flanördür, çünkü sokak salonu değil, iş yeridir. Ve o parlamak ister.

Kotti dünyasını dolaşmak için bir yolu, Sanatçı'ya göre, bir dizi karışık duygunun, keskin soyutlamaların, ışıltı çıkartmaların, ve şekilsel fikirlerin ilişki nasıl kurduğunu bulmak için huysuz ama gittikçe artarak kesin bir gösterici prensip geliştirmektir. (Biraderci bir kavramsal yaklaşım değildir bu; bir çevrenin tutarsızlığını anlamaya çalışmak için sıradan bir stratejidir.) Ayrıca ilişki nasıl kurmadıkları. Sanatçı, farklı türde yakınlıkları deneyerek, çevresini bir arada tutan içselleştirme ve dışsallaştırmanın noktalarını ortaya çıkarır. Maddi bir değer vardır: gerçek altın yani. Duygusal bir değer de vardır: gerçek bir kişiye yönelik güller yani. Sanatçı, yarı şaka bir şekilde "ufacık materyalizm" ismini verdiği bu yöntemi geliştirmiştir: değer alınıp, sönünceye, gerçek hayattan, içinde var olan fantezilerden de dahil, yaklaşılabilinceye kadar, küçültülür. Virtüöz bir ironi gerektirir, değer kolaylıkla alınamaz çünkü: değerden sızan nesnellik kötü bir özel efekttir, hayalidir. Tam tersine, Sanatçı değeri, soyuttan estetiğe, sosyal ilişkilerle iç içe, ve işte tam orada biraz saçma, hayat belirleyici, ve zalim olarak resmeder. İç ve içerideki içsellik, mülkiyet, değer, ve emek taraflarından aracılık edilir—ve aynı zamanda gerçek insanların çevrelerini sahiplediklerinin bir ürünü—olarak parıldar. Ne güzeldir.

Birinin başka bir *trompe-l'oeil* penceresinin diğer tarafından bizim için açtığı trans bayrağı mesela: yaratıcı Monica Helms'in onayladığına göre, bebeklerin cinsiyetlerine atanan renklere dayalı olarak bu da ufacıktır. Paleti iyi yakışan, duygusal doğruluğa nesneleştirilmiş bir referans olabilir. Ama, işaret ettiği bedenselleştirme ve dışlama süreçlerini aslında küçümsese bile, aynı zamanda insanların birbirlerini tanıyabilecekleri sıradan bir sembol olarak da çalışır.

Ayrıca dayanabilecekleri bir şekilde birbirlerini yanlış tanıyabilecekleri. Bazen miniktir, anlamlı bir hale gelmesi için çevresine göre küçültülüp bir cepheye dikkatlice takılır. Trans özgürlüğünün hiç anlamı yoktur, bizce anlamlı oluncaya kadar. Bu nedenle, Sanatçı'nın *cringe* olma riskine girip bildiği bu: kendimiz evindeymiş gibi hissettiğimiz alanları üretmek için, işlek bir sokağın ortasındaki bir yüz bile, ufacık olanı önemlidir. Estetik lüks bir meta değildir, ama olabilir. Kay Gabriel şöyle yazar: "İçgüdülerle gerçeklik arasında aracılık eden [bir] arzu [...], siyasal mücadele ölçeğinde özgürlüğün *bazı* koordinatlarını belirlemeye yardımcı olan, dünyaya yönelik bir estetik duyarlılığı açığa çıkarır."[5] Herkes, değerin sıradan yaşamın giriş ve çıkışlarına aracılık etmelerinin dönüşmesini hak eder. Herkes, daha ev gibi görünen bir bedeni ve burjuva içselliğinden ötesine uzanan bir kişisel alanı hak eder.

5 Kay Gabriel, "Gender as Accumulation Strategy," *Invert Journal*, Issue 1 (online).

Öteki (aşko)

Sonunda Öteki, tarla çevresinde karşılanır. Tarla, ahenksiz bir Kotti'ler birleşmesidir. Öteki, bir kitapçıkta okunduğu gibi, "tarlalardan her şeyin gelişmesine, hem bağlı hem dışında olduğu bir sahneye bakar / artık." Kablo bağlarıyla madeni bir yapıya bağlanmış, ama tamamen başka bir yerde: işte tam orada yuvalanır Öteki.

Elif Saydam'ın "Öteki" adlı eserinde, ya konstrüktivist bir kostüm tasarımının ya da yüzülmüş derinin tam ortasında, kavramsal olanıyla yaşanmış olanın pembe tonlarla sergilendiği bir alanda, Öteki şekline gelir. Yorgan yapılı yüzeyi, bilinmez bir sembolik düzenin unsurlarıyla serpintilidir: indirimli balın kum rengi baskıları, sahte dolar faturaları, tıpkı bazılarının reklam selini uzak tutmak için Berlin posta kutularına koydukları gibi Keine Werbung çıkartmaları. Arka fondaki daha koyu lekeler organik aktiviteye ima eder. Kırmızı kurdelelerle kararlılığını bildirir. Robert Ashley'den alıntı yaparak, Öteki "Kanuna aykırı değilse, şiir değil" der. Sırt ve kasığının tam yerlerine dükkan tabelası katarak aynı zamanda "AÇIK!" der.

Öteki bir insan, dünyayı dolaşmak için bir dizi tekniğin alegorisi, ve bazen de sadece bir hayaldır. Uçluktan Öteki elbette en soyut ve en gıcıktır, yine de soyutlama tarzı, genellikle stresli bir durumda kalmanın ve aynı zamanda ondan vazgeçmenin bir orta yoludur sadece. Her şeyin değişmesindeki ısrarları çok fazla olduğu için, Öteki kötü bir flanördür. Öteki hepsini ister. Bazen cam kapıya çarpar. Öteki, dolaştığı dünyadan tamamen bağımsız bir dünyayla karıştırmadan, diğer dünyanın hayalini kurarak dünyayı dolaşır. Böyle dolaşmak için, Öteki fantezi ortaya çıkaracak kadar dünyayı parçalara ayırır. Öteki'ne göre, ufacık demek, *Ah canım dünyacığım! Cidden böyle olmak zorunda değilsindir* demektir.

Çarşılar Projesi konulu bir yazının en sonunda Walter Benjamin, "Meta ekonomisi sarstıkça, burjuvazinin anıtlarının yıktıntı olması yıkılmadan bile tanınmaya başlar" diye ünlü bir şekilde yazar.[6] Hep hala uyku-uyanıklık arasında olan Öteki bunu tanımaya aslında başlar. Öteki, sadece diğer dünyaların hayalini iyi kurur değildir, aynı zamanda diğer dünyaların hayalini daha iyi kurmaya gerekenleri iyi düzenler. Sonunda barikat da kurmak zorunda kalacağımızı bilir Öteki. Herkes için kaplıca da inşa etmek zorunda kalacağız, sezgilere aykırı bir şekilde farkındalık uygulamalarının gösterdiği pastel renkli sürdürülebilirlik felsefesiyle ilgilenmez bir tür açıklık gerektirse bile. "Çoğu insana göre," Lauren Berlant diye yazar, "boğucu bir bugünün içindeki gizilgücün sürdürülebilir bir hayatın canlandırıcı imajları tarafından sembolize edildiği, tükenmiş pratik özerklik, yanal faillik, ve bazen epizodik tazelemeyle karşı-meşguliyet rejimlerinde gerçekleştiğinden daha azdır. Ya sevişmede gerçekleştiği mesela, ya demlenmede, ya lokmalamada."[7] Öteki'ne katıldığı şekliyle Späti'nin ufacık açıklığı, bu anlamda, ihtiyaçla tatminin ilişkinin dönüştürülebileceğine de ima edebilir. Sevgili arkadaşlar, sanki *Zenginleri ye!* cici bir sloganmış gibi görünür–tam anlamına ne kadar aç olsak da biz sofraya oturuncaya kadar.

6 Walter Benjamin, *The Arcades Project*, çv. Howard Eiland ve Kevin McLaughlin, Harvard Üniversitesi Basımı 1999, s.13.

7 Berlant, *Cruel Optimism*, s.119.

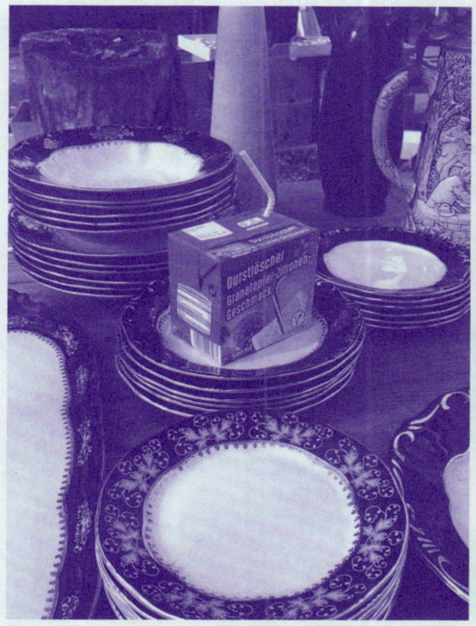

Durstlöscher pomegranate, Charlottenburg flea market

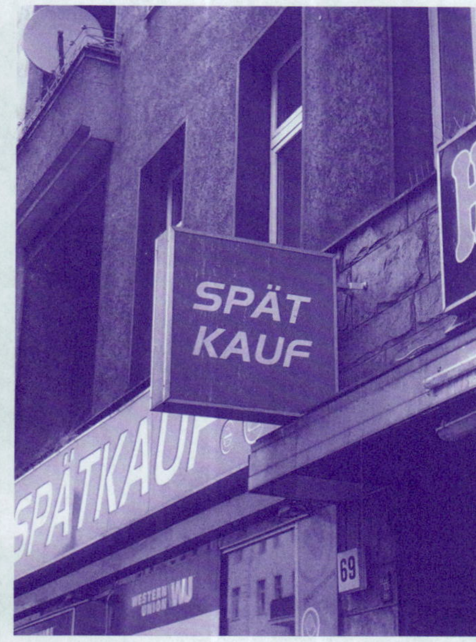

A Späti, anywhere

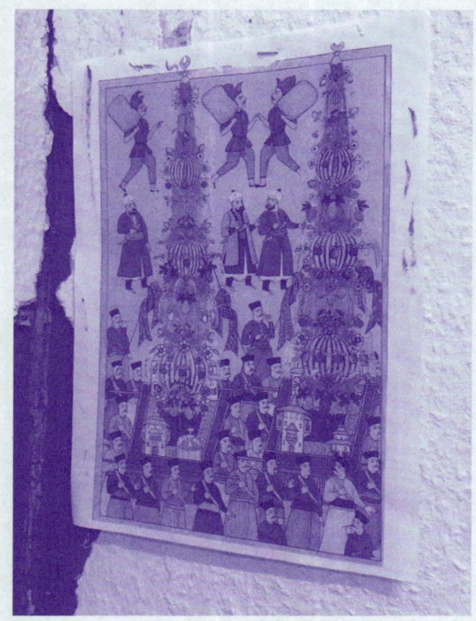

Sixteenth-century Ottoman miniature, VIDEO INN

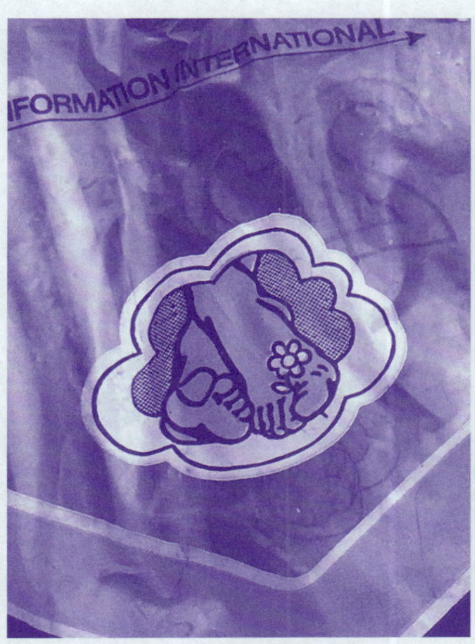

Insole packaging filled with candles, Hansaplatz

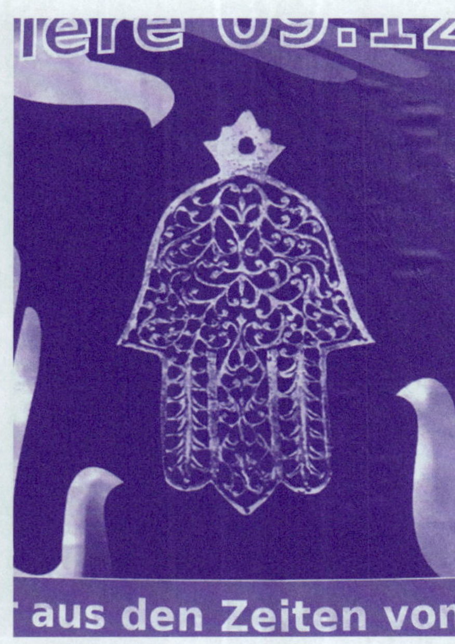

Fatima appears in Moabit

All-Girl Medieval Torture Summer Camp

Asa Seresin

Now I have traveled much farther from our tower, but I have found always that the pattern of our guild is repeated mindlessly . . . in the societies of every trade, so that they are all of them torturers, just as we. His quarry stands to the hunter as our clients to us; those who buy to the tradesman; the enemies of the Commonwealth to the soldier; the governed to the governors; men to women. All love that which they destroy.

—Gene Wolfe, *The Shadow of the Torturer*

It is 1999, I am a six-year-old boy being raised as a girl, and I am obsessed with torture. I watch Disney's *Robin Hood* (1973) every day, ritualistically, like it's a tab of Pornhub. The climax comes in the Sheriff of Nottingham's issuance of a death sentence for Robin. *They're going to put a noose around his neck*, I think, panting. *They're going to tighten it until he chokes. They're going to force him to surrender.*

I draw cartoon fan fiction about myself or my friends being captured, tied up, and hanged. These pornographic drawings contain fantasies of rescue as often as they do defeat. *Robin Hood* initiates me into raging anarcho-sadomasochism via my crush on this outlaw, Fox, who I want to be and want to fuck, whose hands I want to unbind only so I can take him home and tie him up again.

My days and nights are consumed by thoughts of handcuffing, torturing, and fucking girls from my elementary school. In one recurring daydream, I push a girl in fifth grade through the halls of a hospital in a wheelchair, leading her into surgery. *Don't be scared*, I whisper, lying her on the bed, before performing what I've abstracted into a complicated medical procedure. What I know about sex comes from a Danish children's book in which a stick figure Mamma and Pappa make a baby in a hot air balloon. This Crayola reproductivity is so far removed from my own desire that I'm convinced they have nothing to do with one another. *I don't want to* have sex *with girls*, I reassure myself. *I just want to torture them.*

Of course, it turns out that I do want to have sex with girls. But there is more intimacy between this sex and the complicated medical procedures I daydream about—those fantasies of instruments applied to bodies, of my body, dispersed across objects and in total control—than I initially expect. Before I become a man, I understand my gender as an act of domination.

The Lindsay Lohan version of *Parent Trap* (1998) is another trove of fantasy material, particularly the film's opening, in which the twins come for each other's throats in a high-stakes fencing duel only to shed their masks and realize they look exactly the same. Unconvinced by the actual plotline of familial reconciliation, to me this is essentially twincest porn, the sisters' hatred of each other grounded in desire. Their pranks seem patently flirtatious, especially a truth-or-dare striptease card game wherein Hallie's winning hand forces Annie to dive naked into the lake in front of the entire all-girl summer camp. Beaten by her doppelgänger, Annie pays the price of humiliation.

I *desperately* want to play this game.

At my real-life summer camp in the San Bernardino mountains in California, my friend tells a crowd of rapt listeners about how she fills her mouth with ice cubes to suck her boyfriend's dick. The haze of erotic fantasy standing between the world and me is so thick I sometimes wonder how I'm able to see anyone. At night, the twenty girls in my cabin stand around naked in a pink cloud of Herbal Essences, taking turns to step into the cold shower and scream.

Maybe it's because I am the product of an all-girl secondary school (grades six through twelve), but my sexual desire is always on supercharge in what the sociologist Erving Goffman calls total institutions: college, a residency, summer camp.[1] It's embarrassing to admit how much I love these micro-worlds, betraying as it does a certain fantasy of queer and trans people being intrinsically at odds with regimentality and discipline. At the same time, there's surely something queer about the total institution, the same-sex pseudo-commune that provides Western children with their only true respite from the family.

In Leslie Paris' history of summer camp, *Children's Nature*, Paris quotes a brochure advertising the coeducational Camp Kinacamps: "Boys and Girls who are afraid of themselves and afraid of each other are just the types that develop dangerous, unnatural crushes between members of the same sex and that need very badly the wholesome contacts under adequate chaperonage to be found at Kinacamps."[2] Here, gender integration and heterosexuality itself are rendered safe and cute in comparison to the destabilizing, "dangerous" and violent homosexual crushes likely to overwhelm single-sex environments. Afraid of themselves and afraid of each other. As an adult, I question how much of my childhood torture fixation was a kind of revenge fantasy directed at other girls for our supposed categorical similarity. Or maybe I just wanted a tool in my hand. Either way, whoever wrote this brochure might have been peering into my sad little sadist heart.

The emergence of the North American summer camp movement in the early twentieth century was heavily influenced by the psychoanalytic theory of recapitulation, which held that (white) children progress from a state of "savagery" to civilization in a manner supposedly reflective of the fate of humanity as a whole. Boys in particular were thought to be at risk from the feminizing influence of modern urban life and were thus encouraged to set free their inner wildness by courting danger, getting tan, staying dirty, and playing Indian.

It was during this same period, Sianne Ngai argues, that cuteness as a major aesthetic category burst onto the consumer scene via the children's toy market. "The emergence of that particularly exemplary cute object, the stuffed animal or manufactured plush toy, for example, can be easily traced to a newfound awareness of the aggressiveness of children that arose with the advent of twentieth-century psychology."[3] Ngai defines "'cute' toys" as "denoting an aesthetic of accentuated helplessness and vulnerability."[4] While we might be accustomed to associating children and their cute toys as inhabiting the same aesthetic category, Ngai posits a different, more disturbing relation: toys were cute so children could torture them. "It was only once children were no longer imagined as miniature adults [. . .] that manufacturers found the impetus to produce indestructible toys that could survive the violence with which children were increasingly associated."[5]

1 Erving Goffman, *Asylums: Essays on the Condition of the Social Situation of Mental Patients and Other Inmates*, Anchor Books, 1961.

2 Leslie Paris, *Children's Nature: The Rise of the American Summer Camp*, NYU Press, 2008, p. 152.

3 Sianne Ngai, *Our Aesthetic Categories: Zany, Cute, Interesting*, Harvard University Press, 2012, p. 75.

4 Ngai, p. 77.

5 Ngai, p. 75–76.

The notion that children were violent may have been powerful enough to revolutionize the toy market (and help inaugurate the summer camp movement), but it has never been uncontroversial. In *Civilization and Its Discontents,* Sigmund Freud himself mocks Christian sentimentality about childhood innocence that excuses people from acknowledging what he sees as the existence of the death drive: "For 'little children do not like it' when there is talk of the inborn human inclination to 'badness,' to aggressiveness and destructiveness, and so to cruelty as well. God has made them in the image of his own perfection."[6] Heinous to believe that the big smiley face in the sky would create beings with a natural appetite for violence. Instead, children are made loveable by virtue of their being pure, pliable, asexual, cute—hence the appeal of replacing, to use the words of Lauren Berlant, "a nation made for adult citizens [. . .] by one imagined for fetuses and children."[7]

At Elif Saydam's *All-Girl Medieval Torture Summer Camp*—I stole the name for this essay from them—there is no distance between sweetness and sadism. Here, the death drive is cute. In *The Producer*, a denim cross is strapped, spread-eagle, across a rectangular metal grate, fastened at every end with zip ties—the kind of trick Hallie would have pulled at Camp Walden. My eyes voyeuristically wander to the split at the cross's middle, a kind of crotch with a small metal hole through which the zip tie has been threaded and pulled. Other, squatter crosses in the series have larger holes made from folds in the fabric, creating a kind of neckline; above one, a red bow and a sign that reads *OPEN.*

The dried farfalle pasta, orange slices, straw braids, emoticons, and bows with which these fabric crosses are decorated evoke the small, careful hands of children involved in arts and crafts. There is also an unavoidable way in which these sculptures recall crucifixion, as well as the litany of similar practices of torture that tend to fascinate schoolchildren—being ripped apart on the rack or quartered by four horses. Perhaps, in a sense, this is medieval torture as processed through the mind of a child: funny, dainty, and erotic, its violence not absent, but metaphorical.

Lately, my boyfriend, Gray Wielebinski, has been making pornographic ink drawings at the big table in our apartment in Philadelphia. They depict hypermasculine, demi-human beings tied to racks that vaguely recall the metal grates in Saydam's summer camp sculptures. Clad in skimpy athletic armor revealing muscles that vainly—perhaps disingenuously—strain against their own captivity, these creatures seem to have re-entered my life via a direct line from my childhood dreamscape. In their masked faces I see the exact expression that my own torture fantasies strove to elicit: gritted teeth, reluctant surrender, muted pleasure.

I ended up destroying all of my own bondage and torture drawings back in elementary school, stuffing them inside the tall metal bin in the kitchen of our apartment. I would lie awake panicking at the thought of my mother finding them, (correctly) convinced that there was something uncontained, something dangerous and unnatural, in these drawings' power. I wish I could take that little girl to A.G.M.T.S.C., introduce him to all the perverts I love and who love me. I wonder what he would make of it.

6 Sigmund Freud, "Civilization and Its Discontents," from *The Standard Edition of the Complete Works of Sigmund Freud*, translated by James Strachey, Hogarth Press, 1955, p. 120.

7 Lauren Berlant, *The Queen of America Goes to Washington City*, Duke University Press, 1997, p. 1.

Nun hat mich meine Reise weit von unserem Turm fortgeführt, aber stets musste ich feststellen, dass sich das Muster unserer Gilde gedankenlos wiederholt ... in den Kreisen jedes Gewerbes. Sie alle sind daher Folterer, genau wie wir: Dem Jäger ist seine Beute, was uns die Freier sind – dem Händler die Käufer, dem Soldaten die Feinde des Commonwealth, den Regierenden die Regierten, den Männern die Frauen. Alle lieben, was sie zerstören.
—Gene Wolfe, *Der Schatten des Folterers: Das Buch der Neuen Sonne*

Wir schreiben das Jahr 1999, ich bin ein sechsjähriger Junge, der als Mädchen aufwächst, und ich bin geradezu besessen von Folter. Täglich schaue ich mir Disneys *Robin Hood* an, ritualisiert, wie einen Pornhub-Tab. Der Klimax wird erreicht, wenn der Sheriff von Nottingham das Todesurteil über Robin ausspricht. *Sie werden ihm einen Strick um den Hals legen,* denke ich keuchend. *Sie werden ihn enger ziehen, bis er erstickt. Sie werden ihn zwingen aufzugeben.*

Ich zeichne Cartoon-Fan-Fiction darüber, wie ich oder meine Freunde gefangen, gefesselt und aufgehängt werden. Diese pornografischen Zeichnungen beinhalten ebenso oft Fantasien von Rettung wie von Unterwerfung. Robin Hood entfesselt in mir die Lust auf Anarcho-Sadomasochismus, weil ich einen Crush auf den Outlaw Fox habe, der ich sein und den ich ficken möchte und dessen Hände ich nur losbinden will, um ihn mit nach Hause zu nehmen und wieder zu fesseln.

Tag und Nacht verzehre ich mich in Gedanken an das Fesseln, Quälen und Ficken von Mädchen aus meiner Grundschule. In einem wiederkehrenden Tagtraum schiebe ich ein Mädchen aus der fünften Klasse im Rollstuhl durch die Gänge eines Krankenhauses und in den OP. *Hab keine Angst,* flüstere ich ihr zu, während ich sie auf das Bett lege, bevor ich das durchführe, was ich zu einem komplizierten medizinischen Eingriff abstrahiert habe. Mein Wissen über Sex stammt aus einem dänischen Kinderbuch, in dem eine Strichmännchen-Mama und ein Strichmännchen-Papa in einem Heißluftballon ein Baby machen. Diese Buntstift-Fortpflanzung unterscheidet sich so stark von meiner eigenen Begierde, dass ich überzeugt bin, dass sie nichts miteinander zu tun haben. *Ich will keinen Sex mit Mädchen haben,* versichere ich mir. *Ich will sie einfach nur quälen.*

Natürlich stellt sich heraus, dass ich sehr wohl Sex mit Mädchen haben will. Aber zwischen diesem Sex und den komplizierten medizinischen Eingriffen, von denen ich tagtäglich träume – den Fantasien von Geräten, die an Körpern angewendet werden, von meinem auf Objekte verteilten Körper, der totale Kontrolle ausübt – gibt es mehr Berührungspunkte, als ich zunächst erwartet hatte. Noch bevor ich ein Mann werde, verstehe ich mein Gender als einen Akt der Beherrschung.

Lindsay Lohans *Ein Zwilling kommt selten allein* diente mir als weitere Quelle für meine Fantasien, vor allem der Anfang des Films, in dem sich die Zwillinge in einem Fechtduell gegenseitig an die Gurgel gehen, um dann ihre Masken abzulegen und festzustellen, dass sie einander wie aus dem Gesicht geschnitten sind. Der Plot um die familiäre Versöhnung überzeugt mich nicht. Für mich ist der Film ein Zwillings-Porno, der gegenseitige Hass der Schwestern entspringt ihrer Begierde. Ihre Pranks wirken unverhohlen flirty, vor allem das „Wahrheit oder Pflicht"-Striptease-Kartenspiel, bei dem Hallie gewinnt und Annie dazu zwingt, vor den Augen des gesamten Mädchen-Sommercamps nackt in den See zu springen. Geschlagen von ihrer Doppelgängerin, zahlt Annie den Preis der Demütigung.

Ich will dieses Spiel *unbedingt* spielen.

In meinem realen Sommercamp in den kalifornischen San Bernardino Mountains erzählt eine Freundin einer entzückten Zuhörer*innenschaft, wie sie ihren Mund mit Eiswürfeln füllt, wenn sie den Schwanz ihres Boyfriends lutscht. Der Schleier der erotischen Fantasie, der zwischen der Welt und mir hängt, ist so dicht, dass ich mich manchmal frage, wie ich überhaupt noch jemanden sehen kann. Des Nachts stehen die zwanzig Mädchen aus meiner Hütte nackt in einer rosafarbenen Wolke aus Kräuteressenzen herum, um abwechselnd unter die kalte Dusche zu steigen und loszuschreien.

Vielleicht liegt es daran, dass ich das Produkt einer reinen Mädchenschule bin (Klasse sechs bis zwölf), aber mein sexuelles Verlangen wird von den „totalen Institutionen", wie der Soziologe Erving

Goffman sie nennt, immer auf Hochtouren gebracht: College, eine Residency, Sommercamp.[1] Es ist mir peinlich, zuzugeben, wie sehr ich diese Mikrowelten liebe, weil sie im Widerspruch zu der Vorstellung stehen, dass queere und transsexuelle Menschen grundsätzlich Probleme mit Reglementierung und Disziplin haben. Andererseits hat die totale Institution, die gleichgeschlechtliche Pseudo-Gemeinschaft, die westlichen Kindern die einzige wirkliche Alternative zur Familie bietet, sicherlich auch etwas queeres an sich.

1 Vgl. Erving Goffman, *Asylums: Essays on the Condition of the Social Situation of Mental Patients and Other Inmates*, New York 1961.

In *Children's Nature*, Leslie Paris' historischer Abhandlung über amerikanische Sommercamps, zitiert Paris eine Werbebroschüre des koedukativ ausgerichteten Ferienlagers Kinacamps: „Jungen und Mädchen, die sich vor sich selbst und voreinander fürchten, sind besonders anfällig für gefährliche, widernatürliche Neigungen zwischen Angehörigen des gleichen Geschlechts. Daher sind sie dringend auf gesunde Kontakte unter angemessener Aufsicht angewiesen, wie sie in Kinacamps ermöglicht werden."[2] Hier werden Gender-Integration und Heterosexualität als sicher und niedlich dargestellt, im Gegensatz zu den destabilisierenden, „gefährlichen" und gewaltsamen homosexuellen Neigungen, die in monogeschlechtlichen Umgebungen überhandnehmen. Angst vor sich selbst und Angst vor den anderen. Als Erwachsener frage ich mich, wie viel von meiner kindlichen Folterfixierung eine Art Rachefantasie war, die sich gegen andere Mädchen aufgrund unserer vermeintlichen kategorischen Ähnlichkeit richtete, oder ob ich vielleicht nur ein Tool zur Hand haben wollte. Jedenfalls haben die Verfasser*innen dieser Broschüre wohl direkt in mein trauriges kleines Sadistenherz geschaut.

2 Leslie Paris, *Children's Nature: The Rise of the American Summer Camp*, New York 2008, S. 152.

Die Anfänge der nordamerikanischen Sommercamp-Bewegung zu Beginn des zwanzigsten Jahrhunderts waren maßgeblich von der psychoanalytischen Rekapitulationstheorie beeinflusst. Diese besagt, dass der Übergang vom Zustand der „Wildheit" zur Zivilisation, den (weiße) Kinder durchmachen, das Schicksal der gesamten Menschheit widerspiegelt. Insbesondere Jungen galten als besonders gefährdet durch den feminisierenden Einfluss des modernen Stadtlebens und wurden deshalb ermutigt, ihre innere Wildheit freizusetzen, indem sie die Gefahr suchten, sich braun und dreckig machten und Native Americans spielten.

Sianne Ngai zufolge wurde in dieser Zeit auch das Konzept der Niedlichkeit (*cuteness*) in der Konsument*innenszene als zentrale ästhetische Kategorie über den Spielzeugsektor etabliert: „Das Aufkommen von exemplarisch-niedlichen Objekten wie Stofftieren oder industriell gefertigten Plüschtieren lässt sich ohne weiteres auf das neu gewonnene Bewusstsein für die Aggressivität von Kindern zurückführen, das mit der Psychologie des zwanzigsten Jahrhunderts aufkam."[3] Ngai definiert „‚niedliches' Spielzeug" als „Ausdruck einer Ästhetik der akzentuierten Hilflosigkeit und Verletzlichkeit"[4]. Während wir Kinder und ihre niedlichen Spielzeuge üblicherweise in ein und dieselbe ästhetische Kategorie einordnen mögen, stellt Ngai einen anderen, beunruhigenderen Bezug her: Spielzeuge sind niedlich, damit Kinder sie quälen können. „Erst als man Kinder nicht mehr als Miniatur-Erwachsene betrachtete [. . .], sahen sich die Hersteller*innen veranlasst, unzerstörbares Spielzeug zu produzieren, das die Gewalt überstehen konnte, die den Kindern zunehmend zugeschrieben wurde."[5]

3 Sianne Ngai, *Our Aesthetic Categories: Zany, Cute, Interesting*, Cambridge 2012, S. 75.

4 Ebd., S. 77.

5 Ebd., S. 75–76.

Die Vorstellung, dass Kinder gewalttätig sind, mag den Spielzeugmarkt revolutioniert (und die Sommercamp-Bewegung ins Leben gerufen) haben, aber sie war nie unumstritten. In *Das Unbehagen in der Kultur* spottet Freud über die christliche Sentimentalität hinsichtlich der Unschuld von Kindern, die die Menschen davor bewahrt, die Existenz des Todestriebs anzuerkennen: „Denn die Kindlein, sie hören es nicht gerne, wenn die angeborene Neigung des Menschen zum ‚Bösen', zur Aggression, Destruktion und damit auch zur Grausamkeit erwähnt wird. Gott hat sie ja zum Ebenbild seiner eigenen Vollkommenheit geschaffen [. . .]."[6] Dass das große lächelnde Gesicht im Himmel Wesen mit einem natürlichen Appetit auf Gewalt erschaffen könnte, ist eine abscheuliche Vorstellung. Stattdessen werden Kinder als liebenswert dargestellt, indem man ihre Reinheit, Biegsamkeit,

6 Sigmund Freud, *Das Unbehagen in der Kultur*, GW XIV, Wien 1930, S. 419.

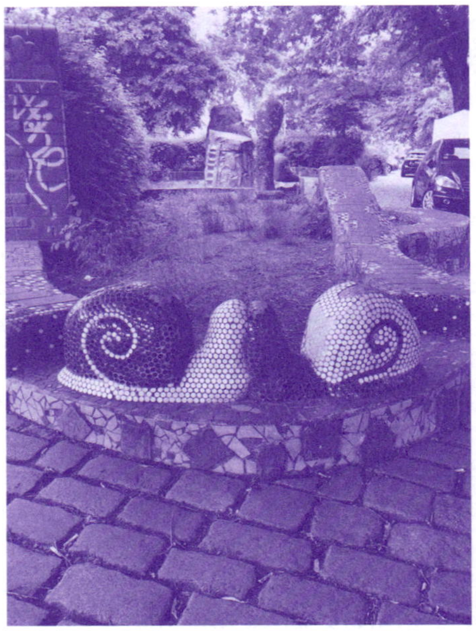

Snail meeting point, Alt-Moabit

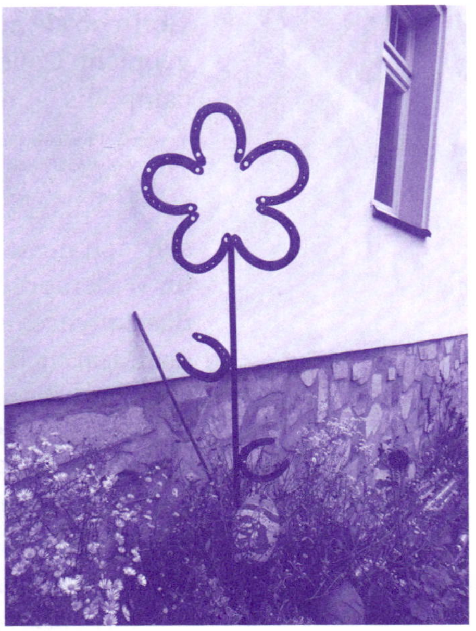

Horseshoe flowers, Brandenburg

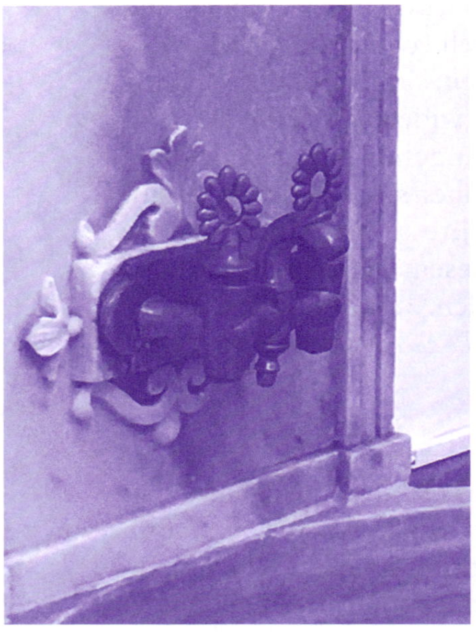

Hamam faucet at Dolmabahçe Palace, Istanbul

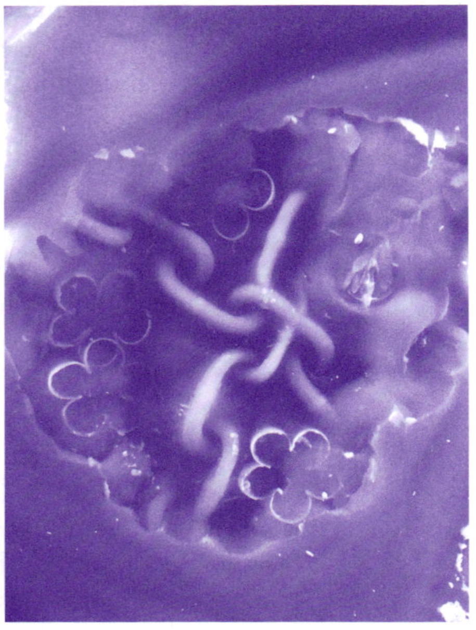

Silicon chains, VIDEO INN

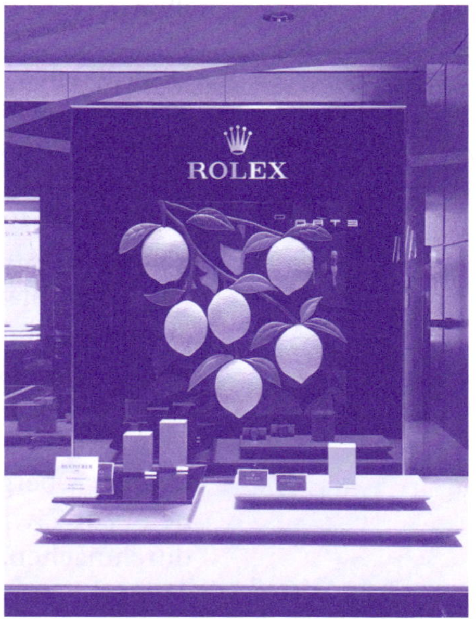

1st wave lockdown Rolex store, Checkpoint Charlie

Asexualität und Niedlichkeit hervorhebt. Und daher rührt auch die Motivation „eine Nation, die für erwachsene Bürger*innen geschaffen wurde […], durch eine Nation zu ersetzen, die für Föten und Kinder erdacht wurde“[7], um es mit den Worten Lauren Berlants zu sagen.

7 Lauren Berlant, *The Queen of America Goes to Washington City*, New York 1997, S.1.

In Elif Saydams *All-Girl Medieval Torture Summer Camp* – den Titel habe ich für diesen Aufsatz geklaut – wird kein Unterschied zwischen Süße und Sadismus gemacht. Hier ist selbst der Todestrieb niedlich. Für *The Producer* wird ein Kreuz aus Jeansstoff mit gespreizten Beinen auf ein rechteckiges Metallgitter geschnallt und an den Enden mit Kabelbindern fixiert – das Ganze mutet wie einer von Hallies Streichen im Camp Walden an. Mein Blick wandert voyeuristisch zum Spalt im Zentrum des Kreuzes, einer Art Schritt mit einem kleinen Metallloch, durch das der Kabelbinder gefädelt und gezogen wurde. Andere, gedrungenere Kreuze aus der Serie wiederum haben größere Löcher. Sie kommen durch Falten im Stoff zustande und formen eine Art Ausschnitt; über einem prangen eine rote Schleife und ein Schild mit der Aufschrift *OPEN*.

Die getrockneten Farfalle, Orangenscheiben, Strohzöpfe, Emoticons und Schleifen, mit denen diese Stoffkreuze verziert sind, lassen an kleine, sorgfältige Kinderhände beim Basteln denken. Außerdem erinnern diese Skulpturen unweigerlich an Kreuzigungen und eine ganze Reihe verwandter Foltermethoden, die eine große Faszination auf Schulkinder ausüben: das Zerreißen auf der Streckbank oder das Vierteilen durch Pferde. Vielleicht entspricht dies in gewisser Weise der kindlichen Vorstellung von mittelalterlicher Folter: lustig, anmutig und erotisch, wobei die Gewalt nicht abwesend, sondern metaphorisch ist.

Neuerdings fertigt mein Boyfriend Gray Wielebinski am großen Tisch in unserer Wohnung in Philadelphia pornografische Tuschezeichnungen an. Sie zeigen hypermaskuline, halb-menschliche Wesen, gefesselt an Gestelle, die vage an die Metallgitter von Saydams Sommercamp-Skulpturen erinnern. Gehüllt in knappe athletische Monturen, die Muskeln offenbaren, die sich vergeblich – und vielleicht unaufrichtig – gegen ihre eigene Gebundenheit stemmen, scheinen diese Kreaturen aus der Traumwelt meiner Kindheit über einen bestimmten Kanal wieder in mein Leben getreten zu sein. In ihren maskierten Gesichtern erkenne ich genau den Ausdruck, den meine eigenen Folterfantasien hervorrufen wollten: zusammengebissene Zähne, widerwillige Kapitulation, stumme Wollust.

Noch in der Grundschule zerstörte ich sämtliche meiner Bondage- und Torture-Zeichnungen und stopfte sie in den großen Mülleimer in der Küche unserer Wohnung. Ich lag panisch wach bei dem Gedanken, dass meine Mutter sie finden könnte, weil ich (zu Recht) davon überzeugt war, dass die Macht dieser Zeichnungen etwas Unbändiges, Gefährliches und Unnatürliches barg. Ich wünschte, ich könnte das kleine Mädchen zu A.G.M.T.S.C. mitnehmen und ihm all die Perversen vorstellen, die ich liebe und die mich lieben. Ich frage mich, was er davon halten würde.

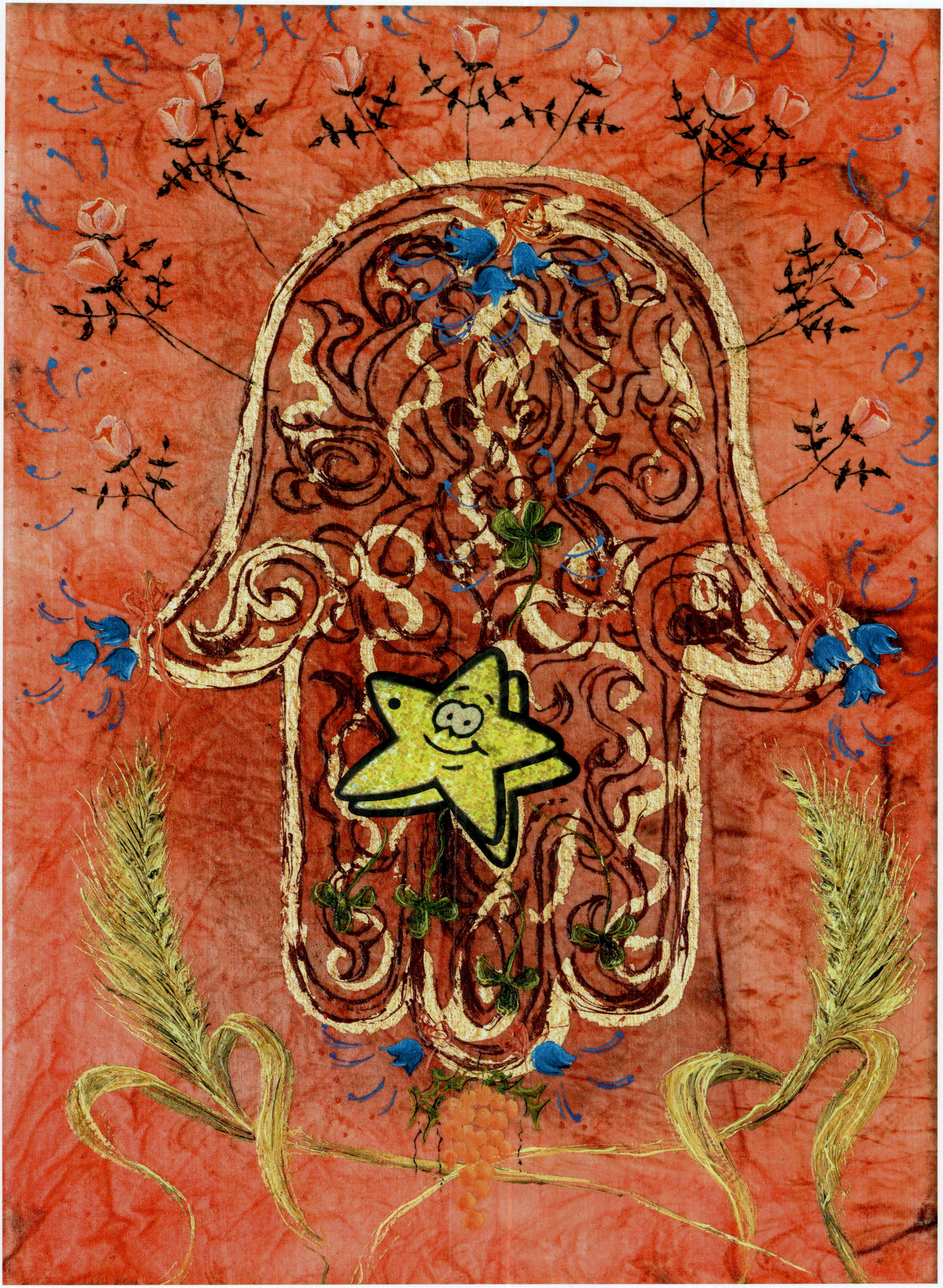

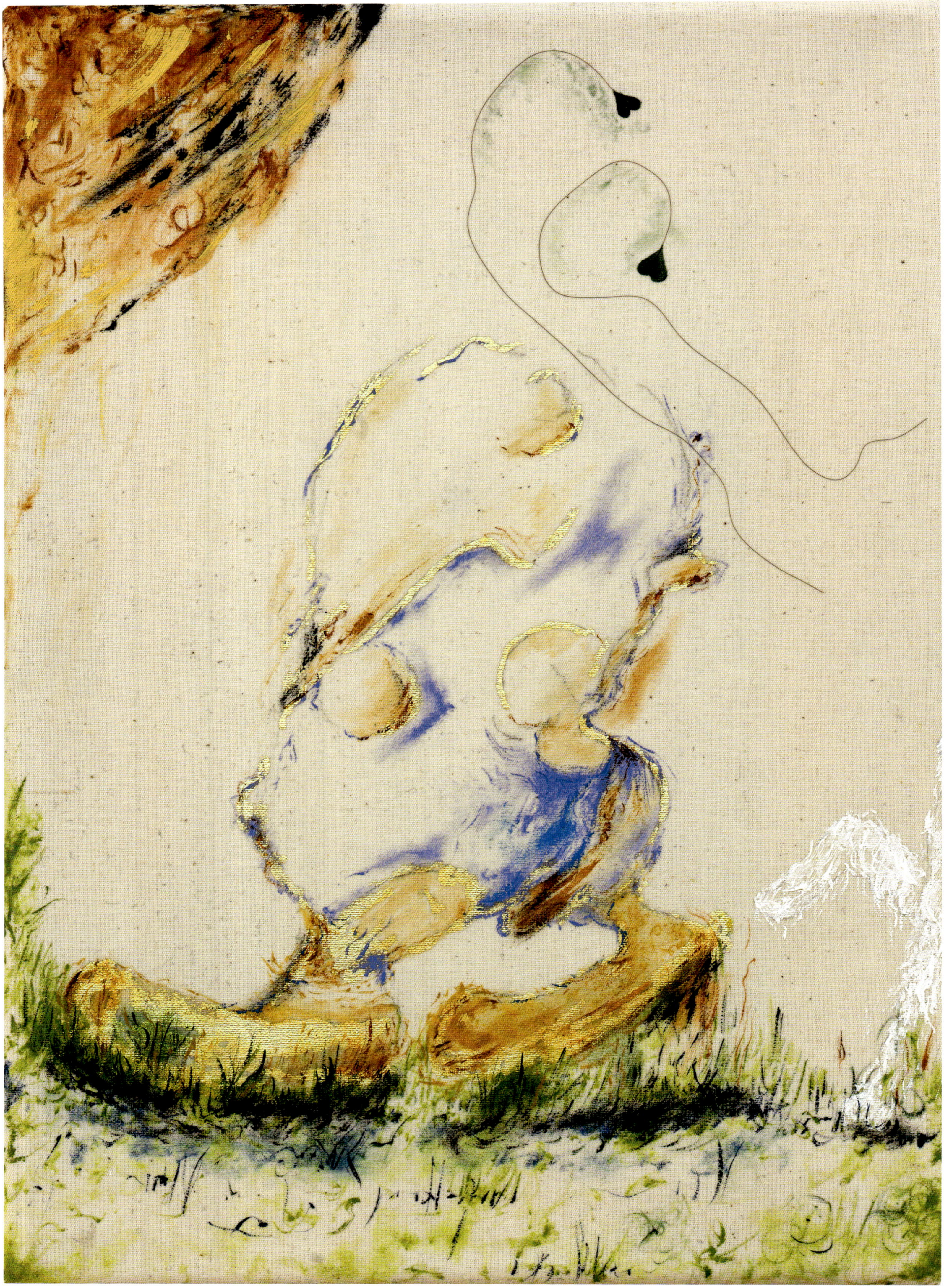

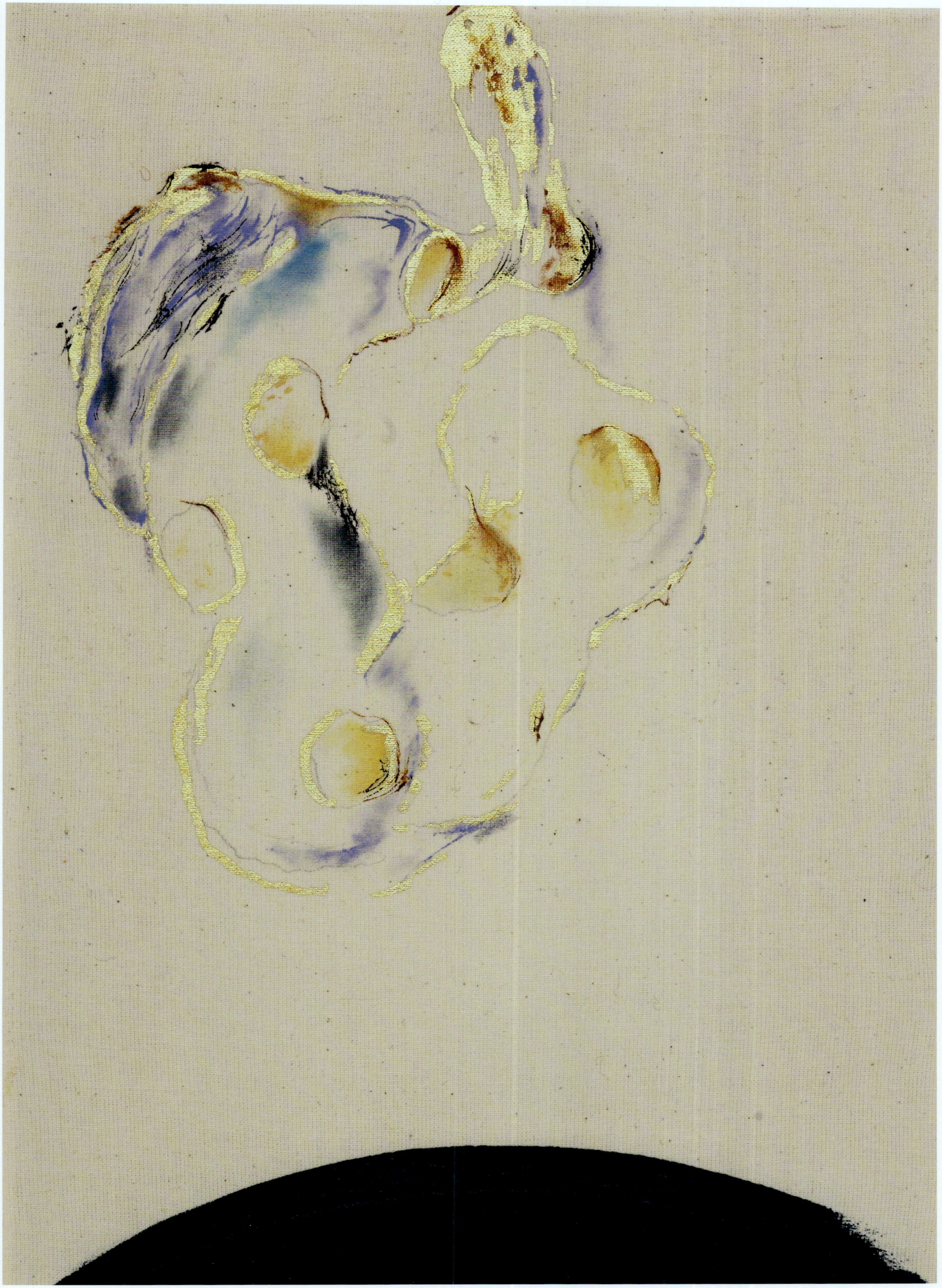

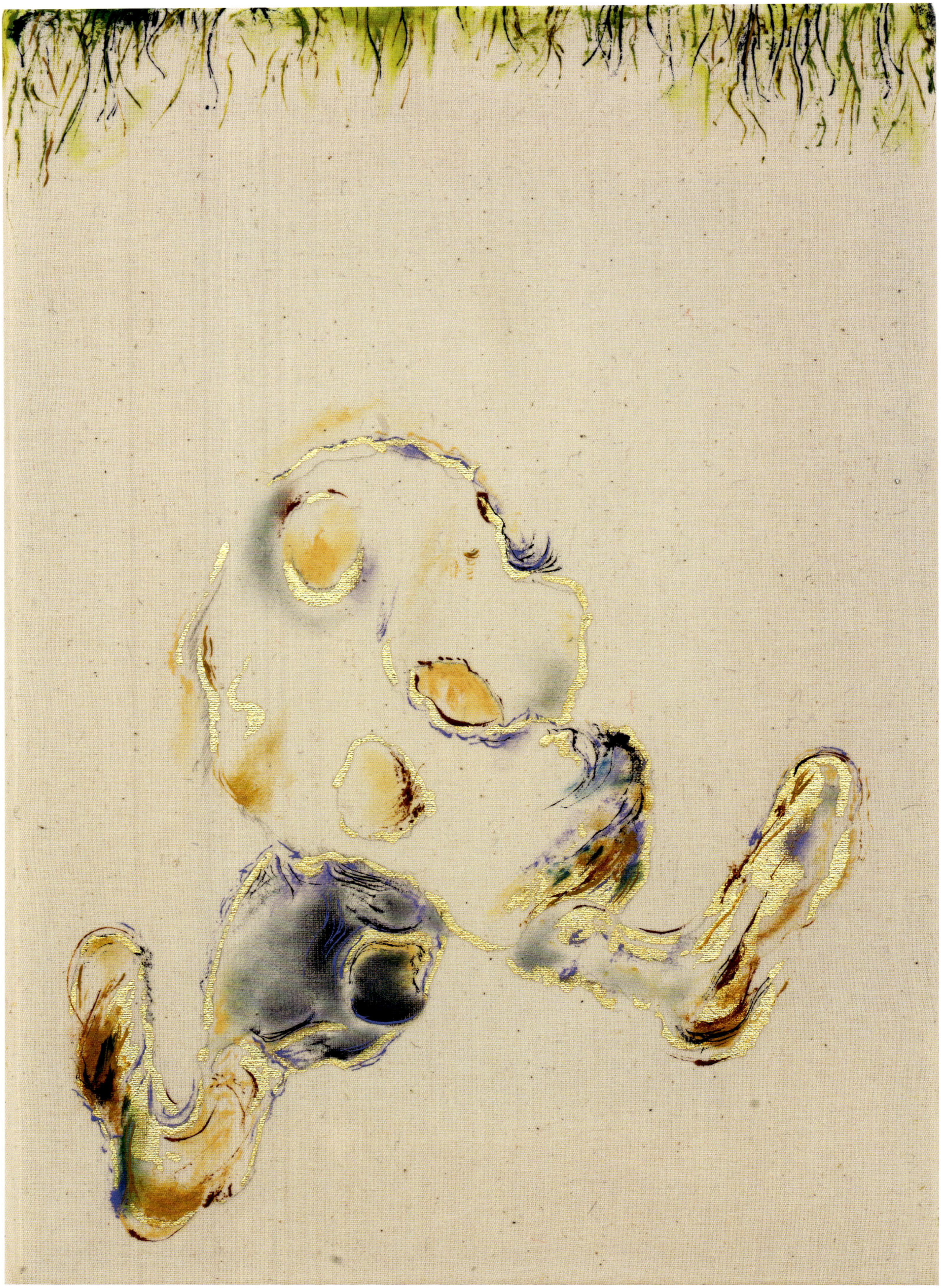

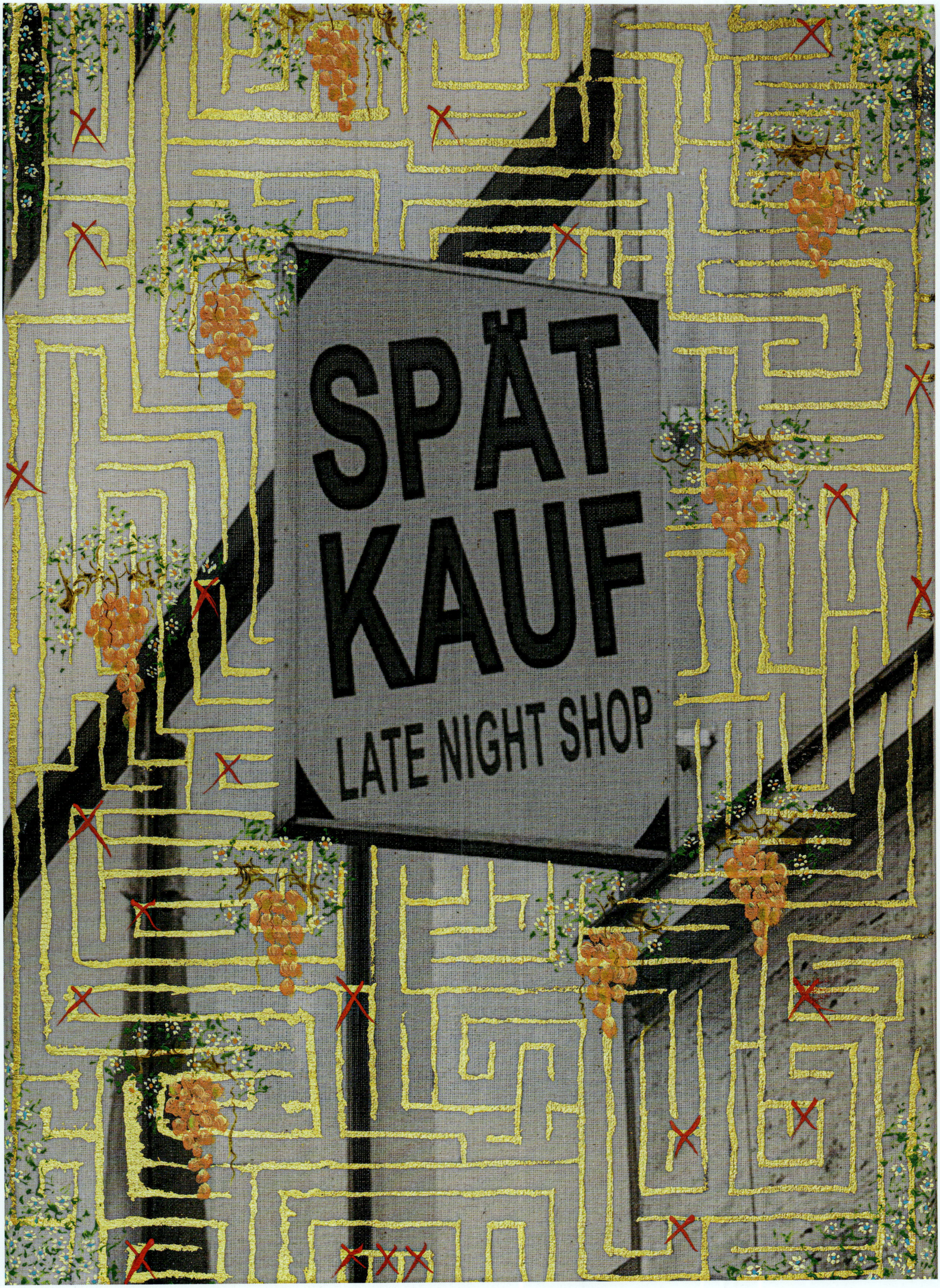
SPÄT
KAUF
LATE NIGHT SHOP

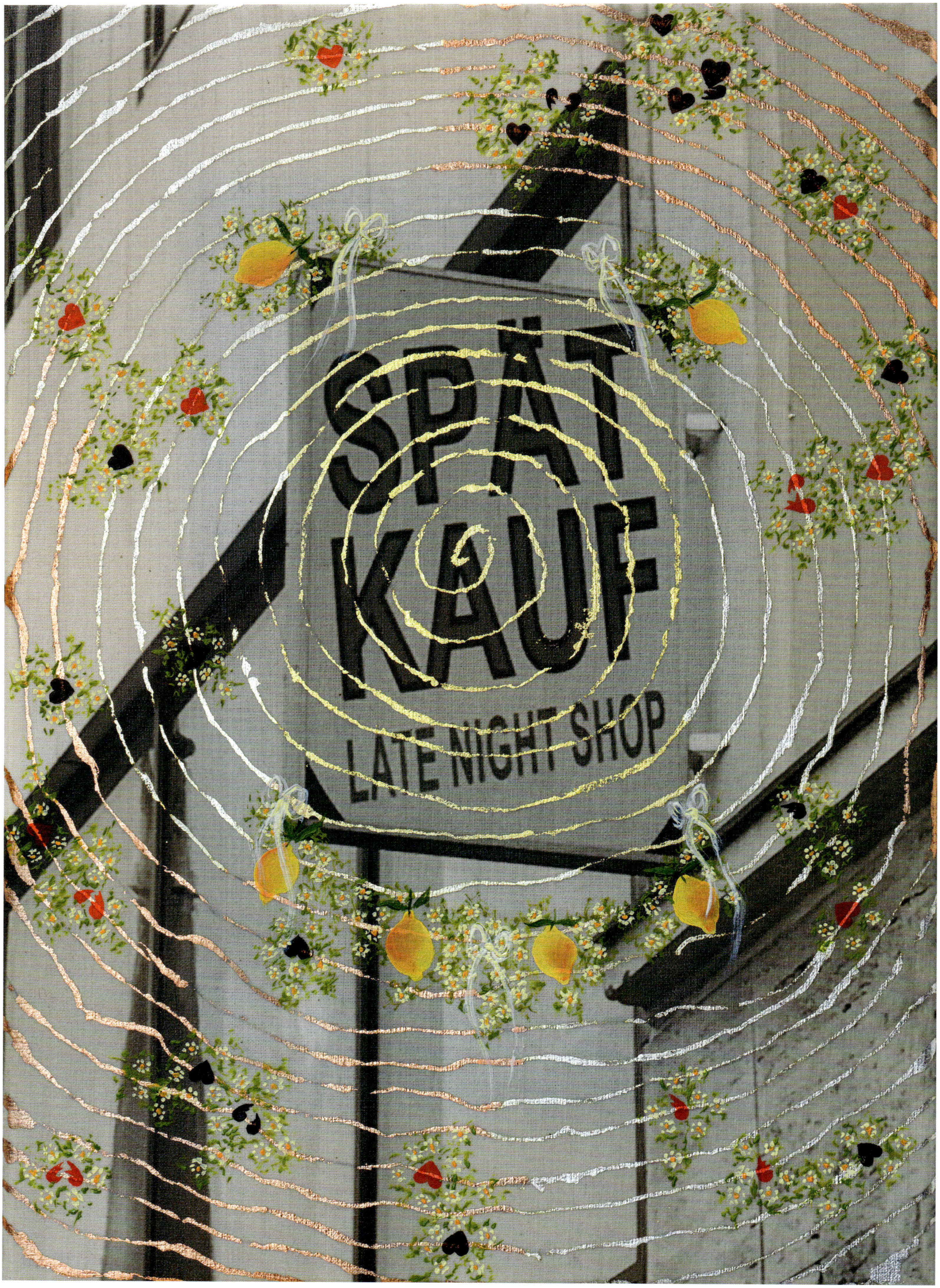
SPÄT
KAUF
LATE NIGHT SHOP

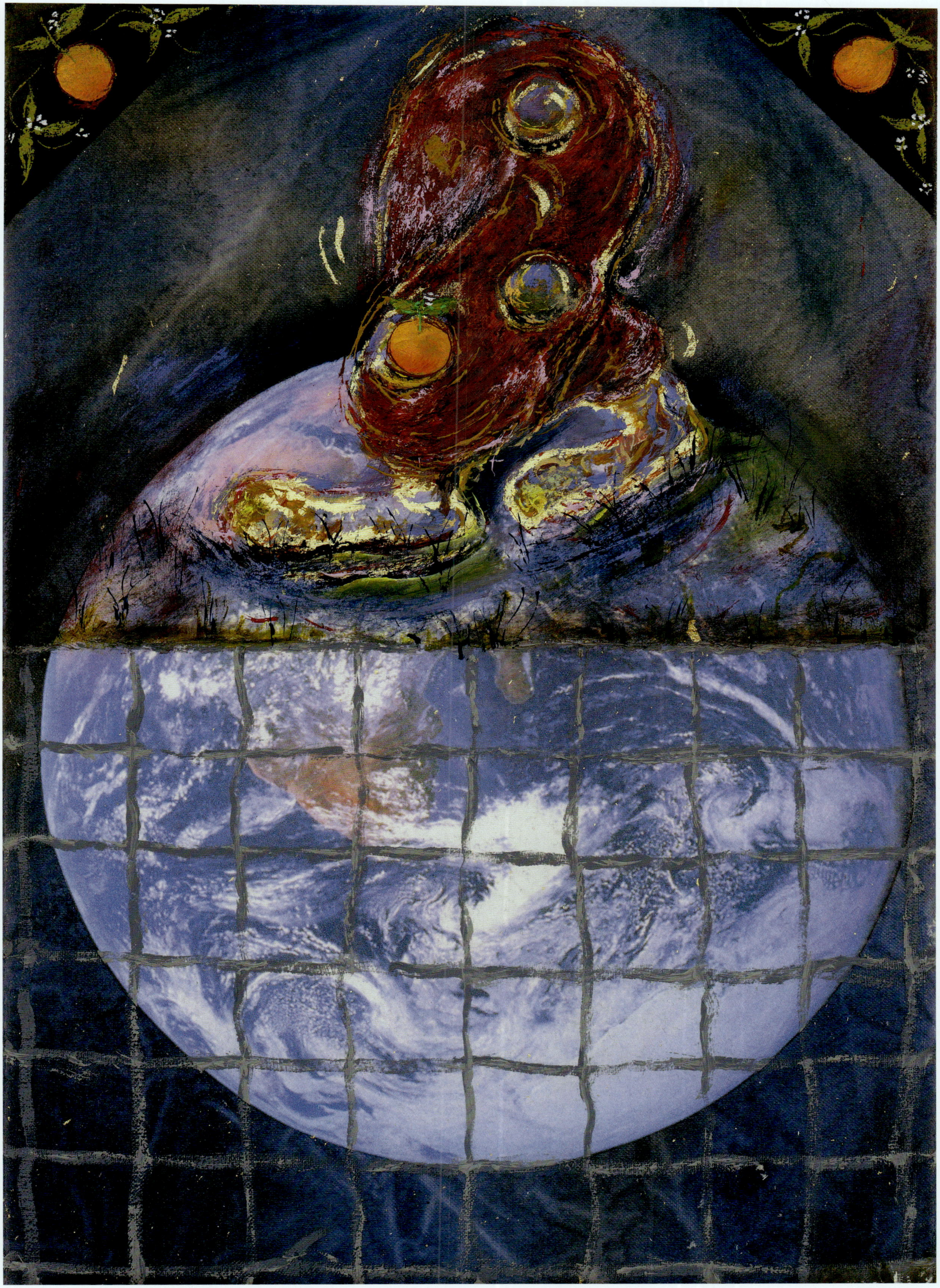

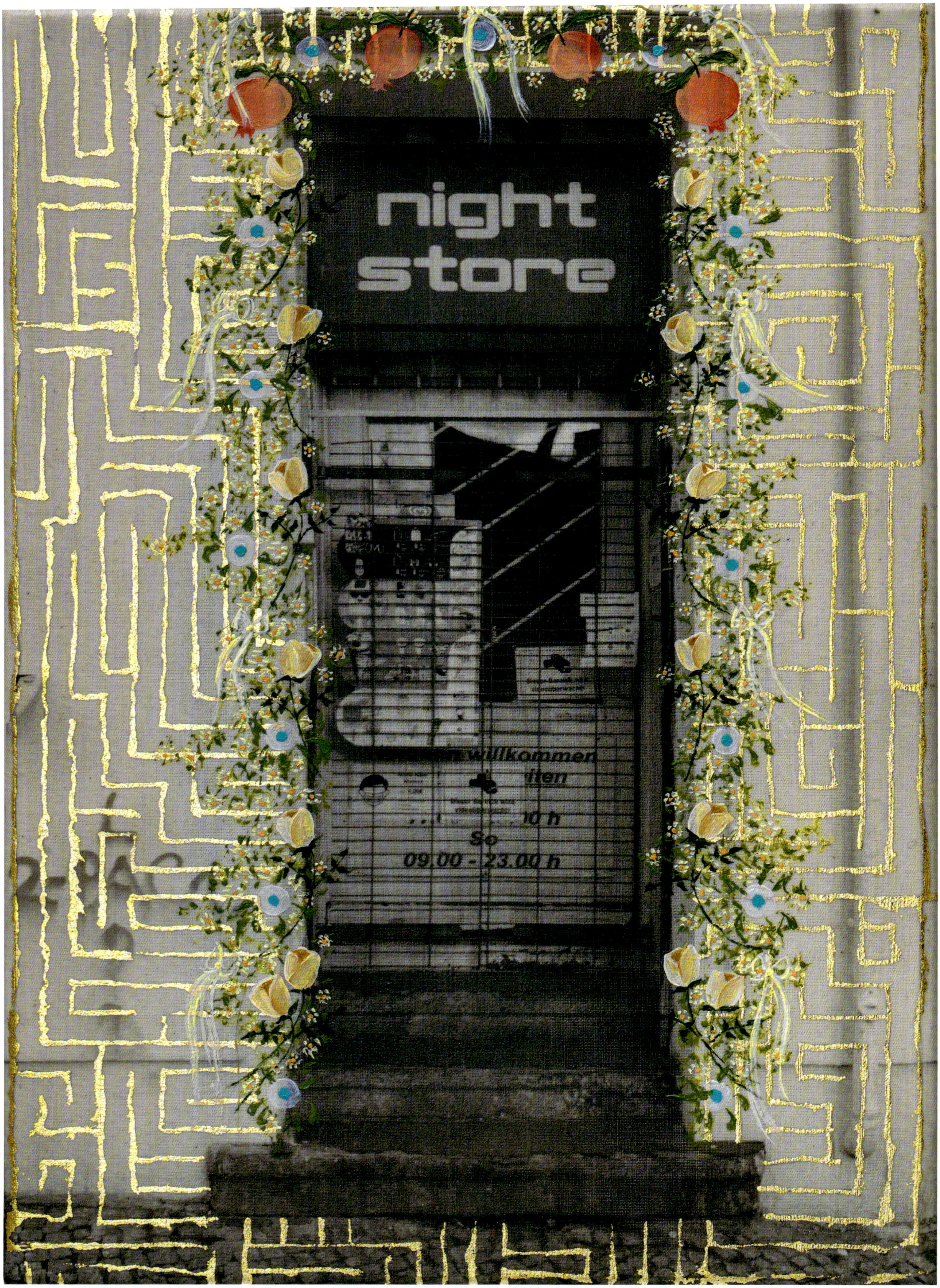
night
store
willkommen
So
09.00 - 23.00 h

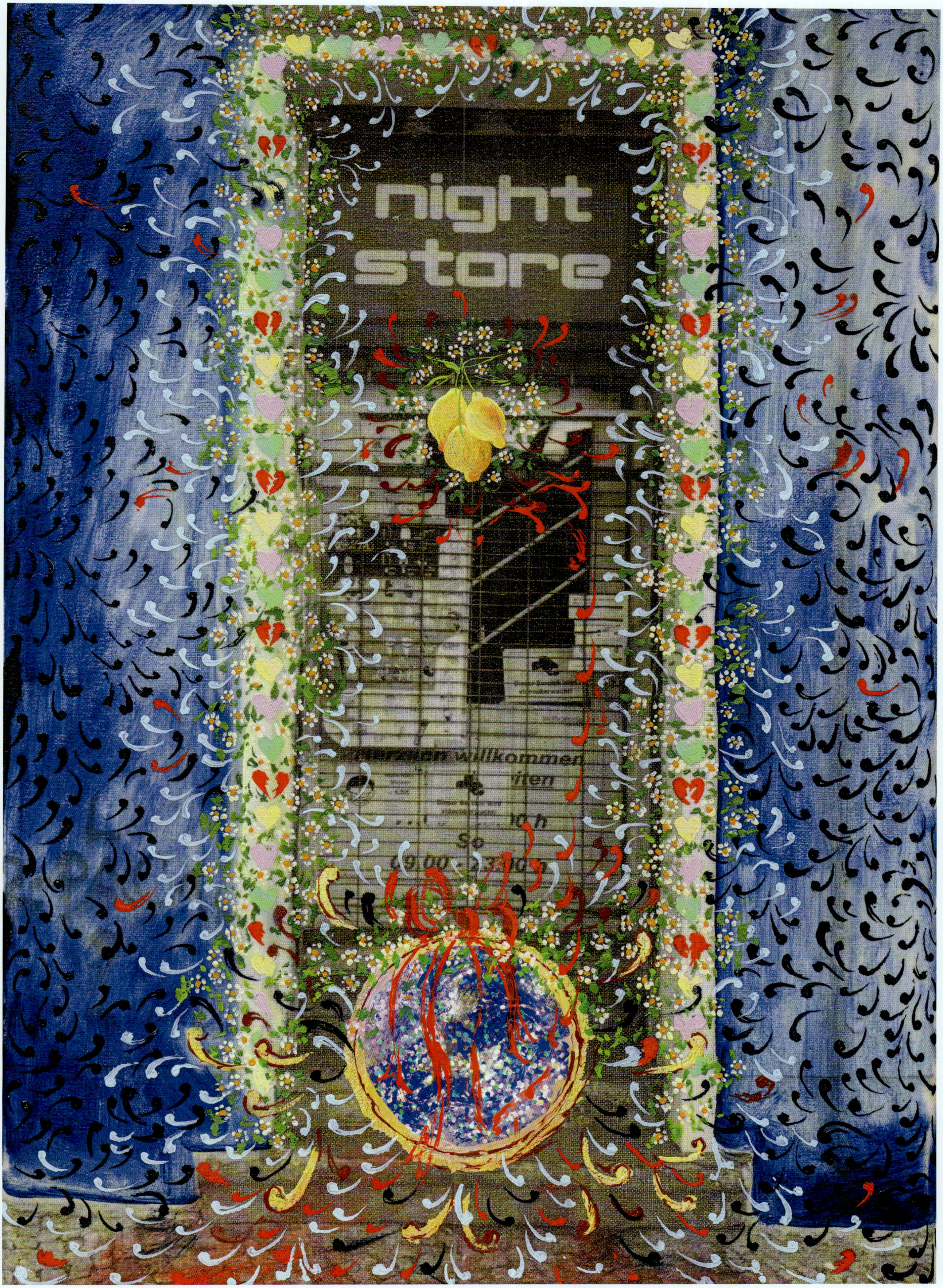
night
store
willkommen

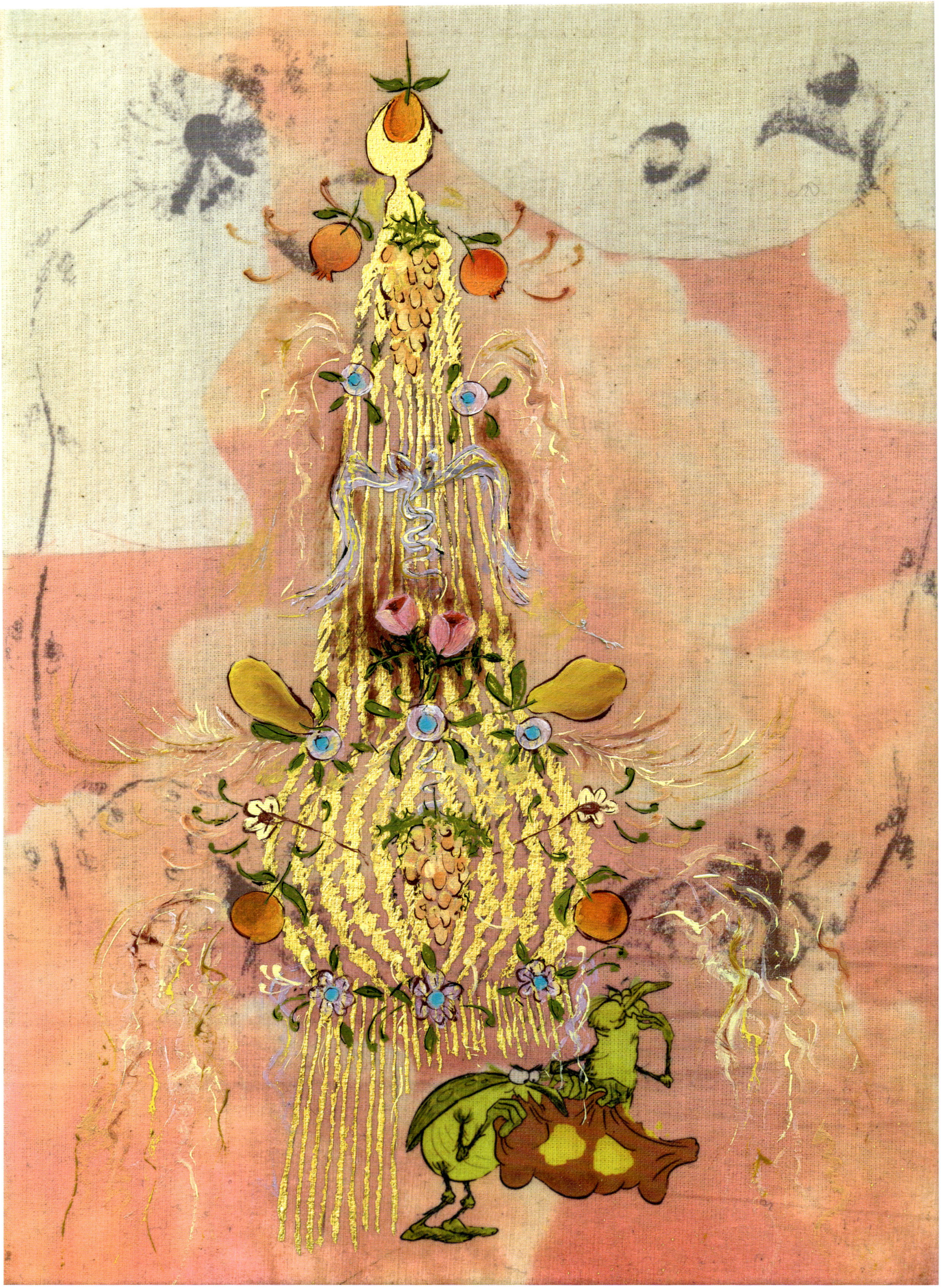

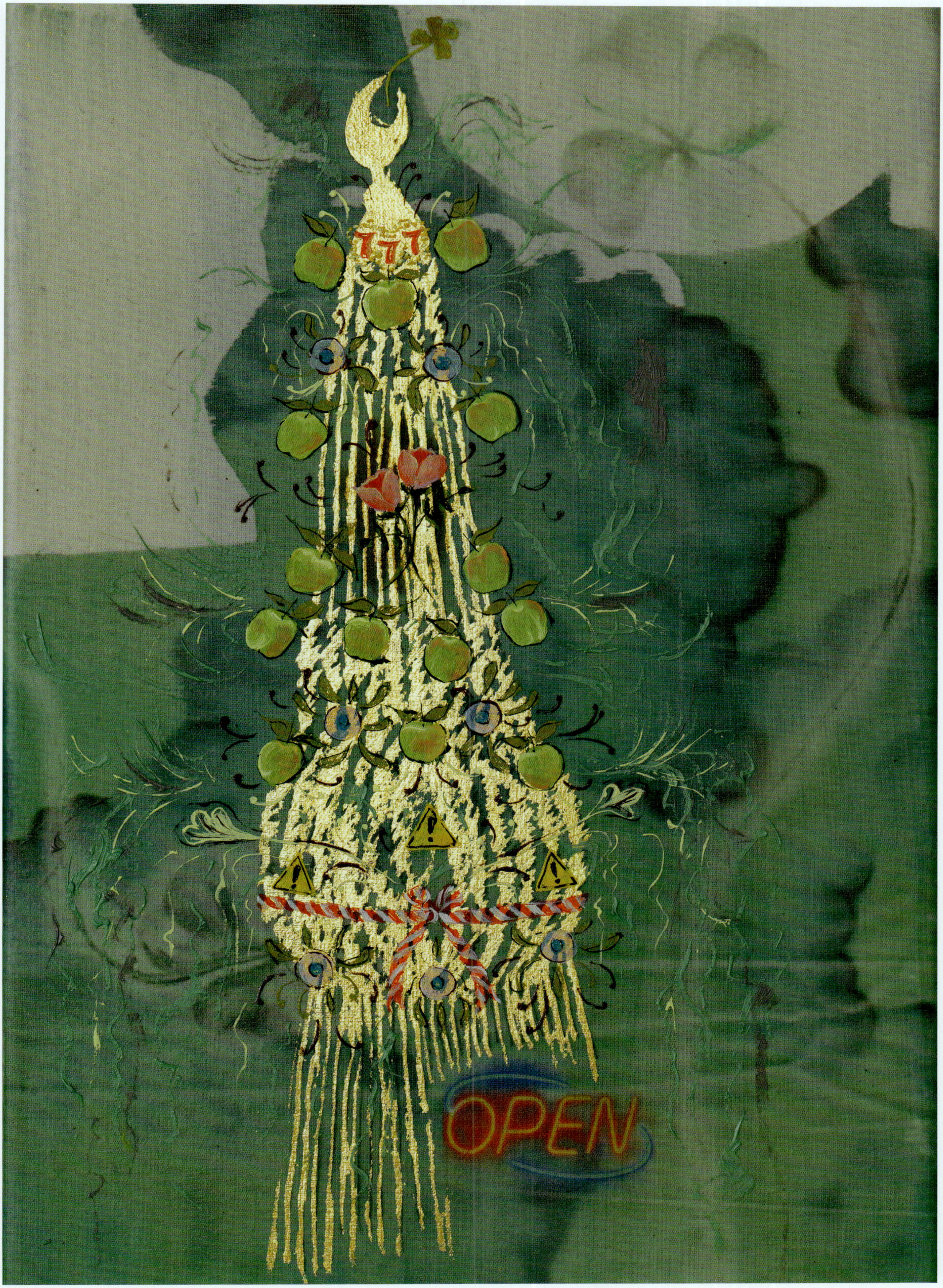
OPEN

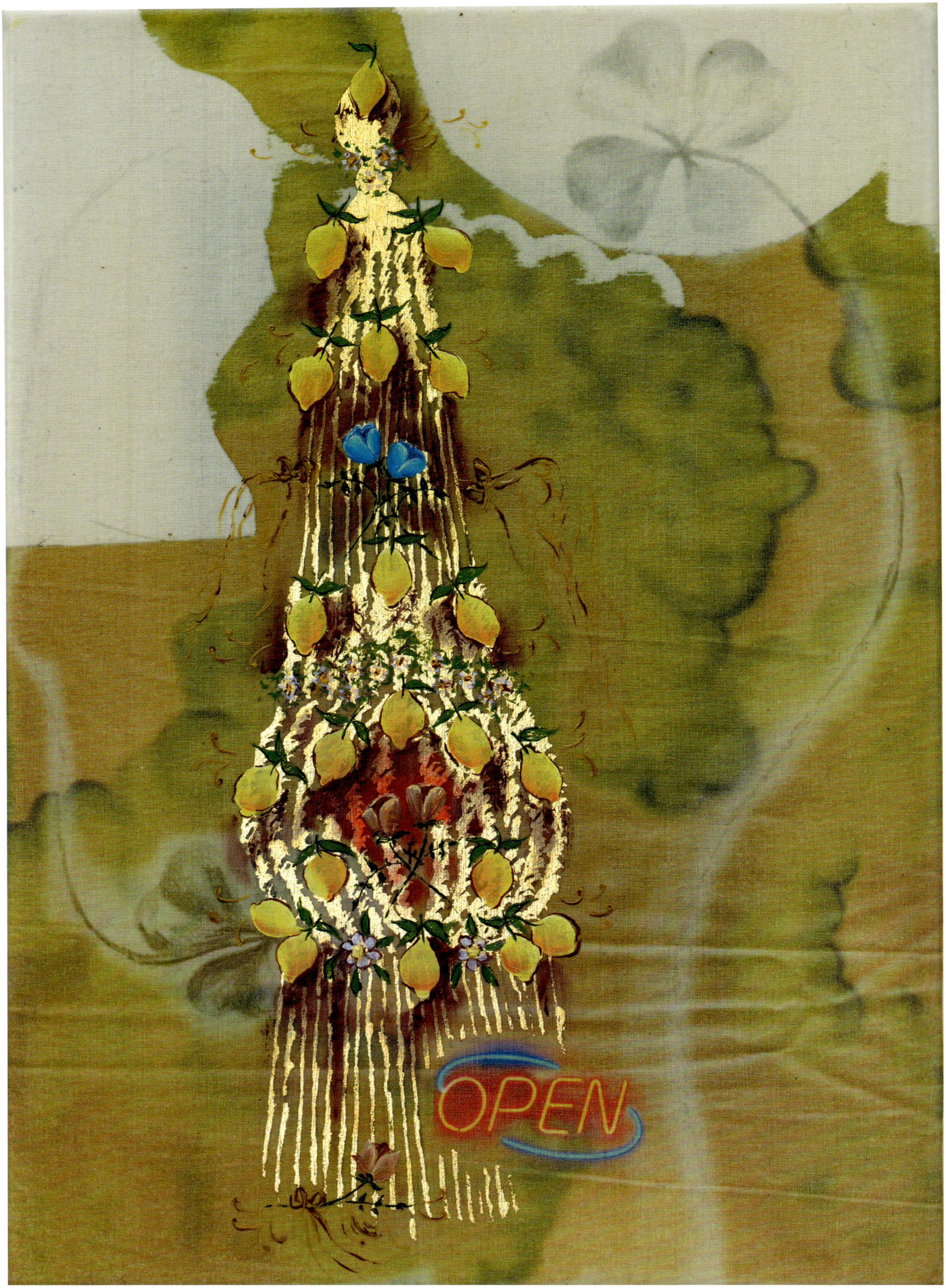
OPEN

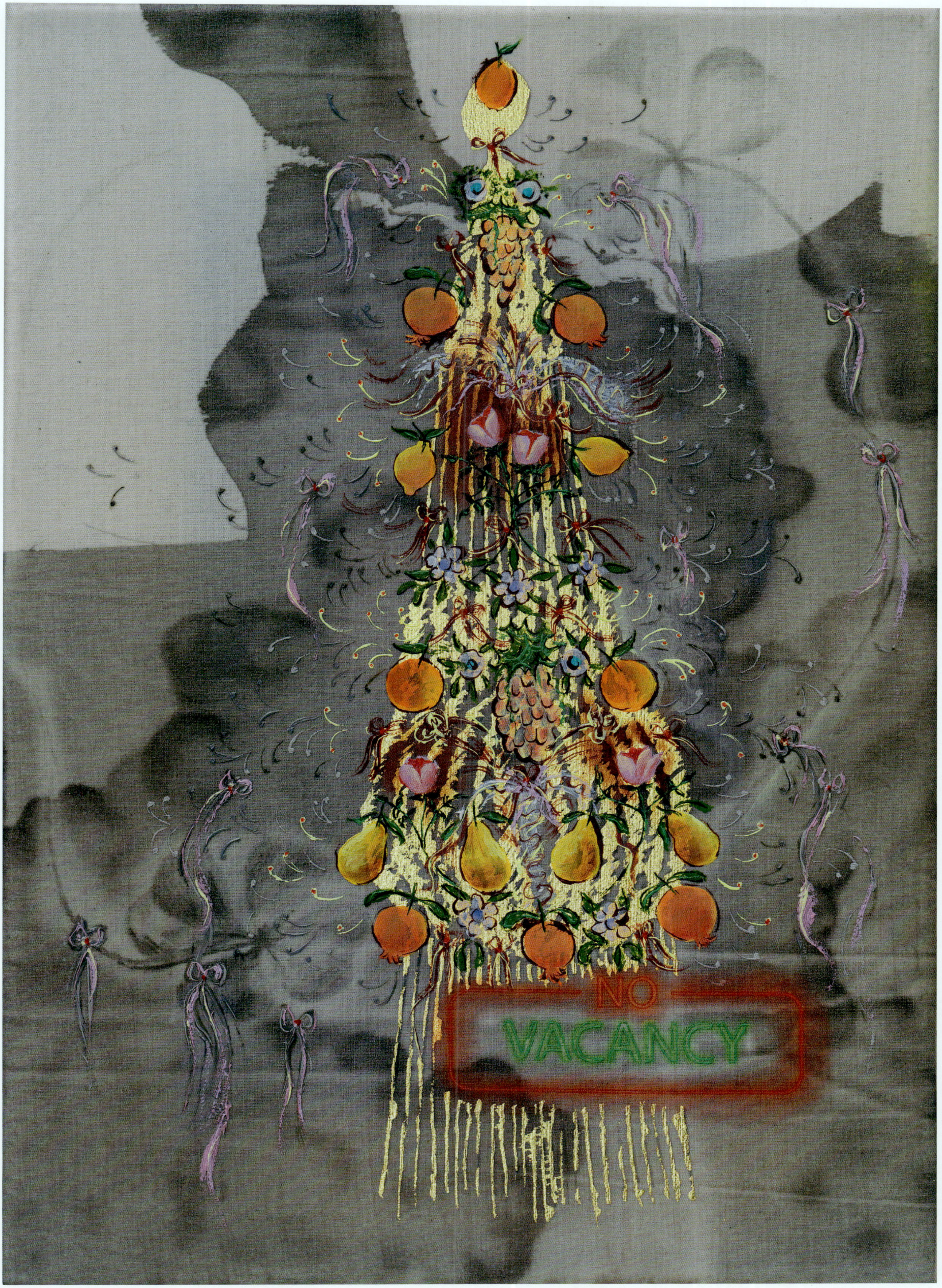
NO
VACANCY

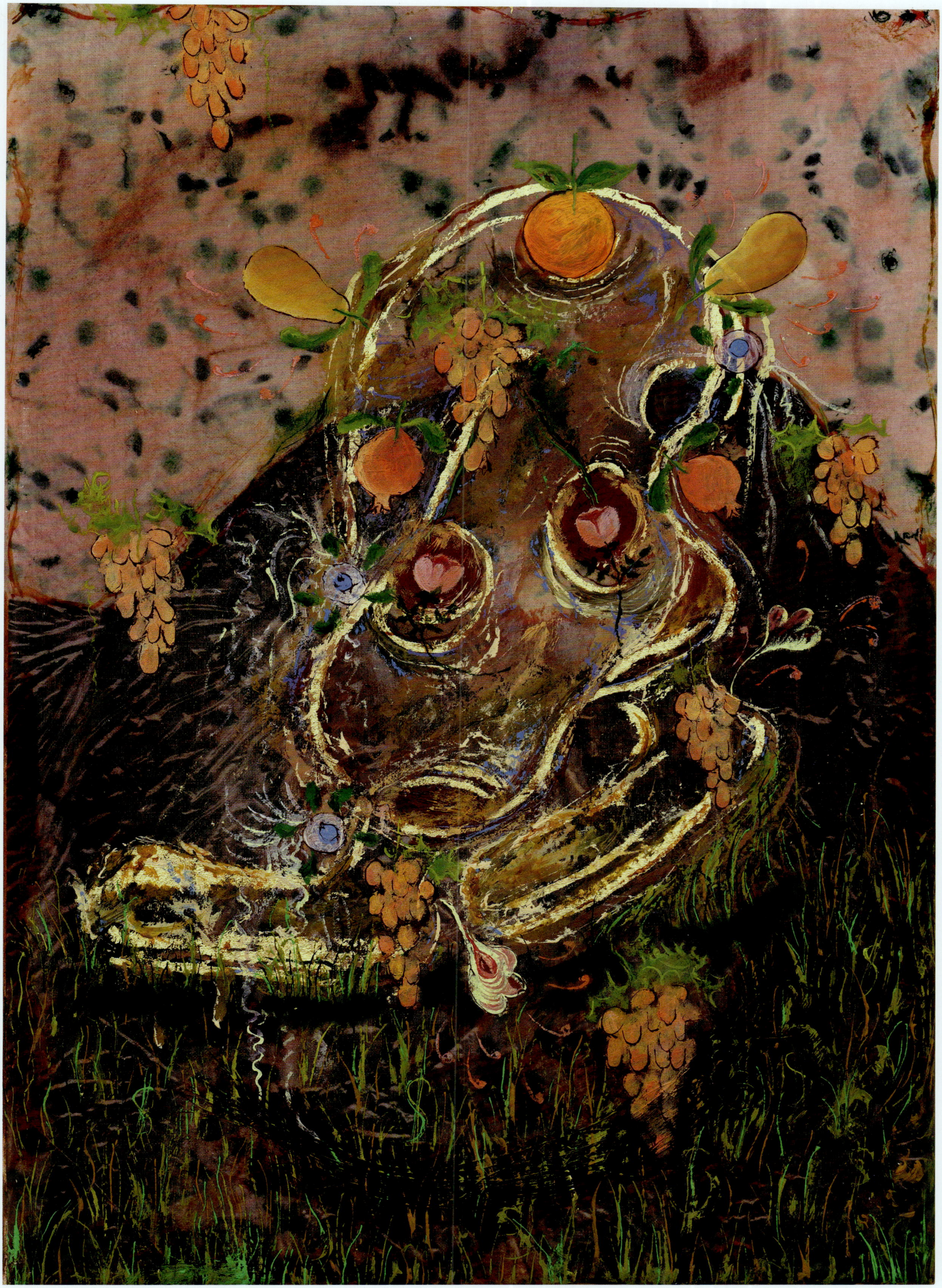

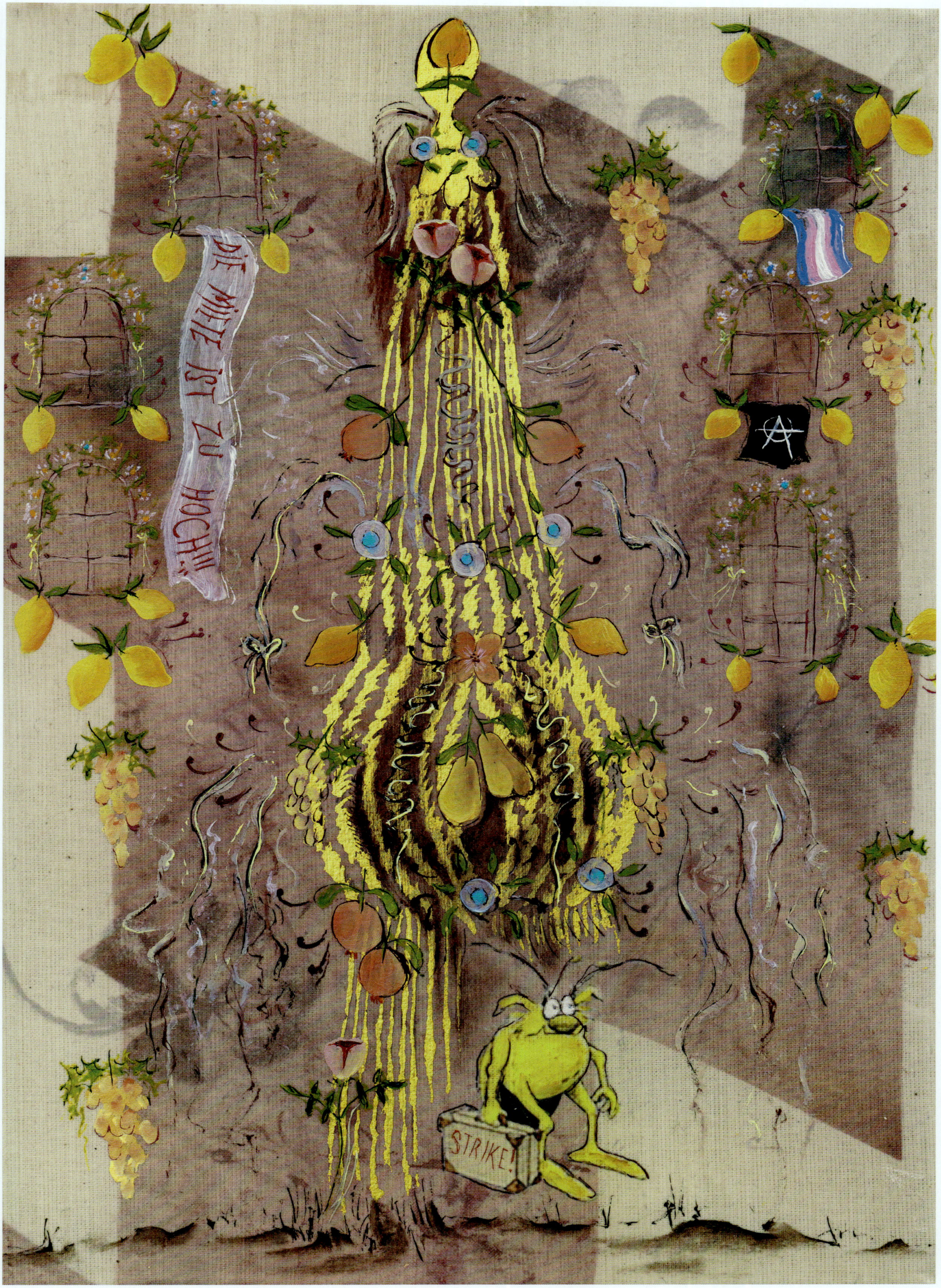
DIE MIETE IST ZU HOCH!!!
STRIKE!

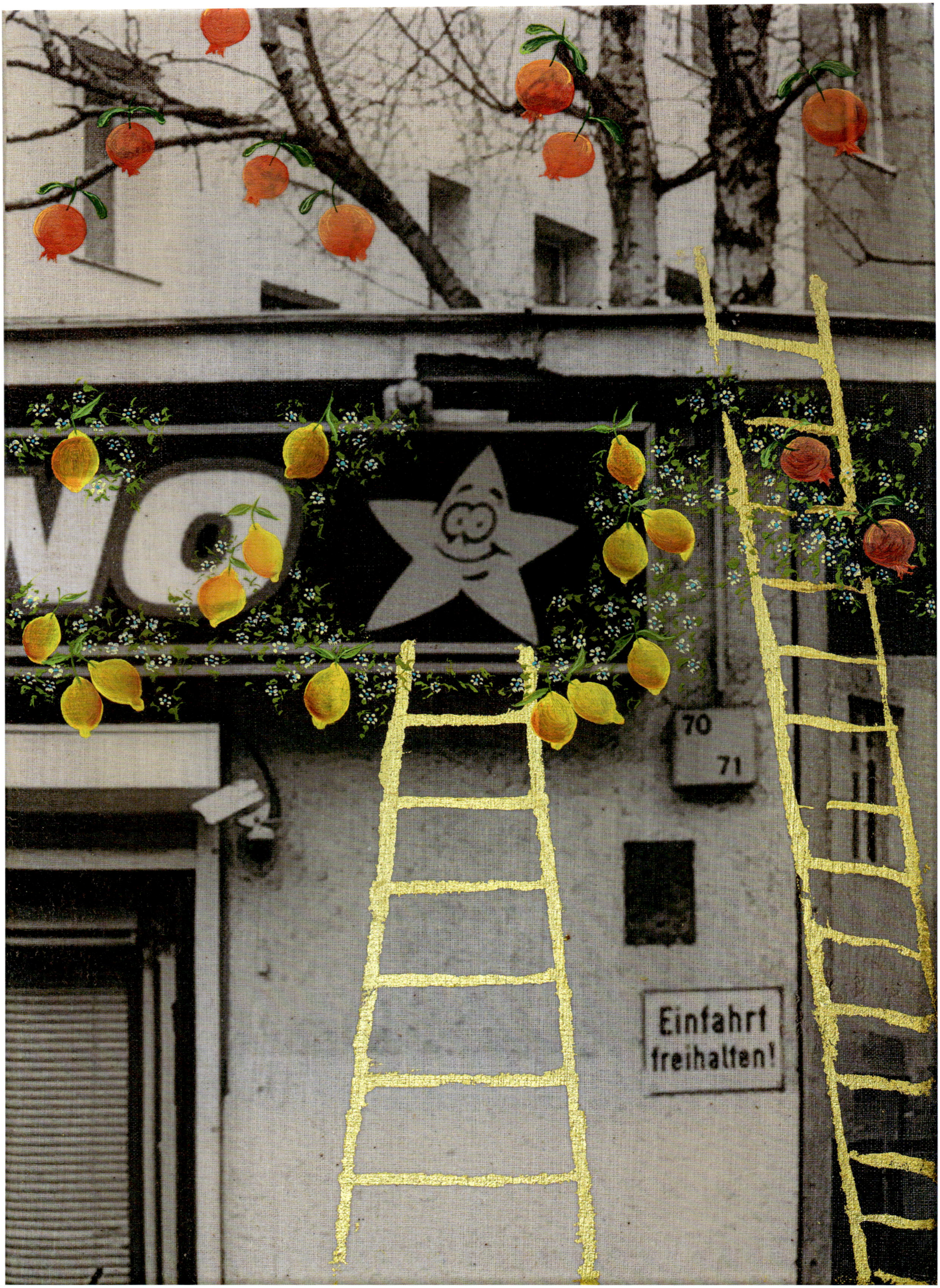
WO
70
71
Einfahrt
freihalten!

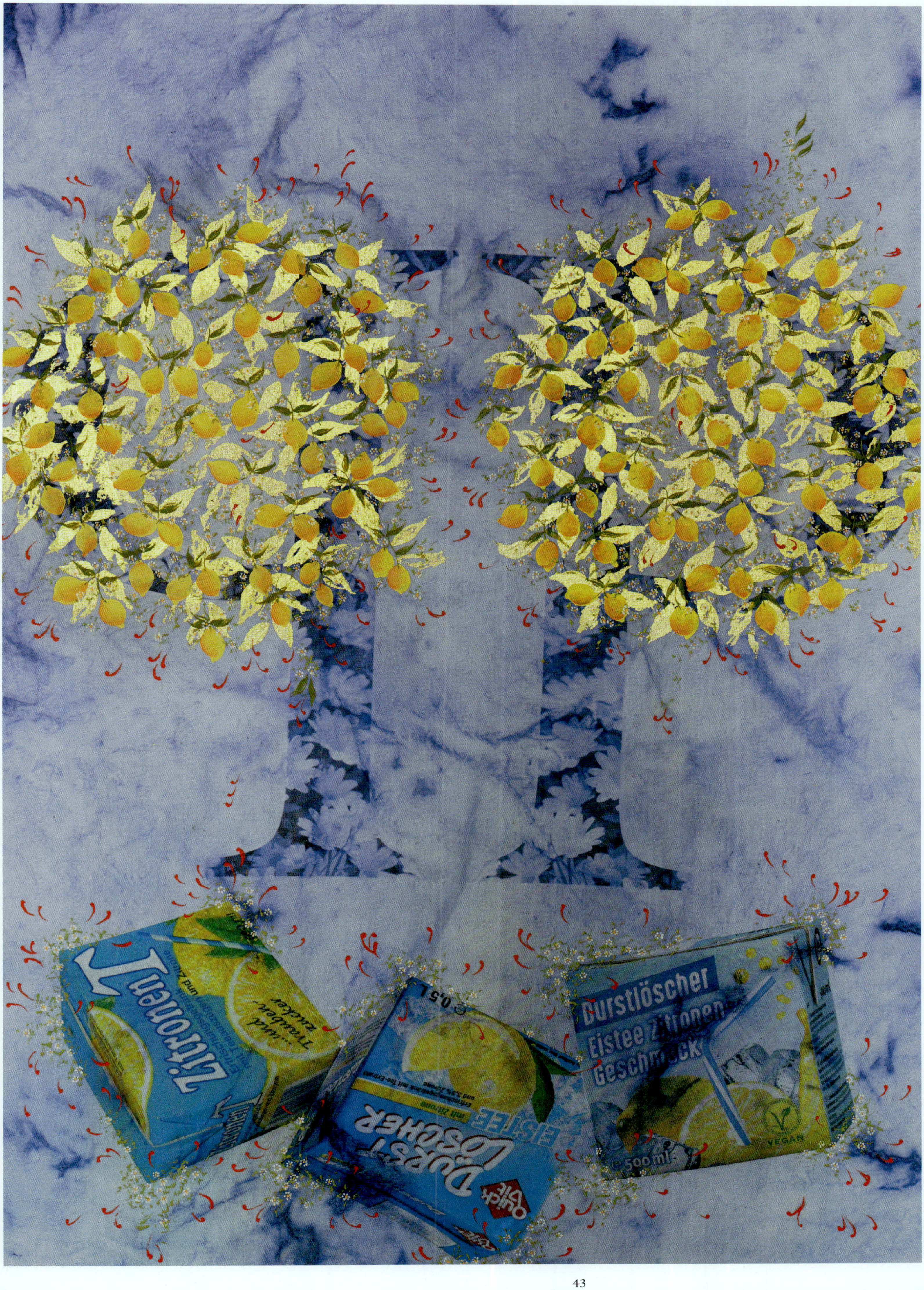

Durstlöscher
Eistee Zitronen Geschmack
500 ml
VEGAN
0,5 L

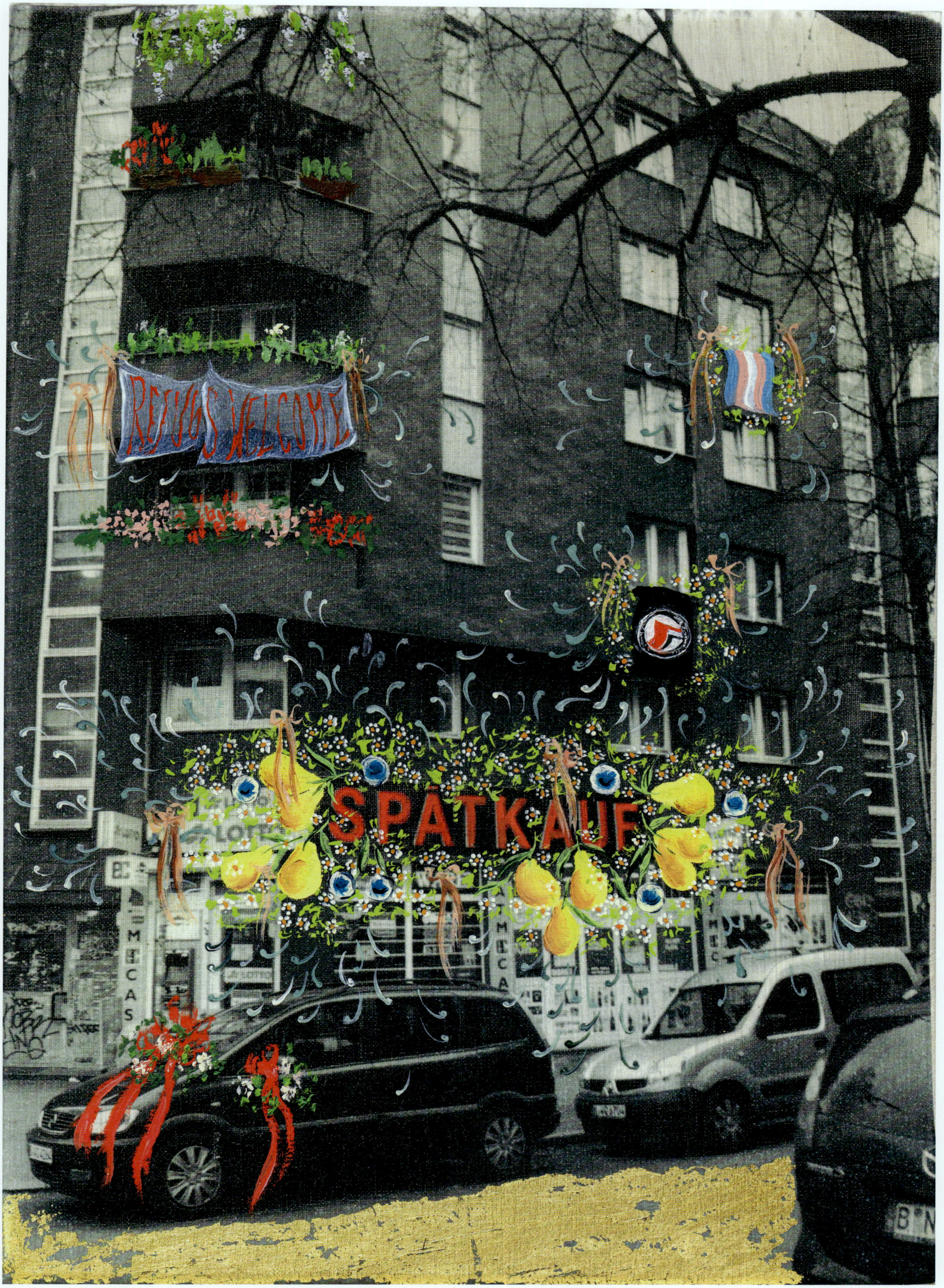
REFUGS WELCOME
SPÄTKAUF

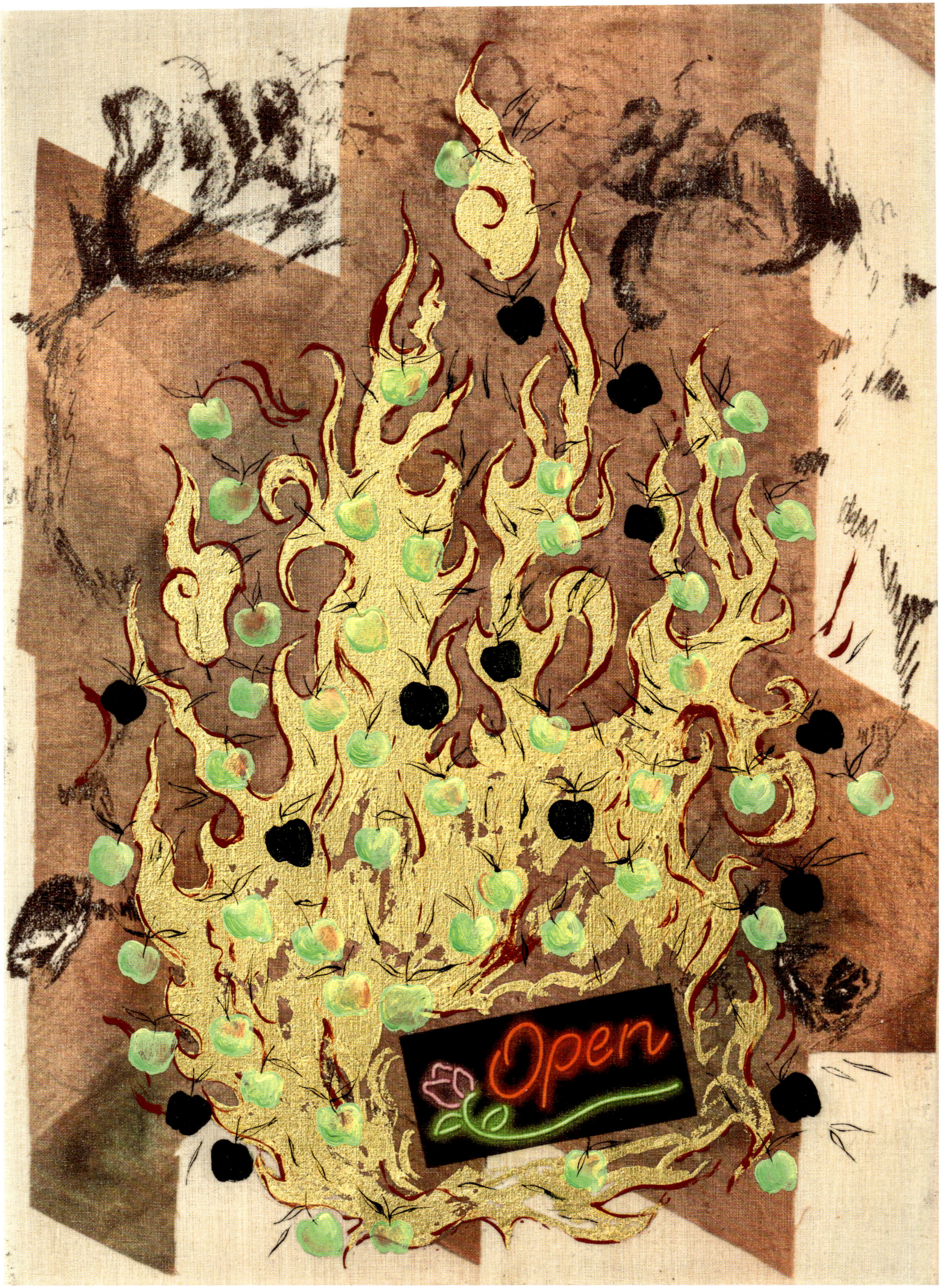
Open

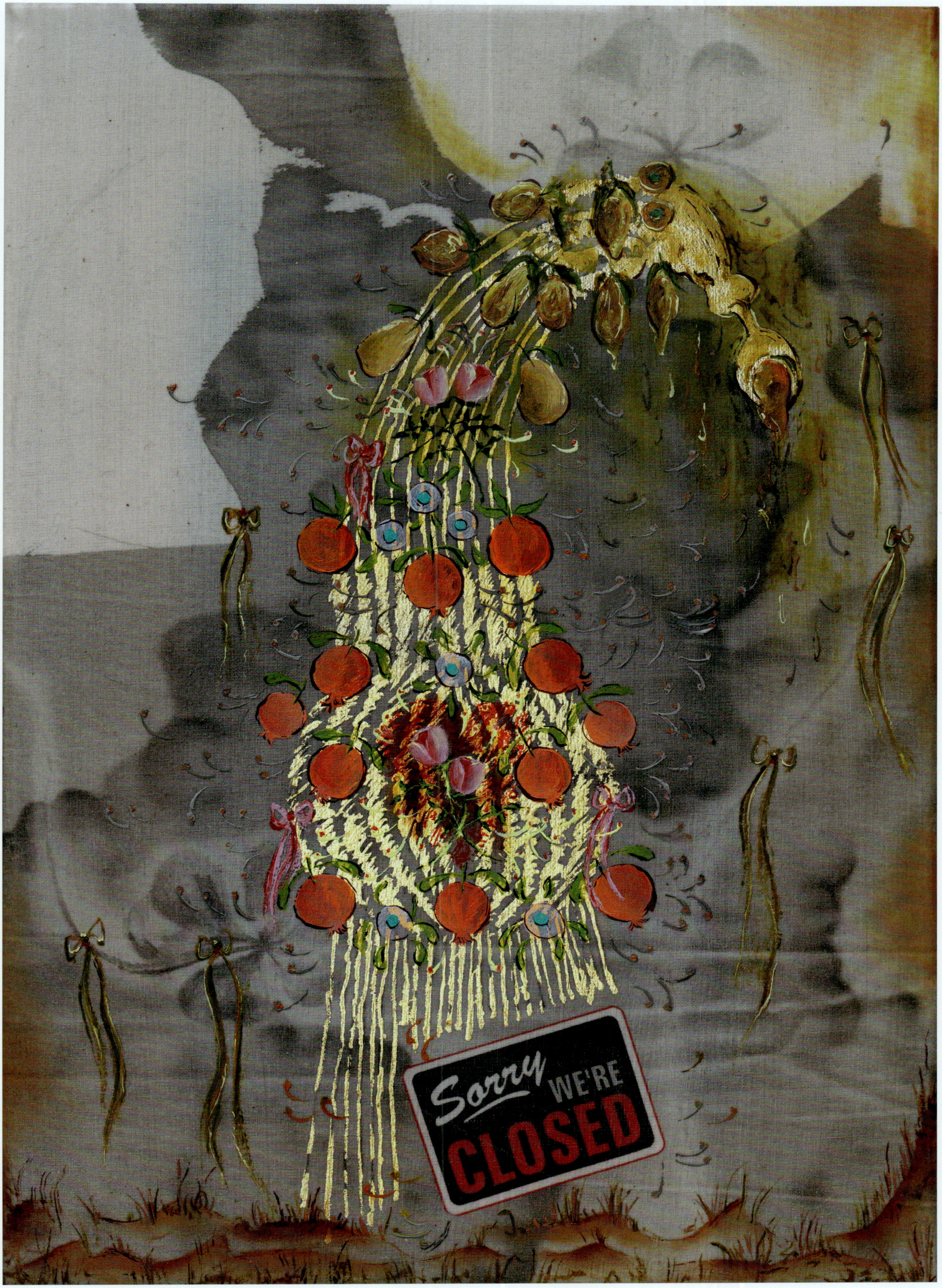
Sorry WE'RE
CLOSED

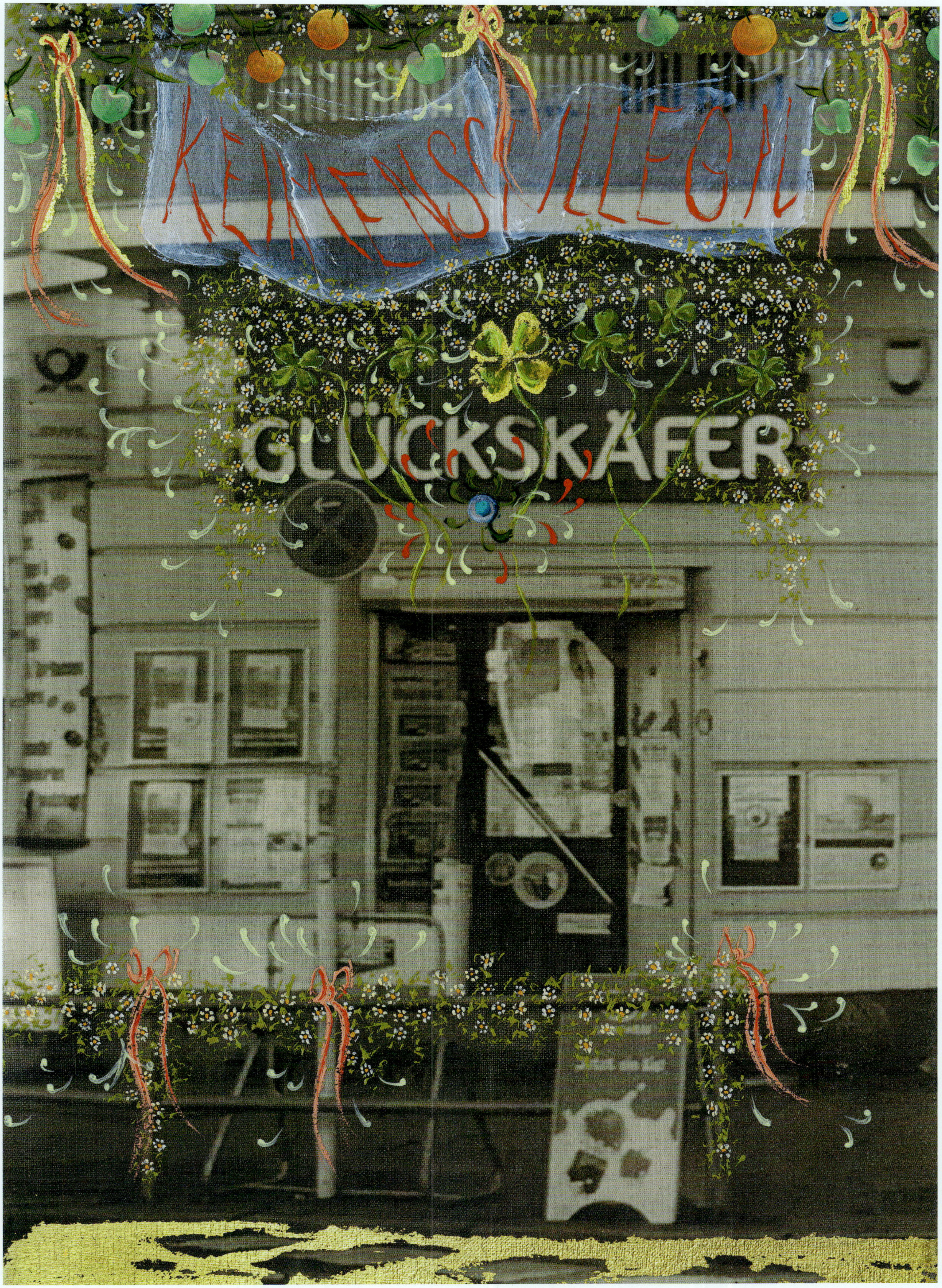
KEIMENSCHLEGH
GLÜCKSKÄFER

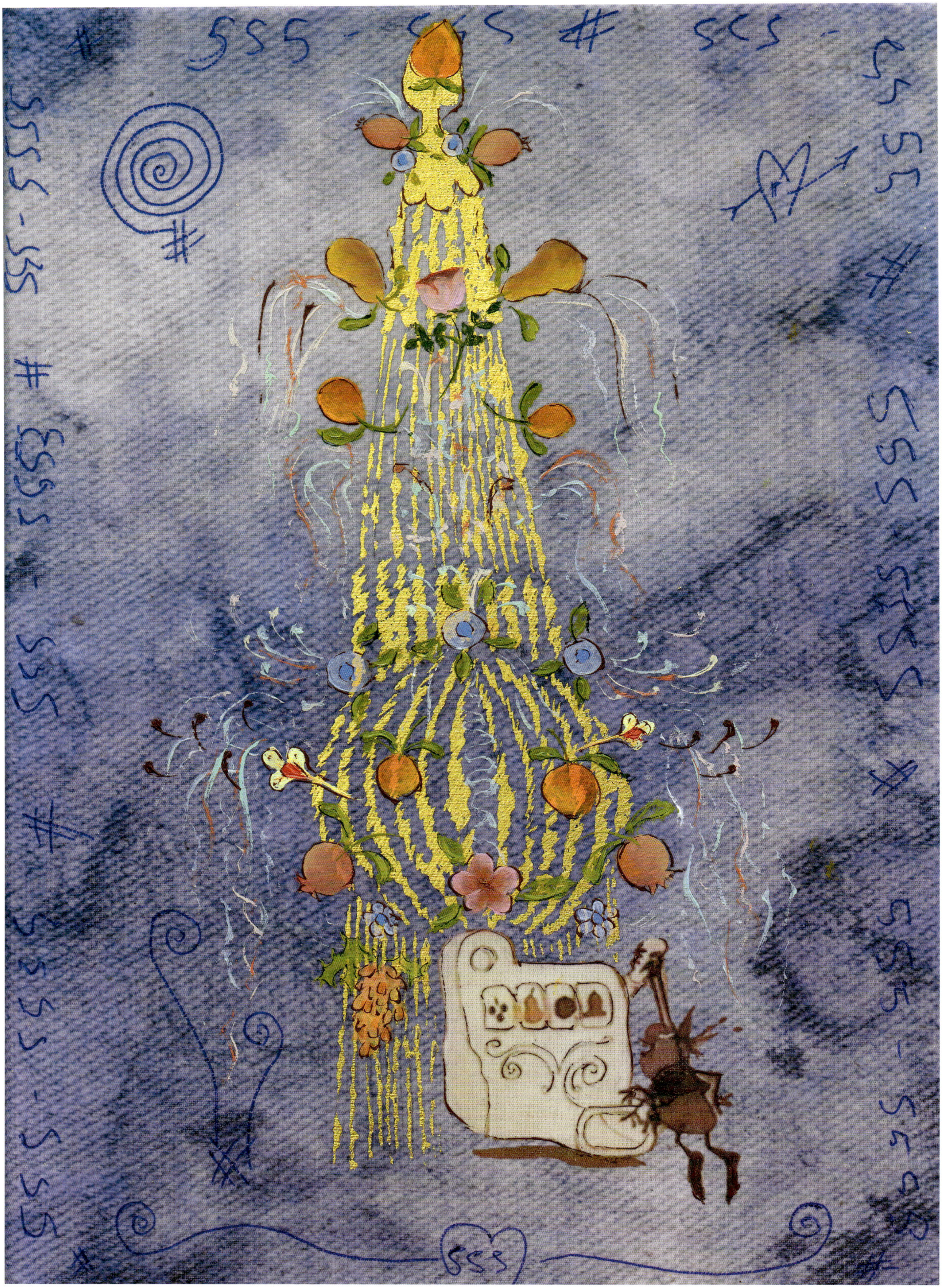

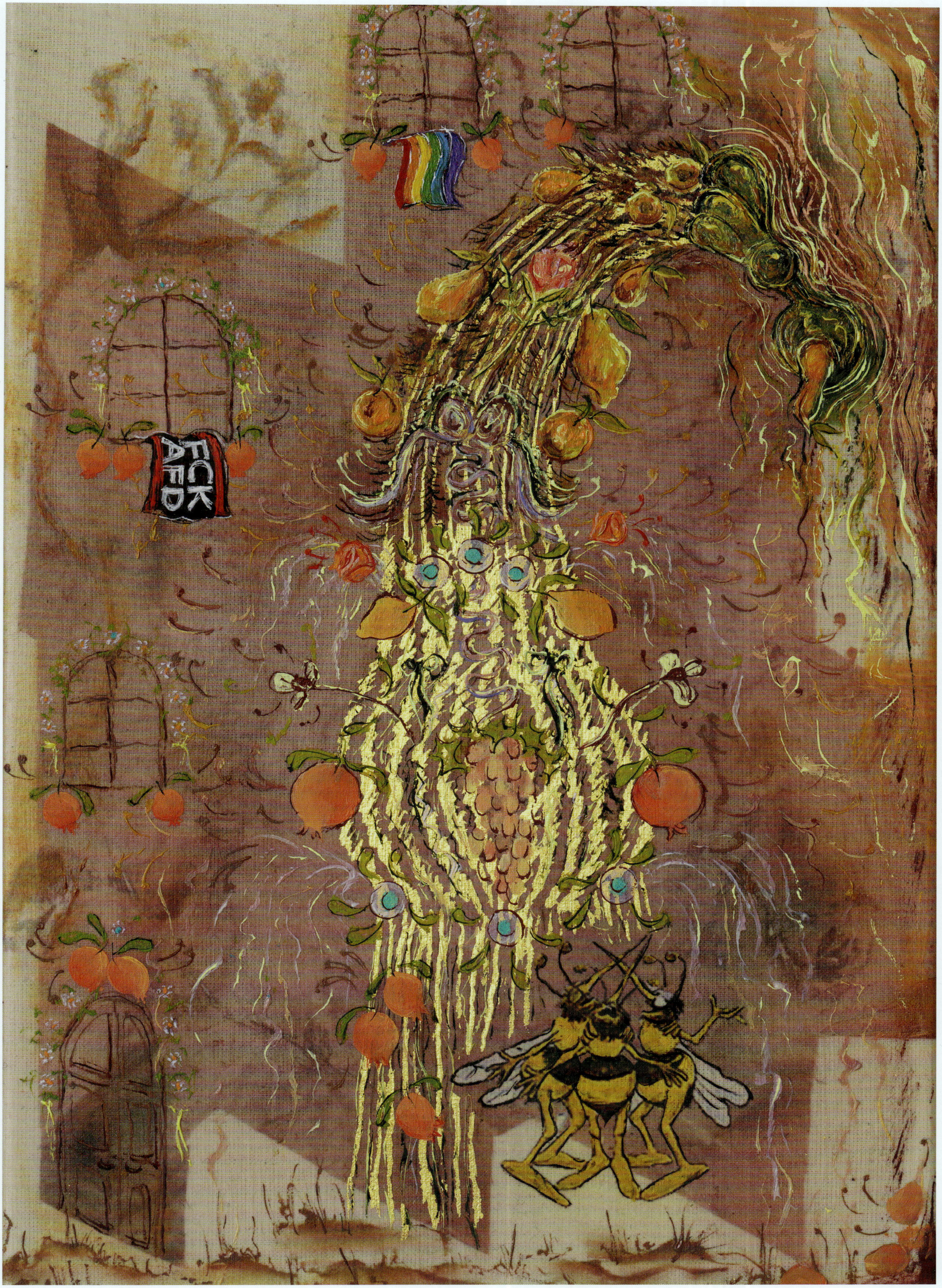
FCK
AFD

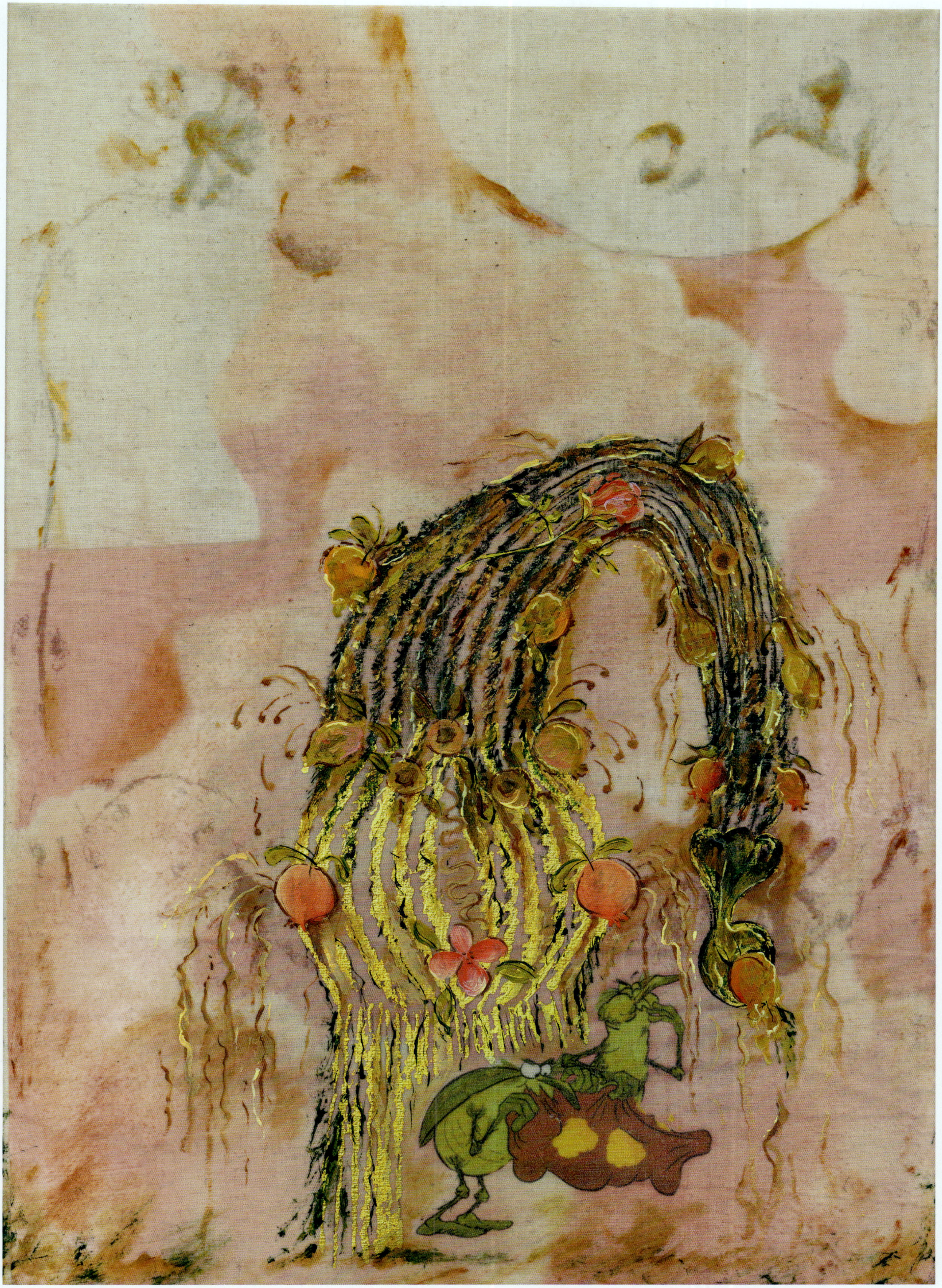

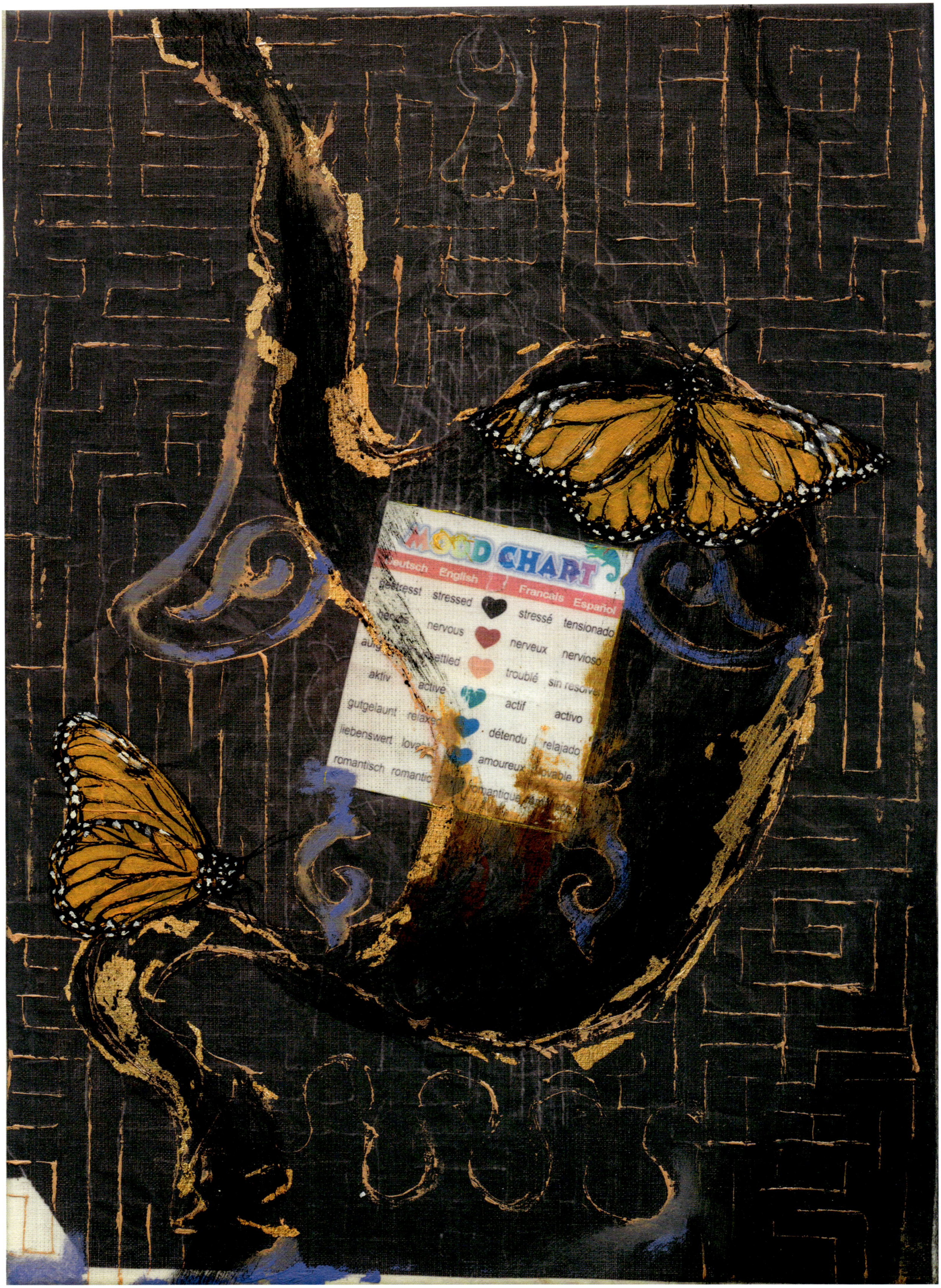
MOOD CHART
Deutsch English Francais Español
stressed stressé tensionado
nervous nerveux nervioso
troublé
aktiv active actif activo
gutgelaunt détendu relajado
liebenswert amoureux
romantisch romantic

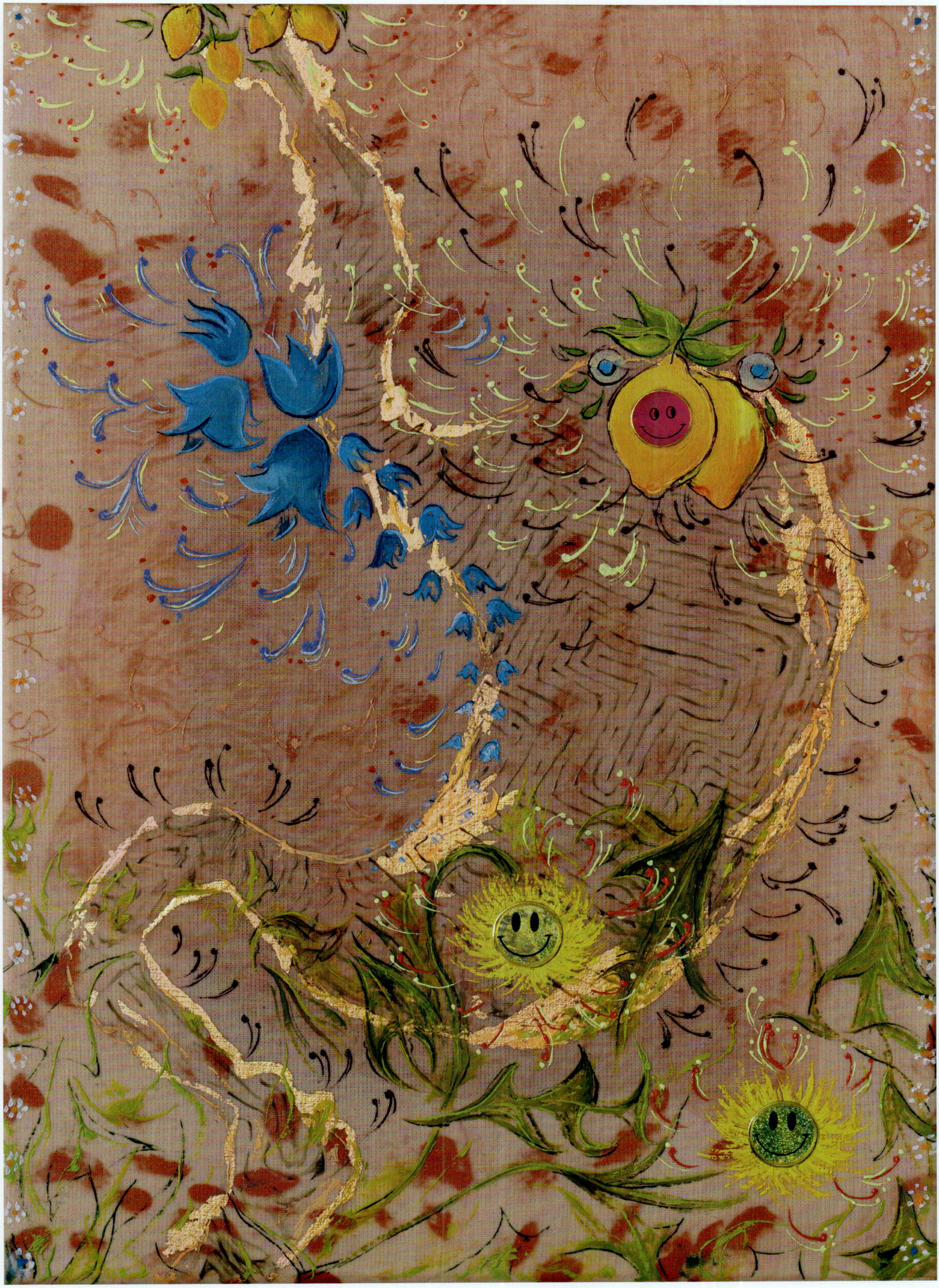

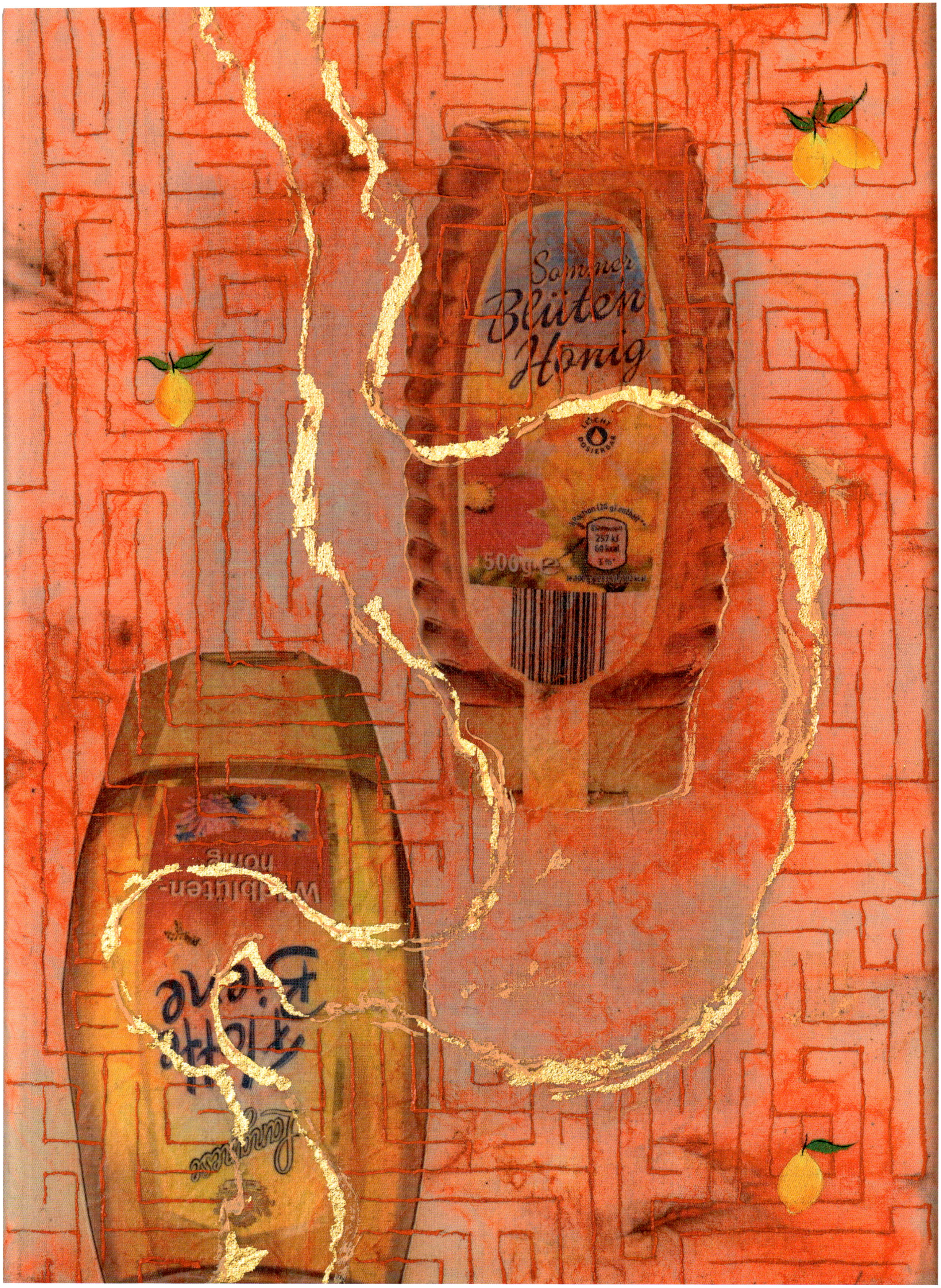
Sommer
Blüten
Honig
500 g

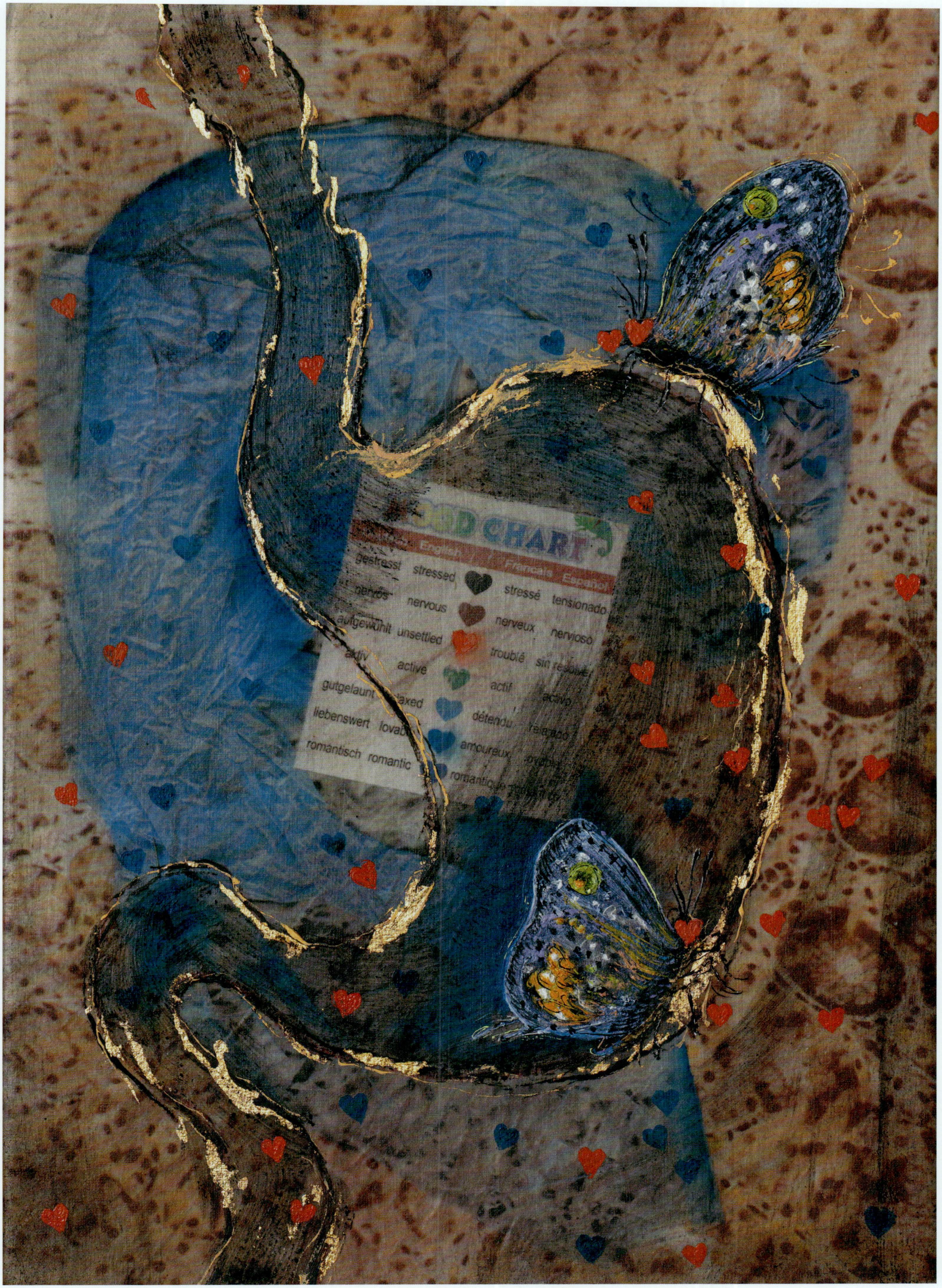

CHART
English
gestresst stressed stressé tensionado
nervous nerveux nervioso
unsettled troublé
active actif
gutgelaunt
liebenswert détendu
romantisch romantic amoureux

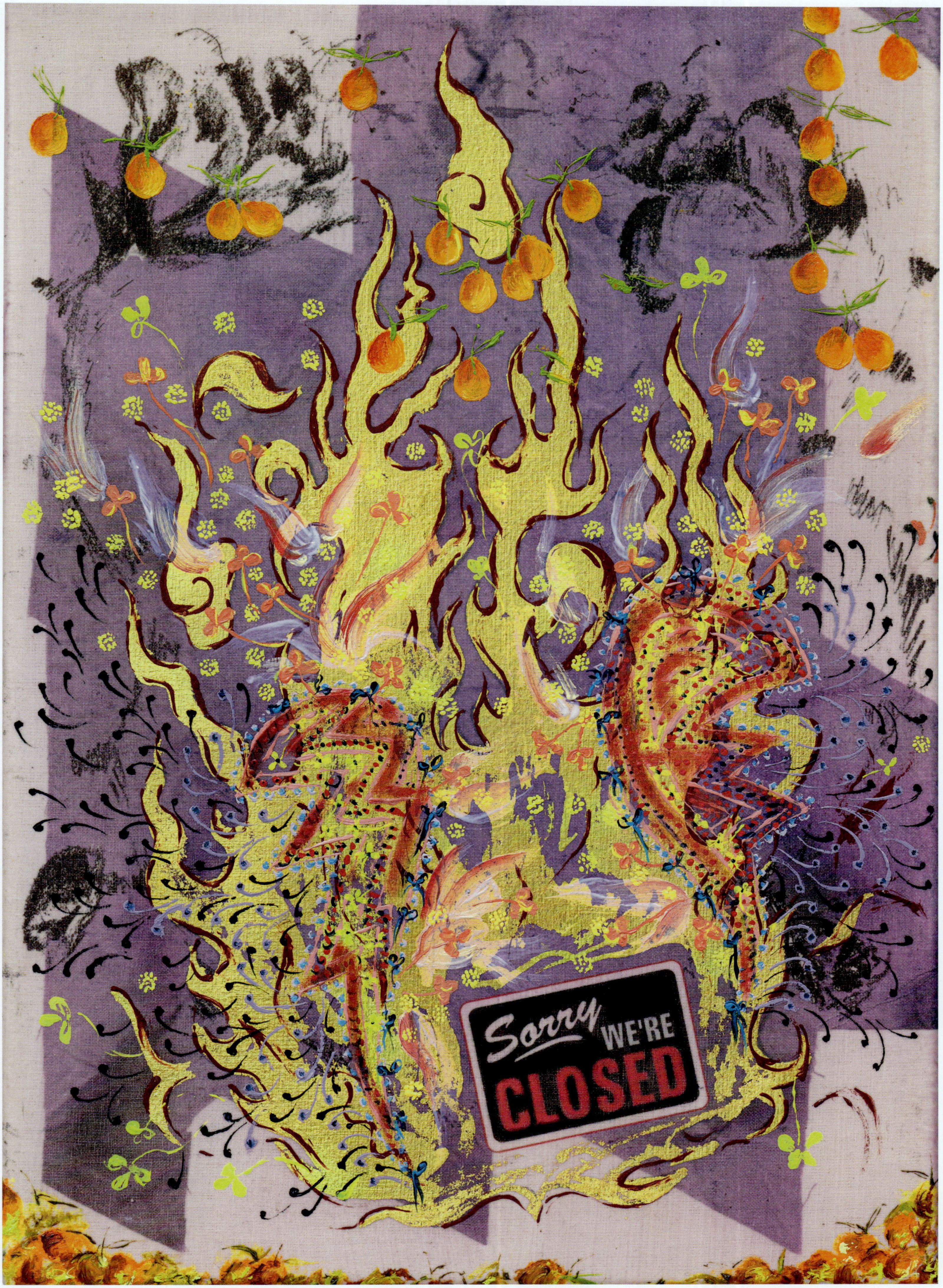
Sorry WE'RE
CLOSED

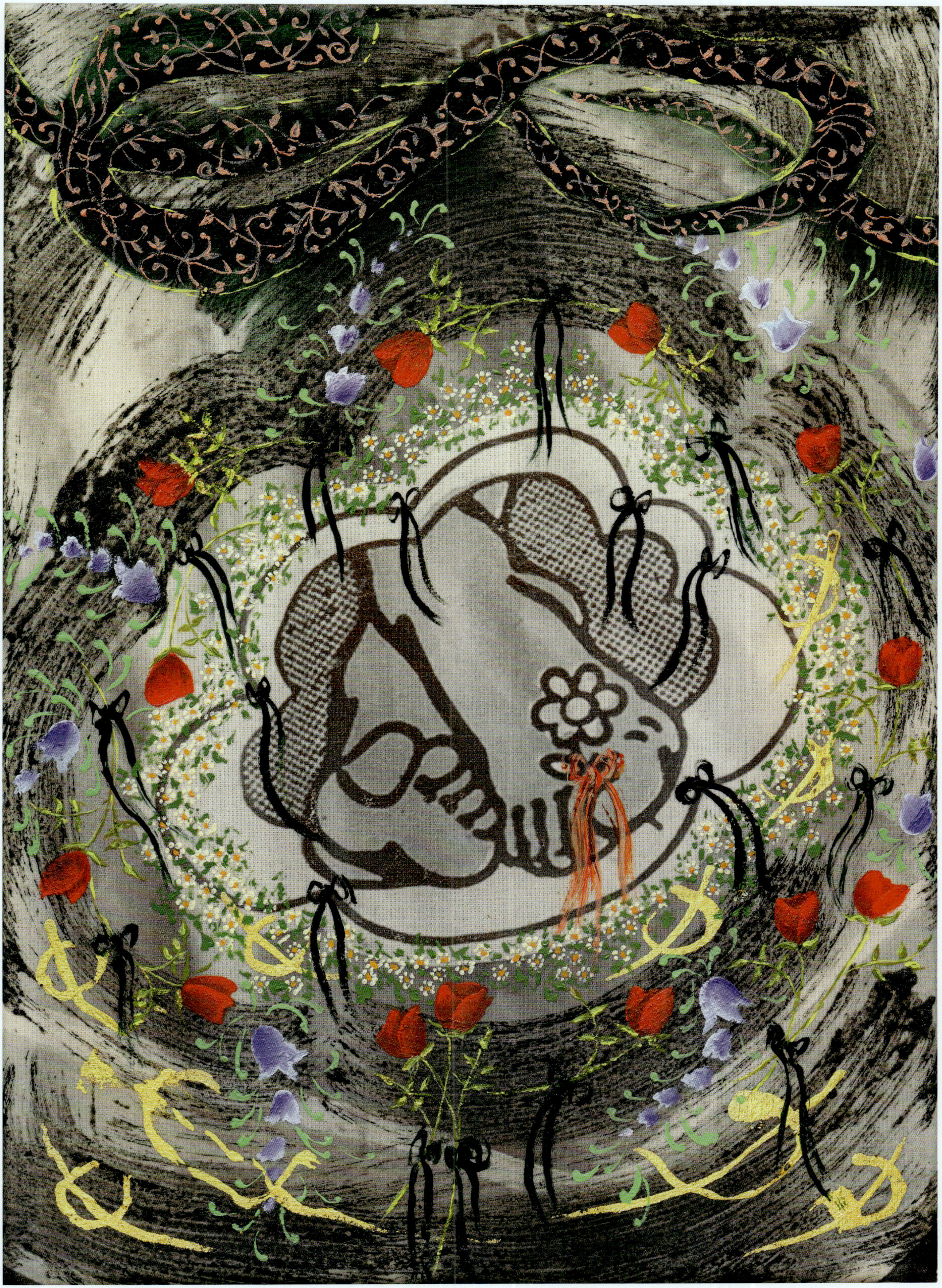

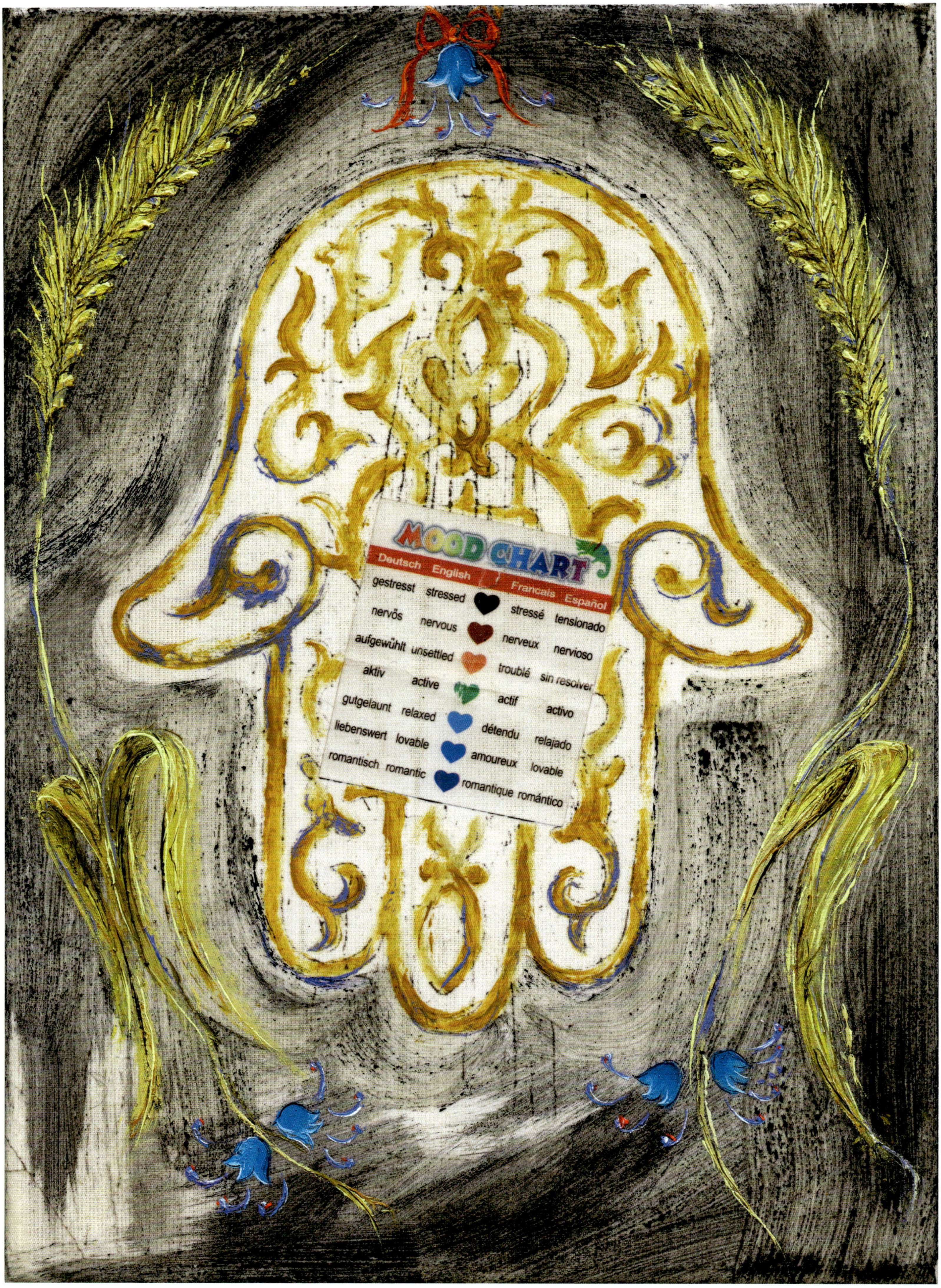
MOOD CHART
Deutsch English Francais Español
gestresst stressed stressé tensionado
nervös nervous nerveux nervioso
aufgewühlt unsettled troublé sin resolver
aktiv active actif activo
gutgelaunt relaxed détendu relajado
liebenswert lovable amoureux lovable
romantisch romantic romantique romántico

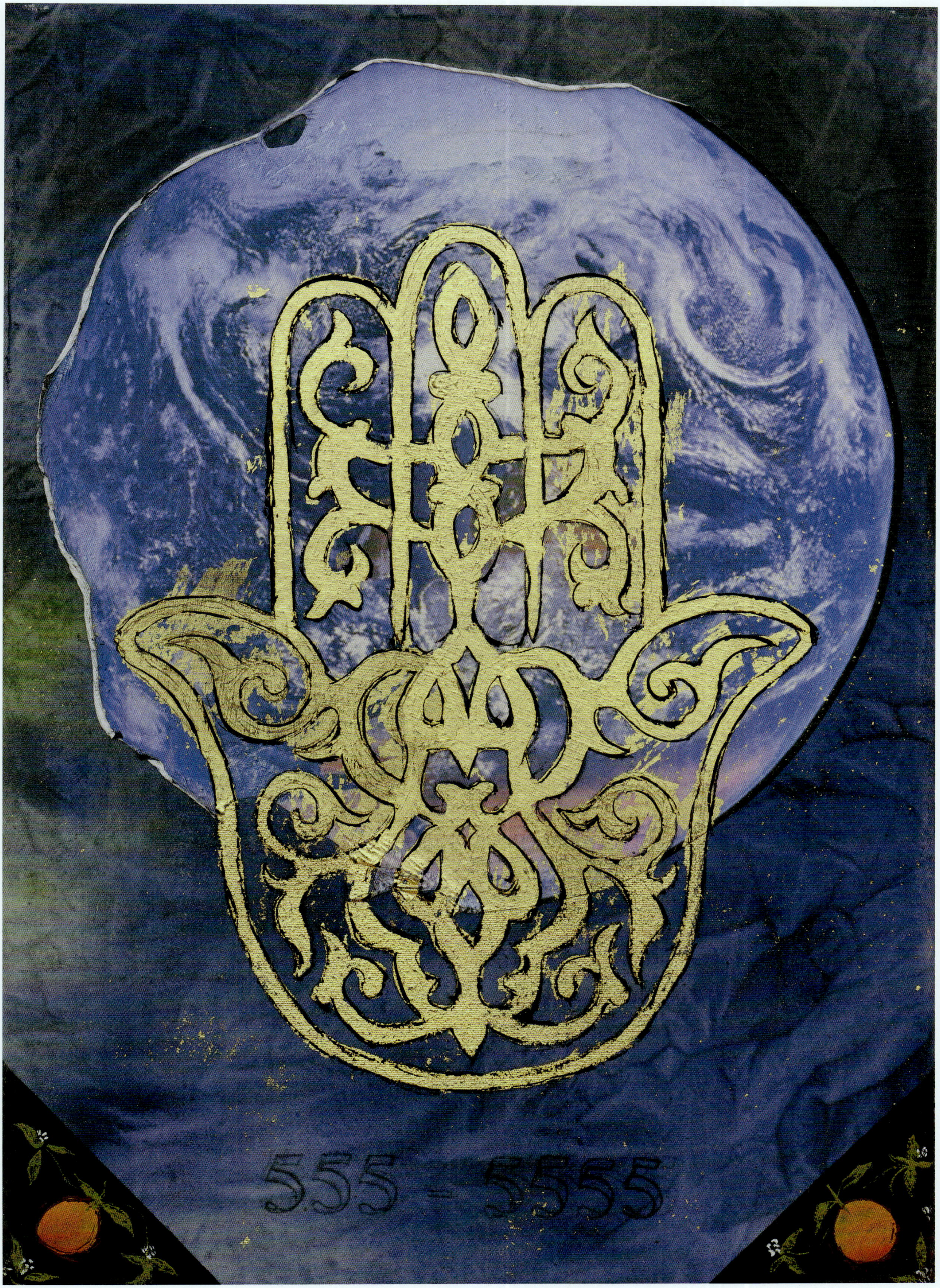
555 - 5555

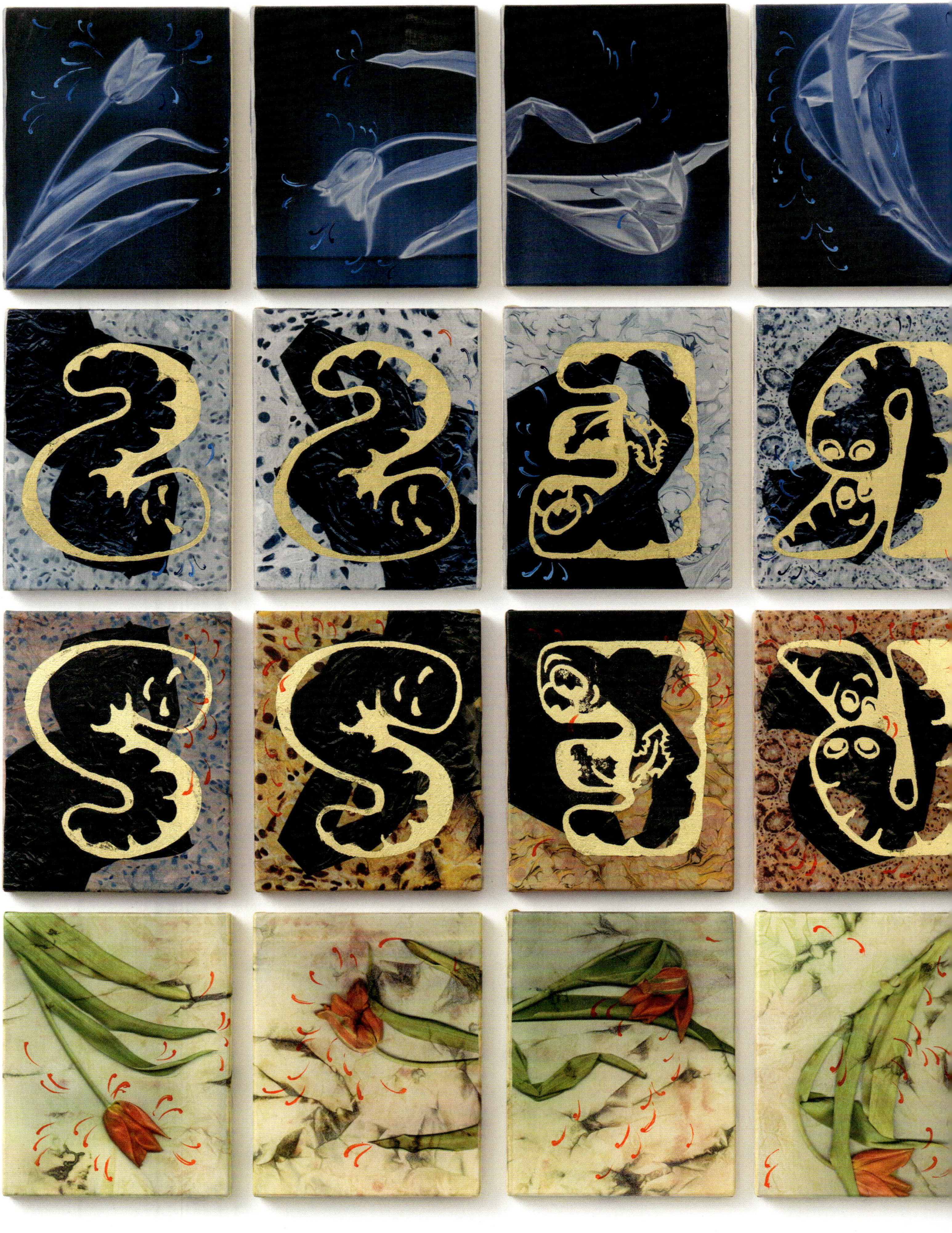

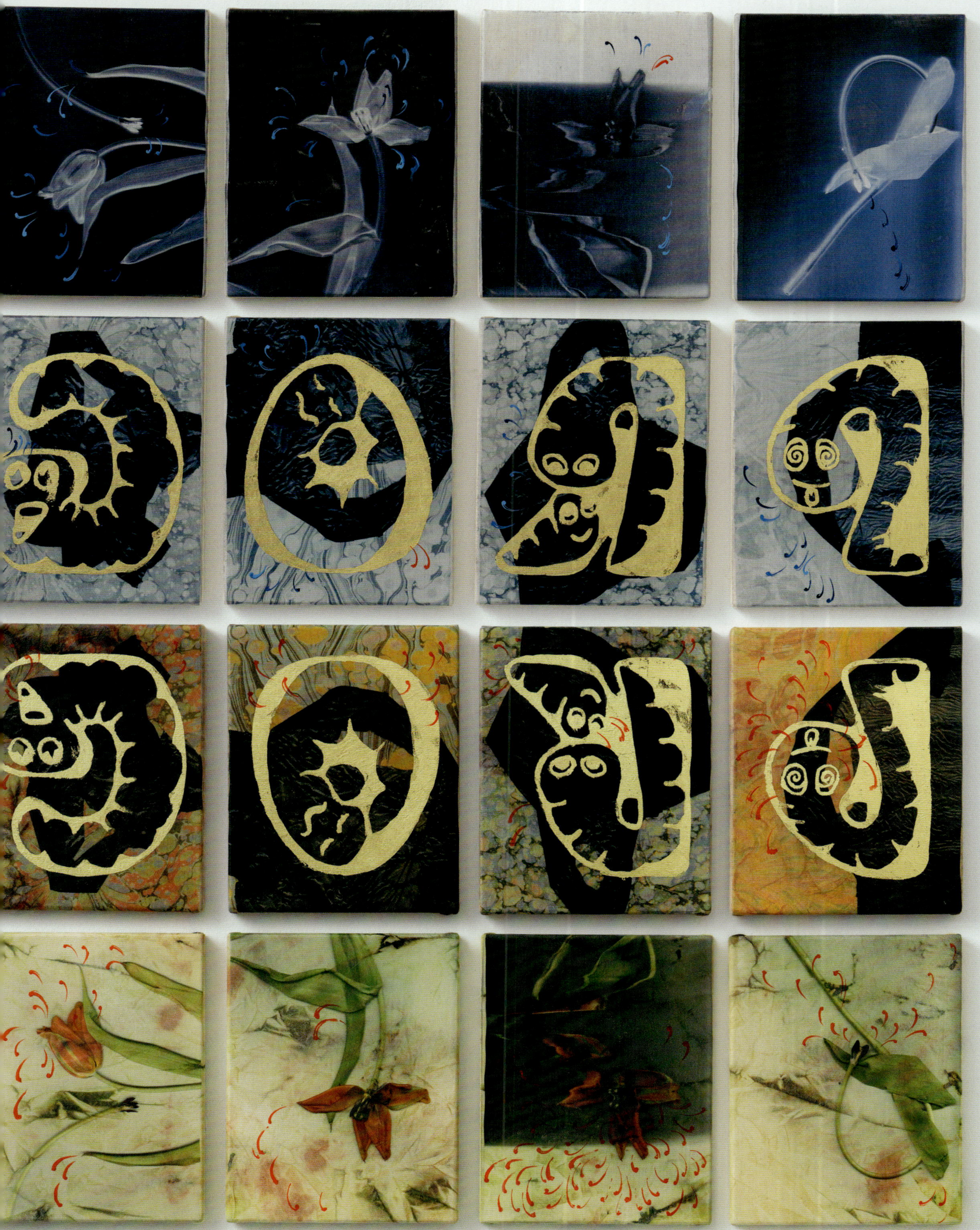

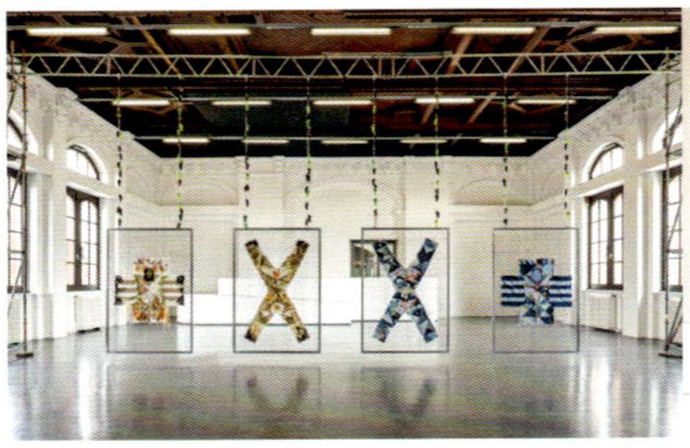

Installation view
...schläft sich durch
Kunstverein Harburger
Bahnhof, Hamburg, 2021
Courtesy of the artist
and Kunstverein Harburger
Bahnhof, Hamburg
Photo: Fred Dott

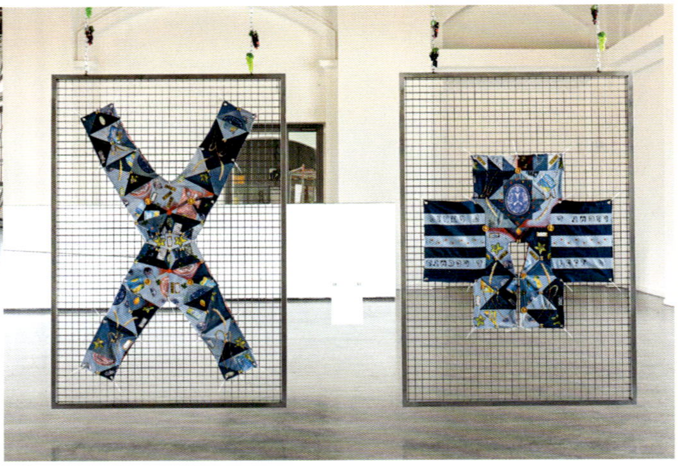

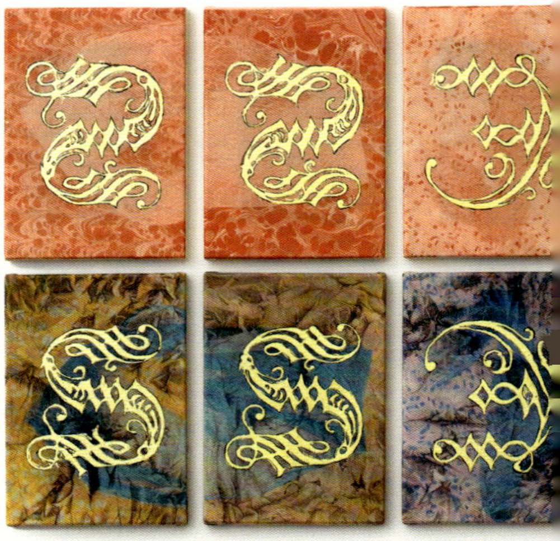

Bind, 2020
16 canvases, 23k gold, inkjet
transfer and oil on dyed canvas
62 × 182 cm
Courtesy of the artist
and Tanya Leighton, Berlin
Photo: Gunter Lepkowski

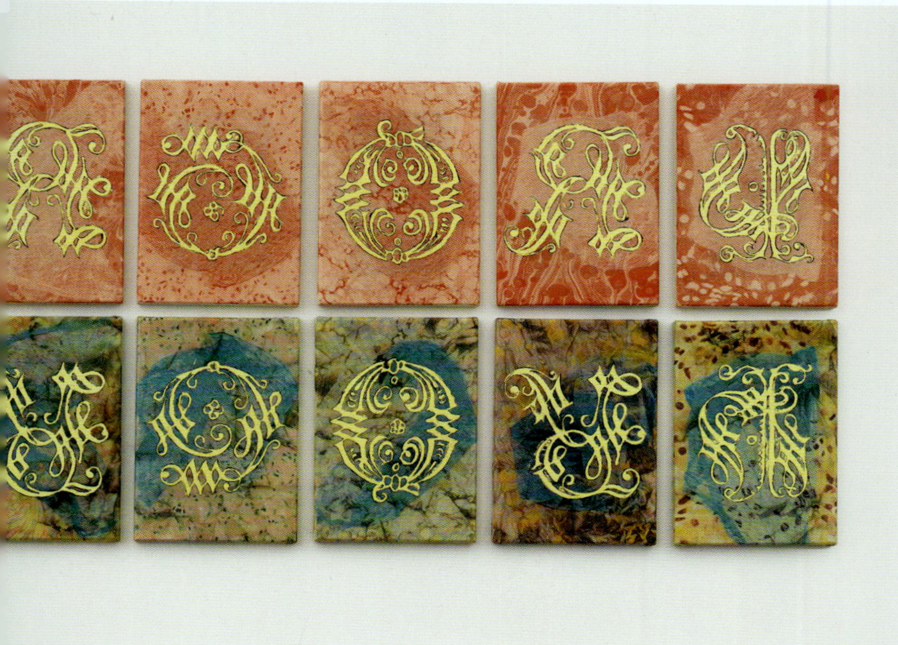

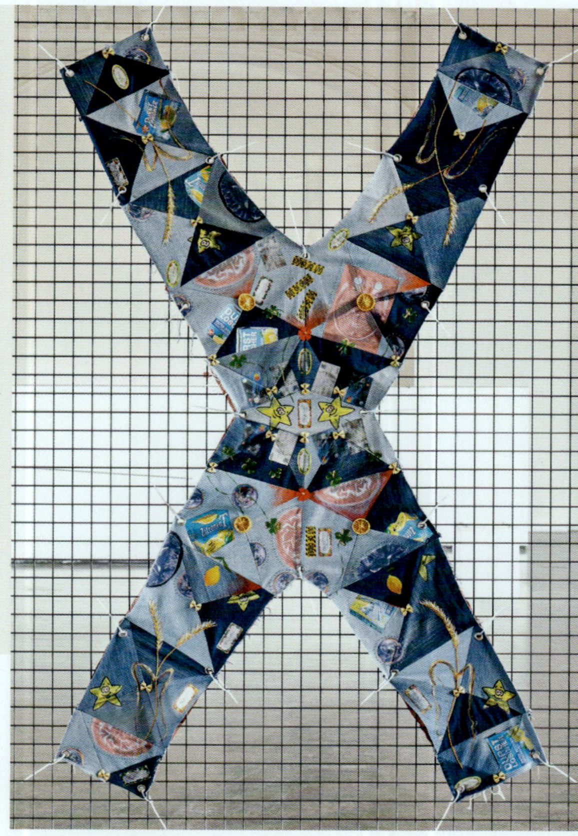

The Producer, 2021
Mixed media, denim on steel
250 × 170 × 6 cm
Courtesy of the artist
and Kunstverein Harburger
Bahnhof, Hamburg
Photo: Fred Dott

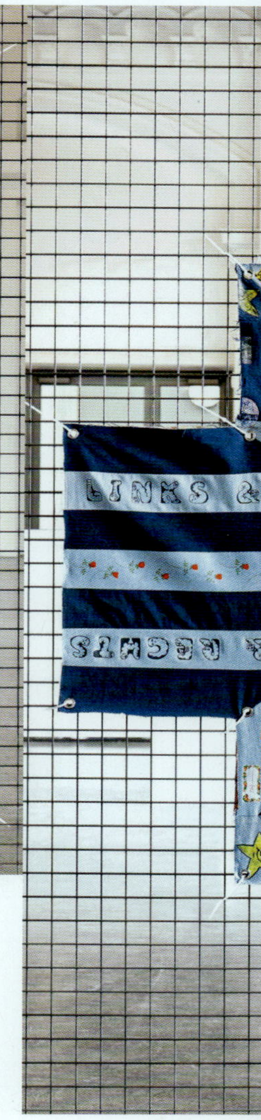

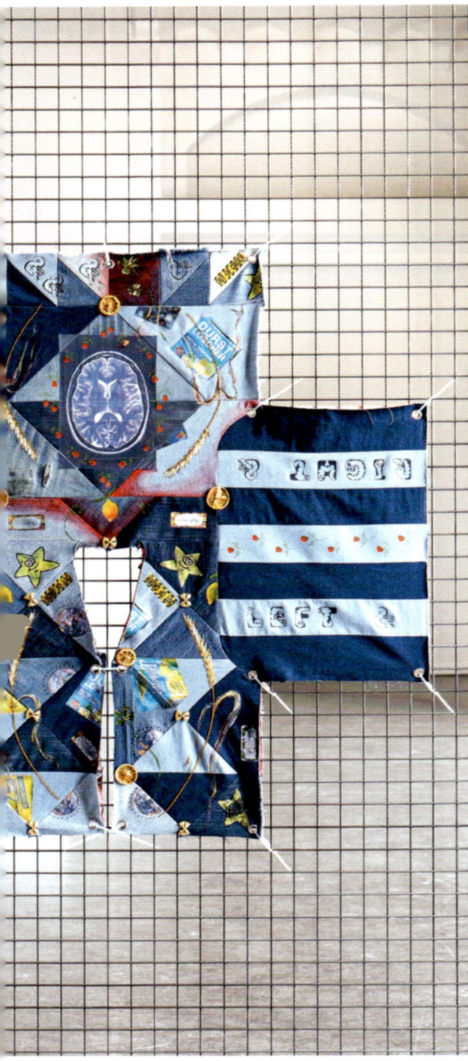

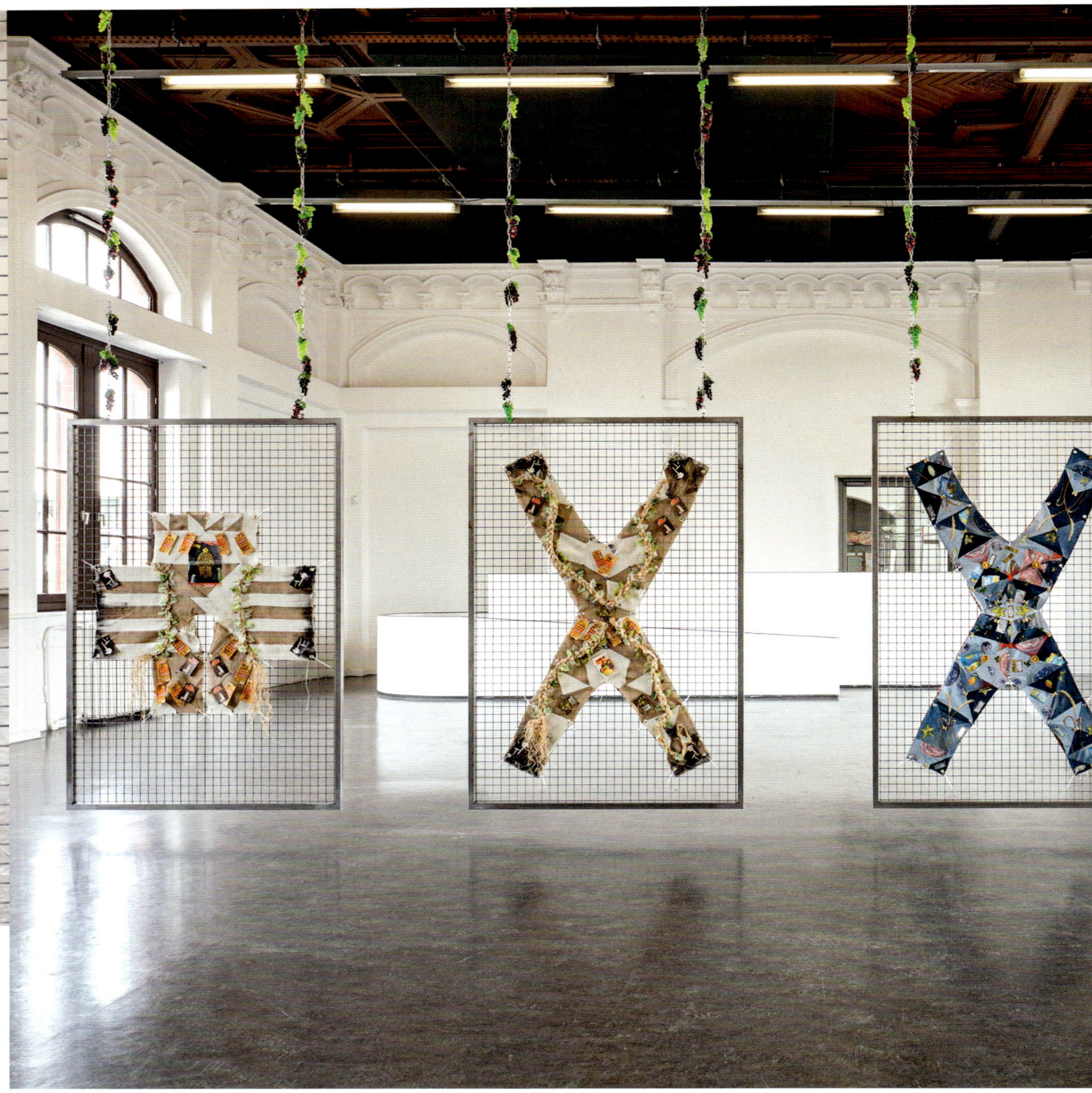

Installation view
...schläft sich durch
Kunstverein Harburger
Bahnhof, Hamburg, 2021
Courtesy of the artist
and Kunstverein Harburger
Bahnhof, Hamburg
Photo: Fred Dott

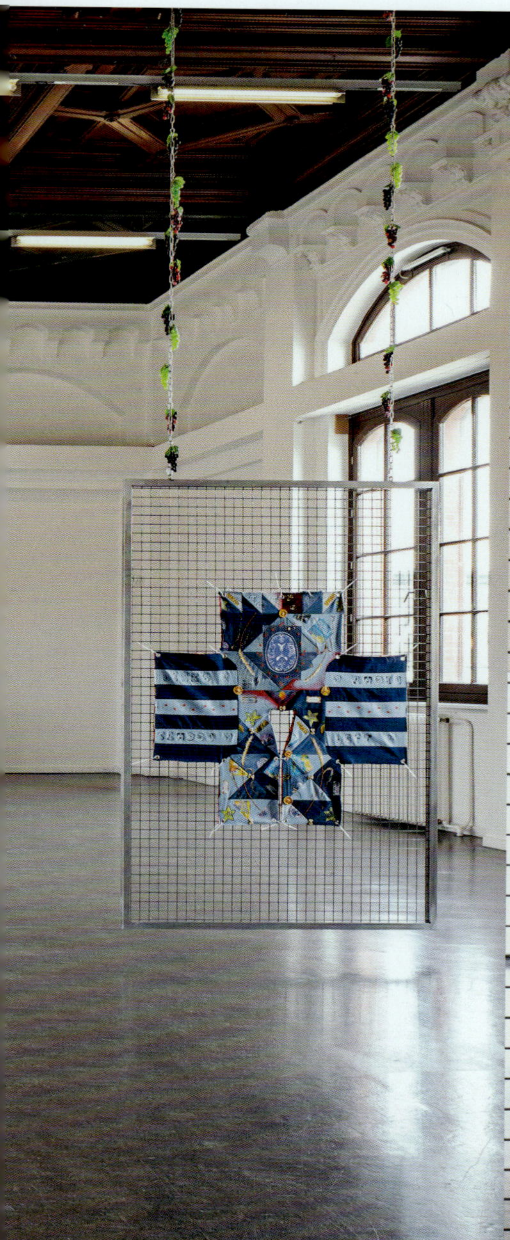

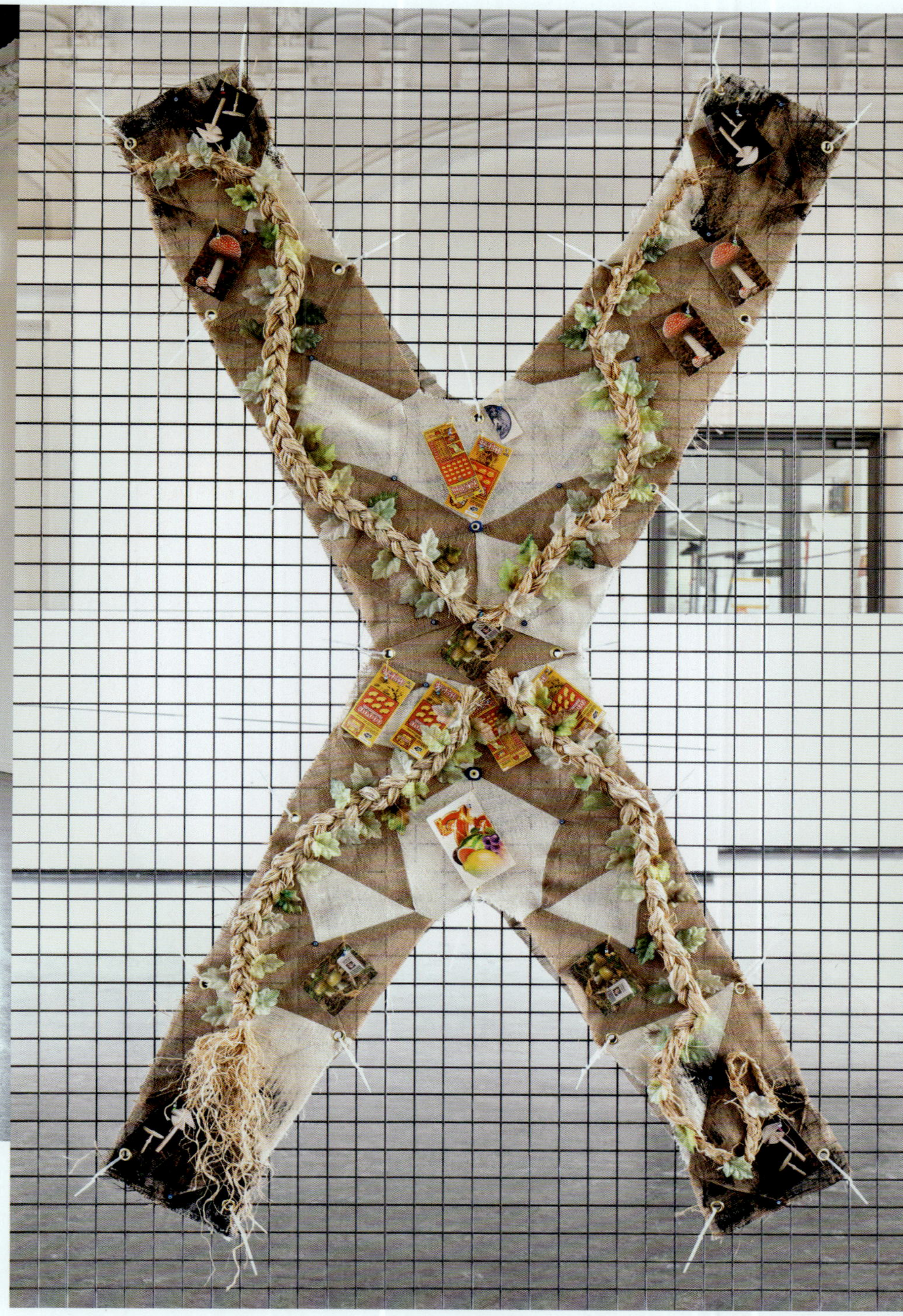

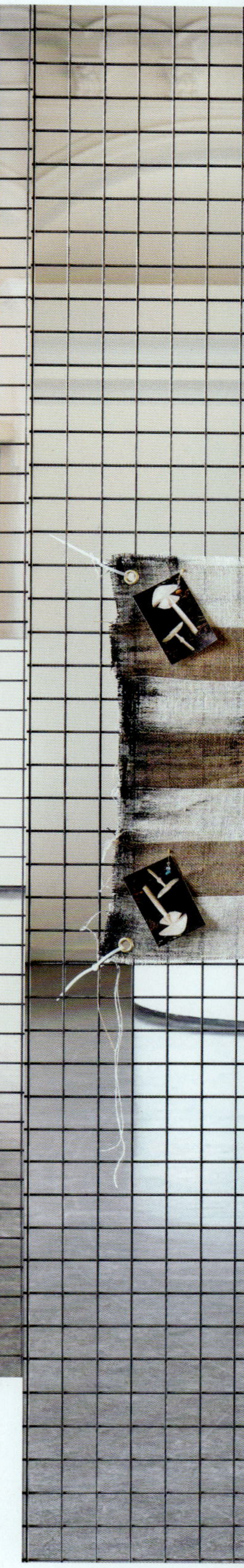

The Drone, 2021
Mixed media, burlap on steel
250 × 170 × 6 cm
Courtesy of the artist
and Kunstverein Harburger
Bahnhof, Hamburg
Photo: Fred Dott

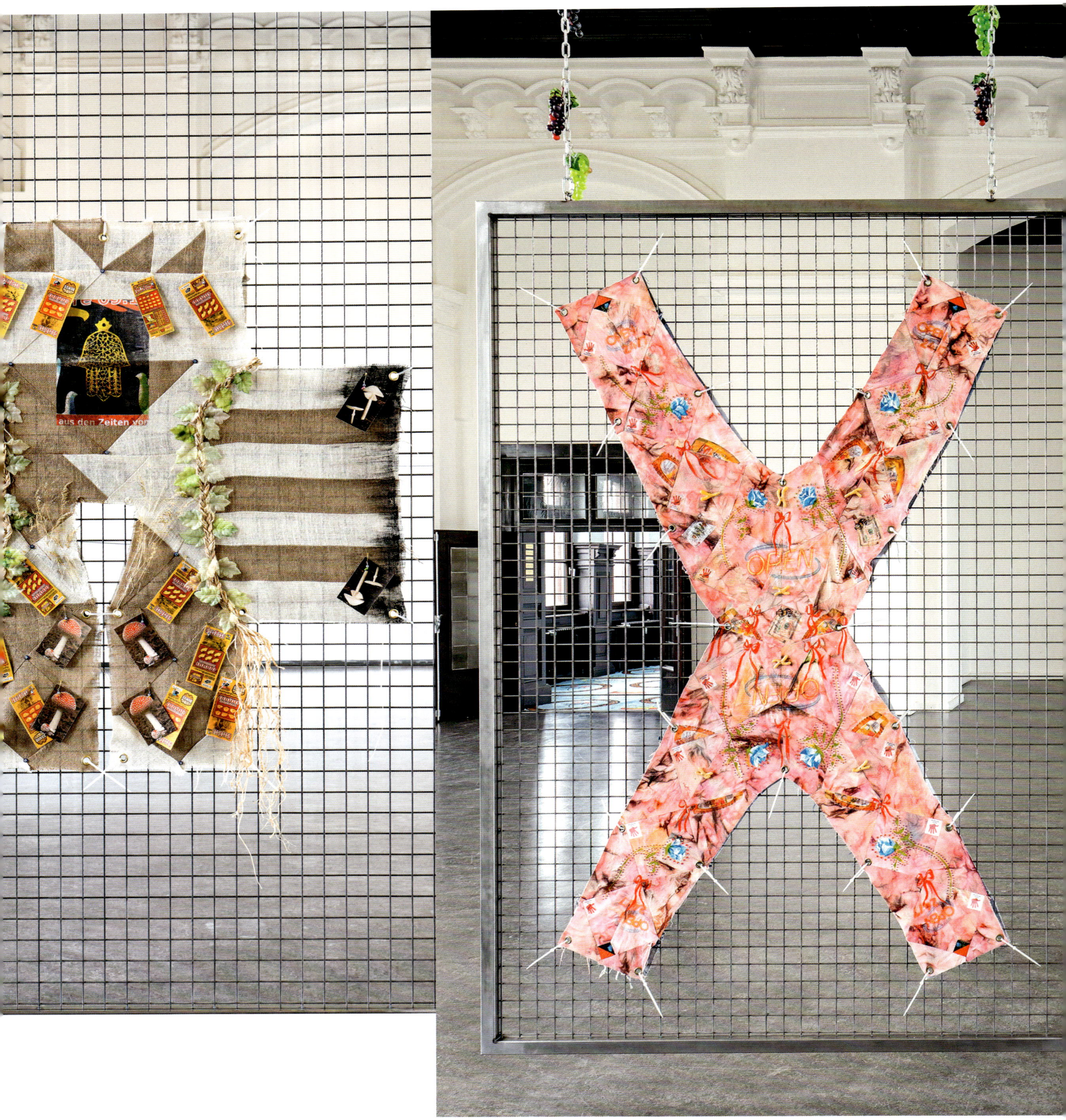

Installation view
...schläft sich durch
Kunstverein Harburger
Bahnhof, Hamburg, 2021
Courtesy of the artist
and Kunstverein Harburger
Bahnhof, Hamburg
Photo: Fred Dott

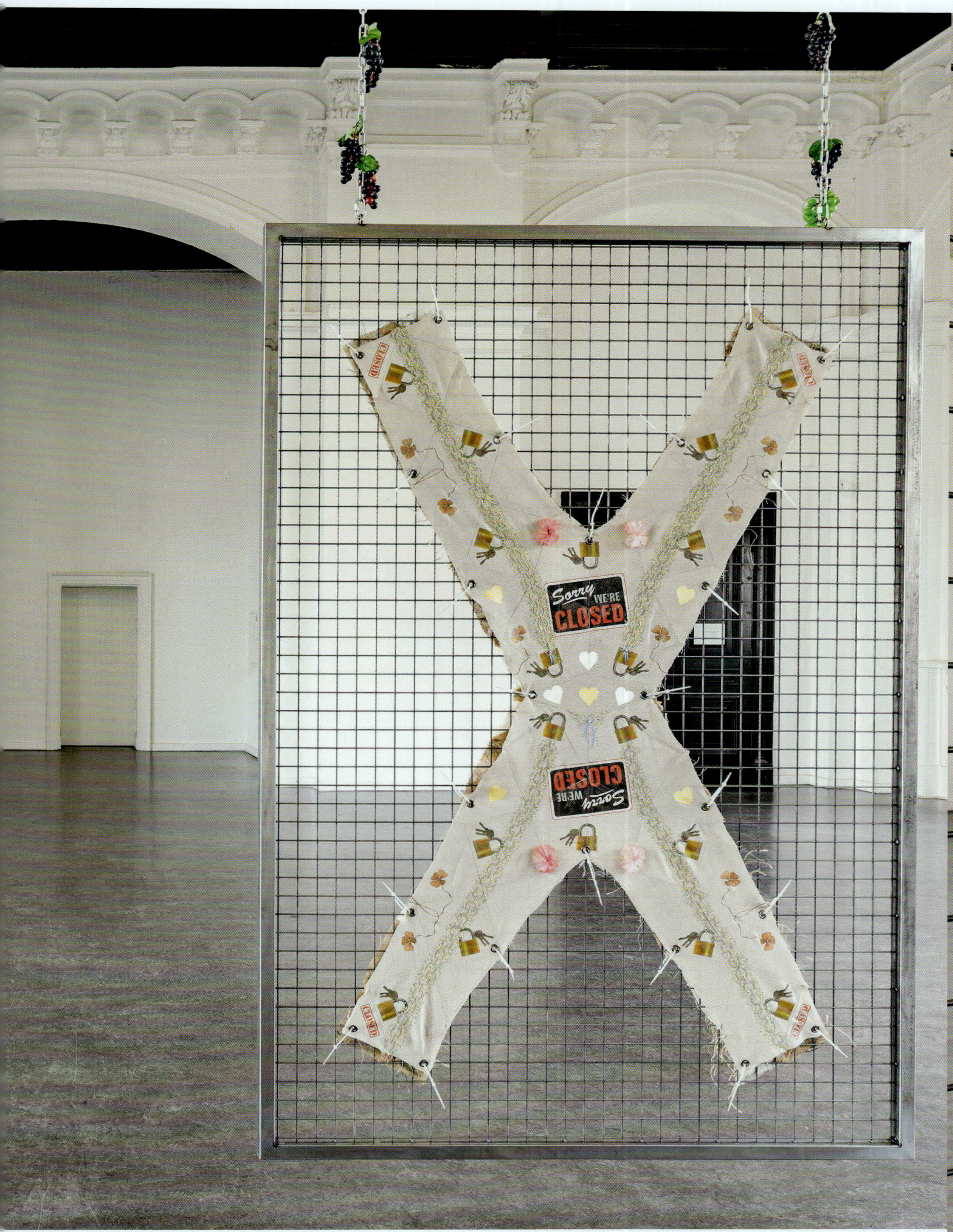

The Producer, 2021
Mixed media, denim on steel
250 × 170 × 6 cm
Courtesy of the artist
and Kunstverein Harburger
Bahnhof, Hamburg
Photo: Fred Dott

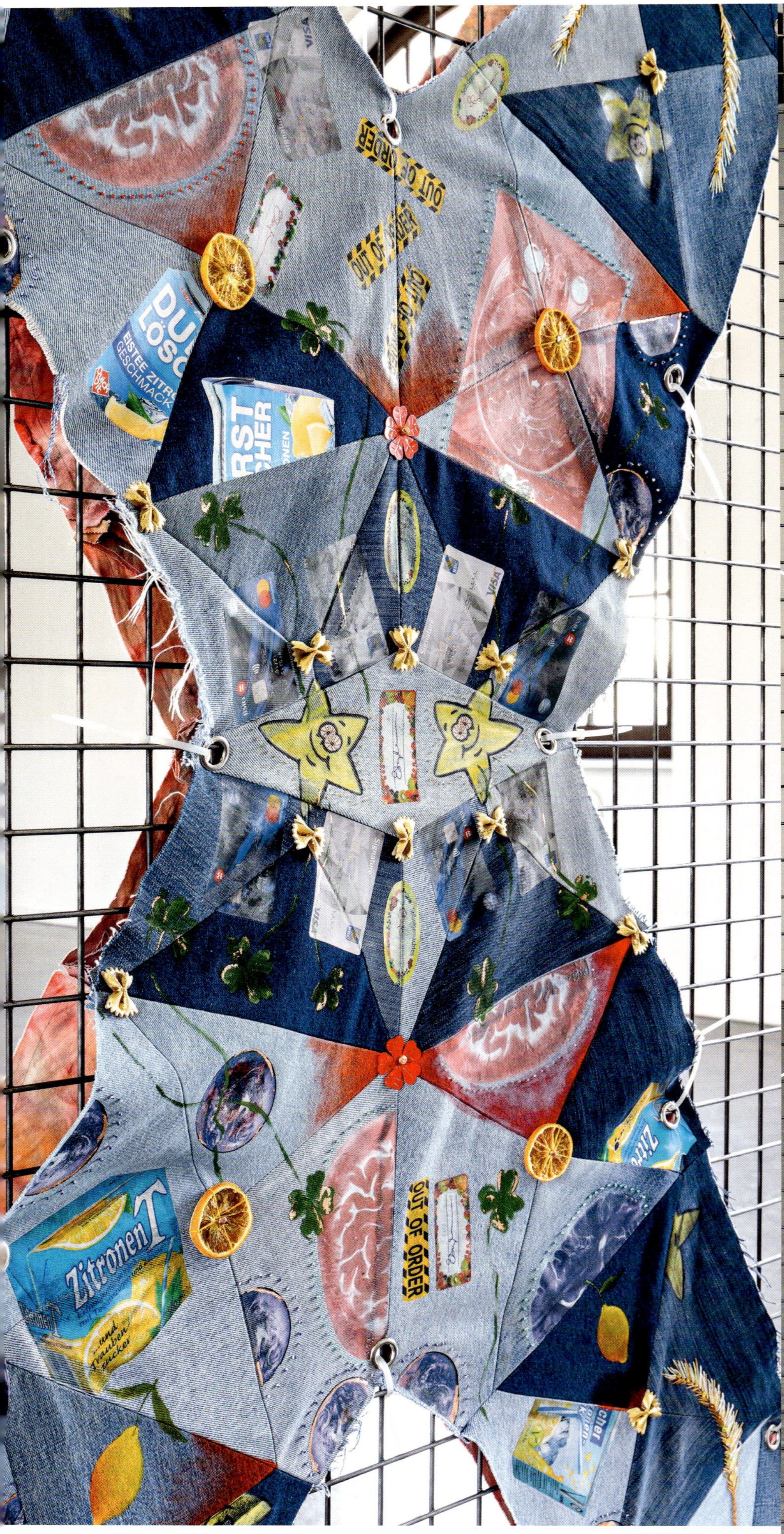

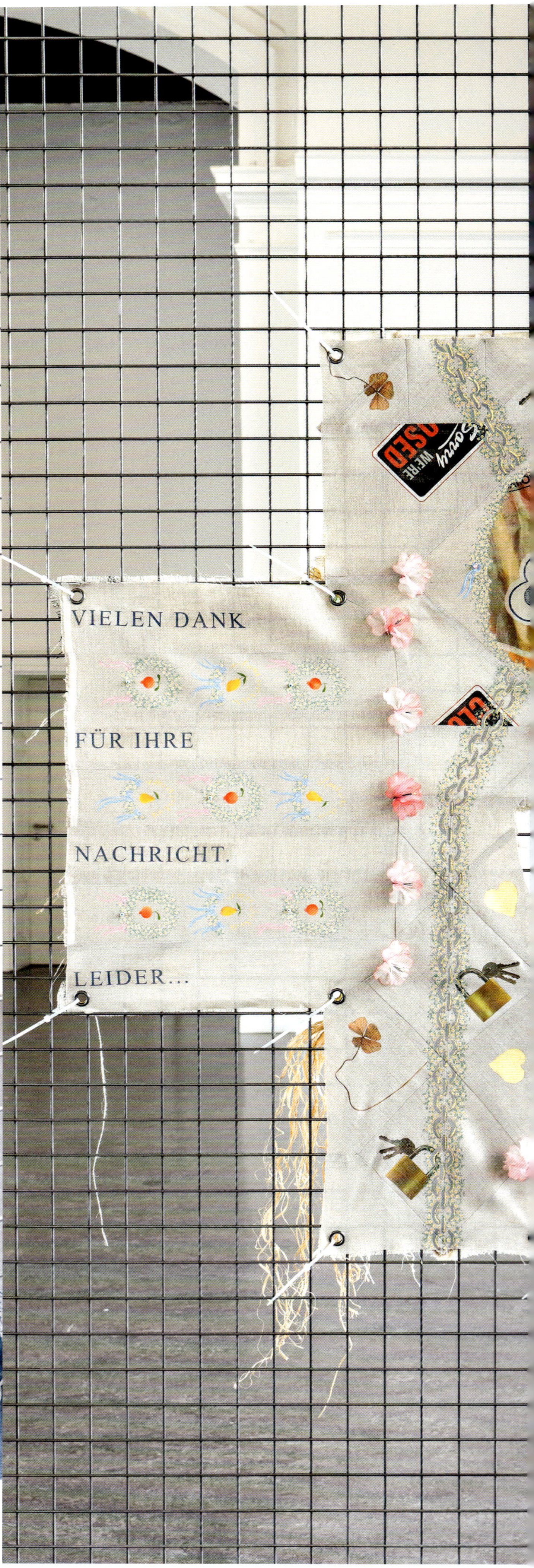

The Landlord, 2021. Mixed media, linen on steel, 250 × 170 × 6 cm
Courtesy of the artist and Kunstverein Harburger Bahnhof, Hamburg. Photo: Fred Dott

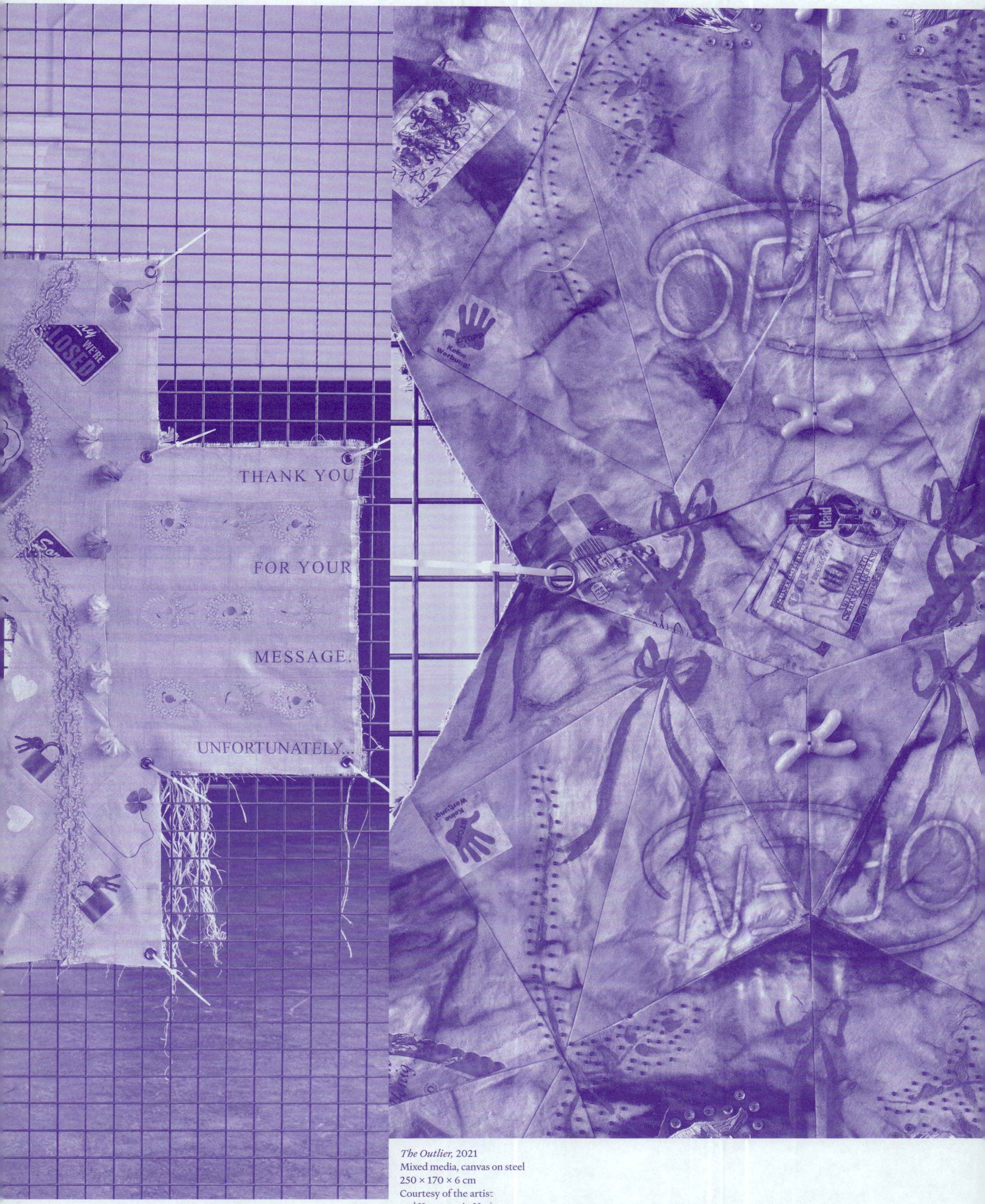

The Outlier, 2021
Mixed media, canvas on steel
250 × 170 × 6 cm
Courtesy of the artist
and Kunstverein Harburger
Bahnhof, Hamburg
Photo: Fred Dott

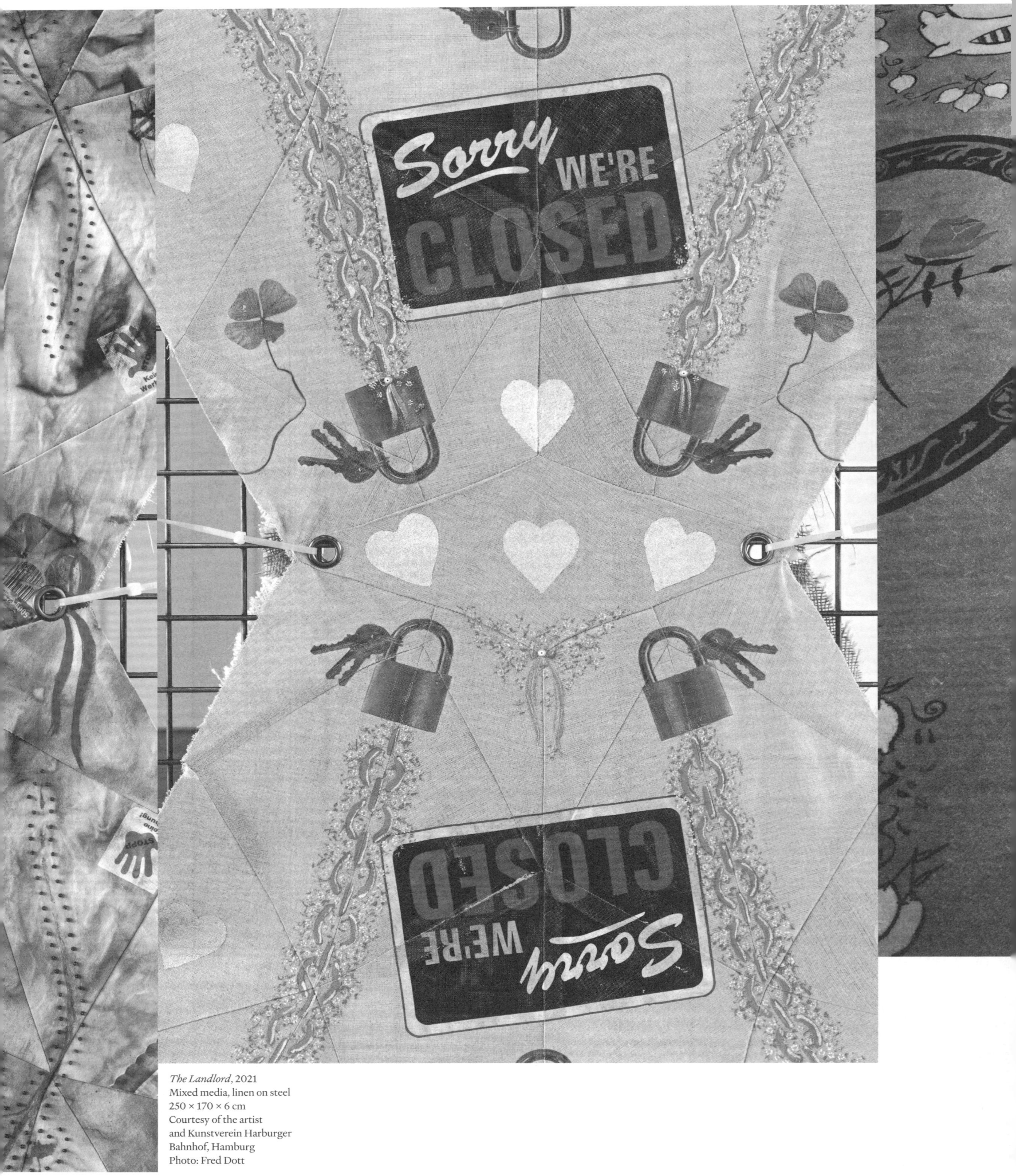

The Landlord, 2021
Mixed media, linen on steel
250 × 170 × 6 cm
Courtesy of the artist
and Kunstverein Harburger
Bahnhof, Hamburg
Photo: Fred Dott

Blue Saloon, 2021
Custom plush printed carpet
540 × 463 cm
Courtesy of the artist
and Kunstverein Harburger
Bahnhof, Hamburg
Photo: Fred Dott

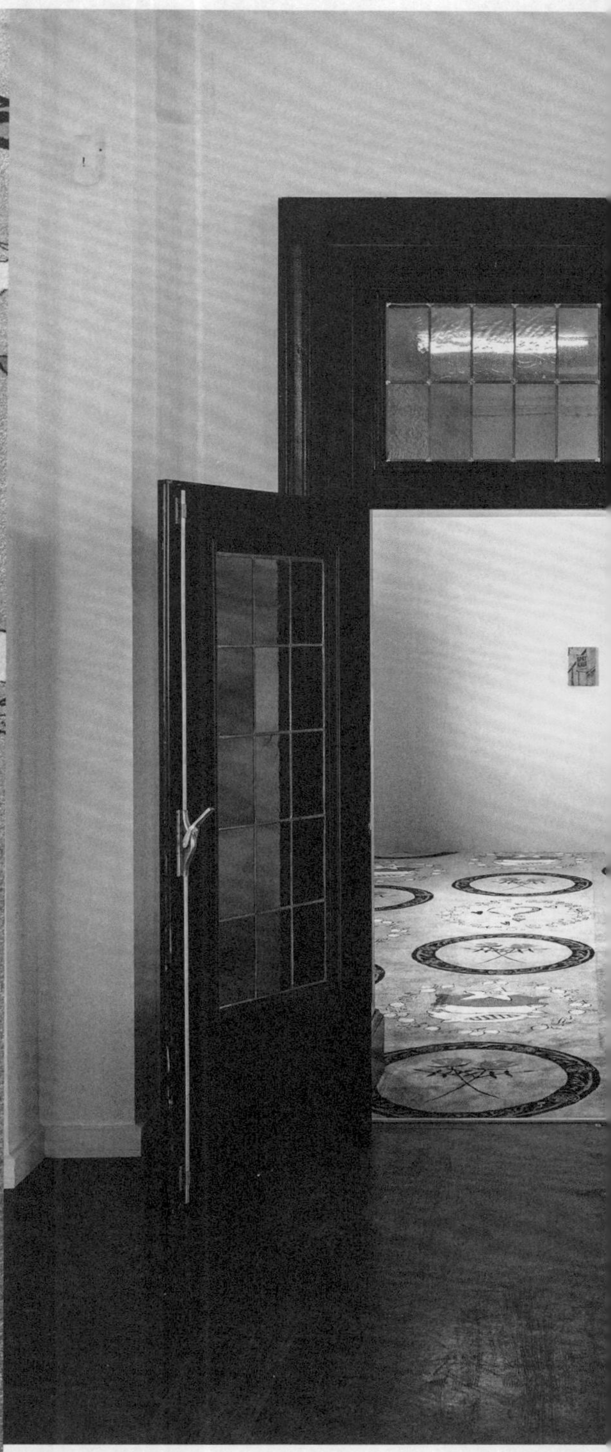

Installation view
...schläft sich durch
Kunstverein Harburger
Bahnhof, Hamburg, 2021
Courtesy of the artist
and Kunstverein Harburger
Bahnhof, Hamburg
Photo: Fred Dott

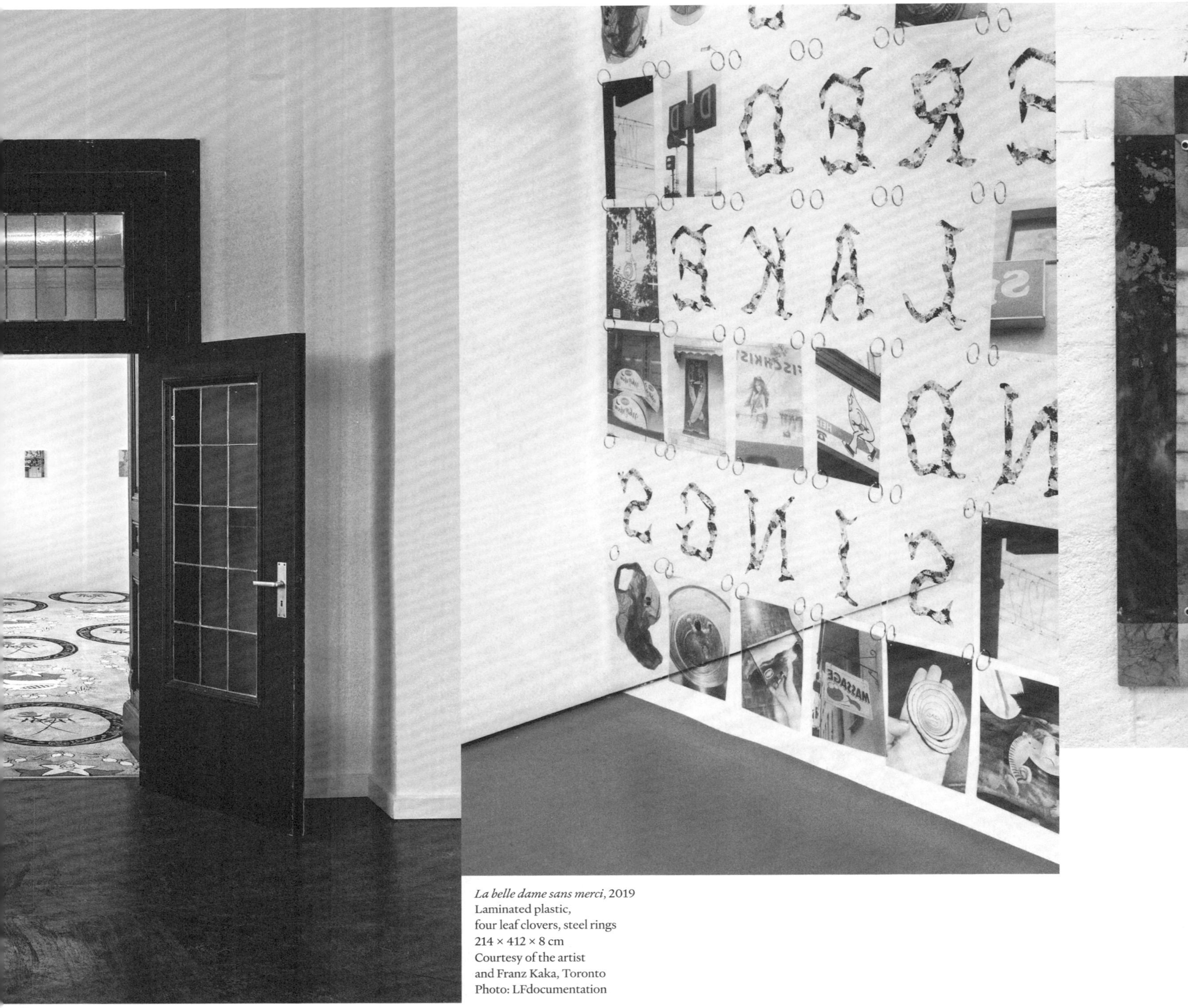

La belle dame sans merci, 2019
Laminated plastic,
four leaf clovers, steel rings
214 × 412 × 8 cm
Courtesy of the artist
and Franz Kaka, Toronto
Photo: LFdocumentation

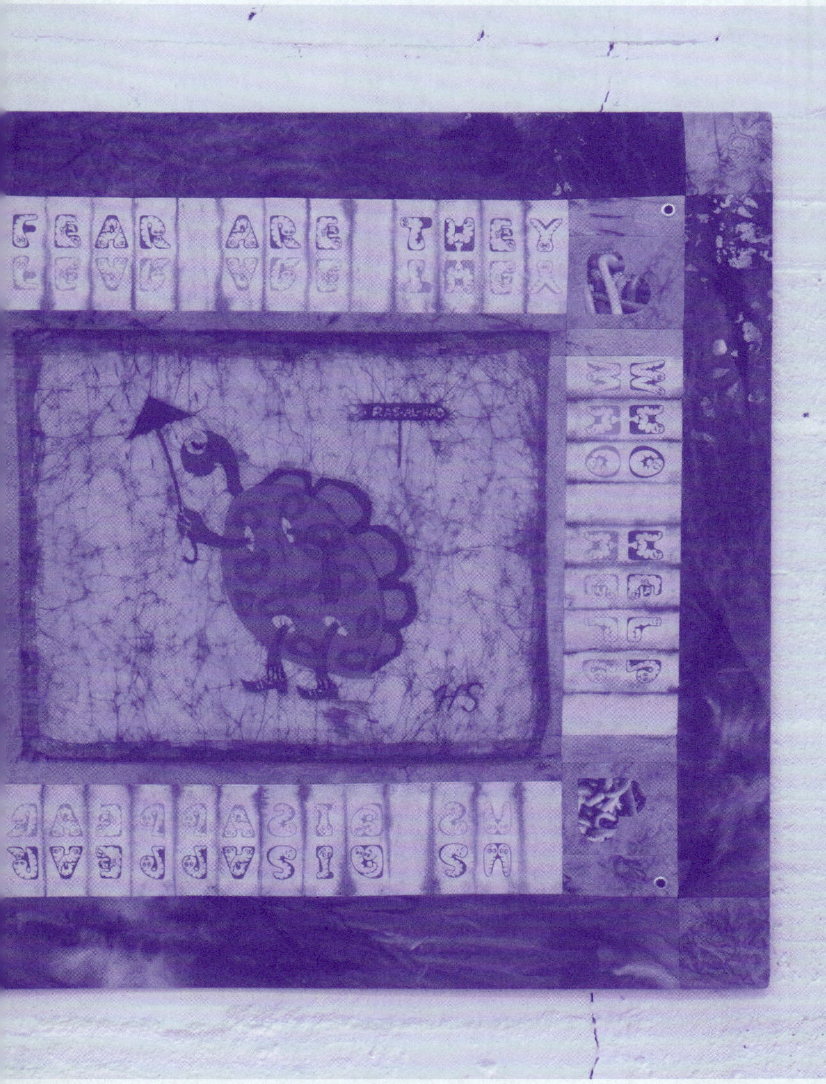

Mutter Natur, 2019
Inkjet transfer, aluminium and oil on dyed canvas, mounted on wood; Batik print by the artist's mother, Hülya Saydam, c. 1988
86.5 × 92.5 cm
Courtesy of the artist and Franz Kaka, Toronto
Photo: LFdocumentation

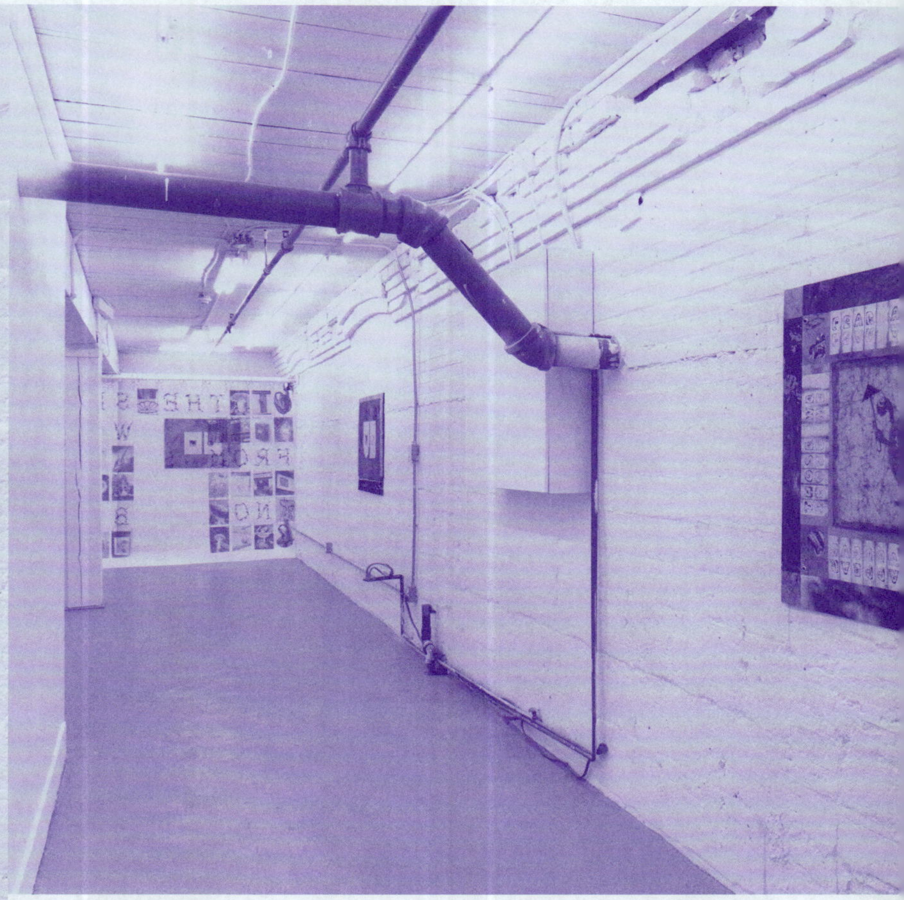

Installation view
La belle dame sans merci
Franz Kaka, Toronto, 2019
Courtesy of the artist and Franz Kaka, Toronto
Photo: LFdocumentation

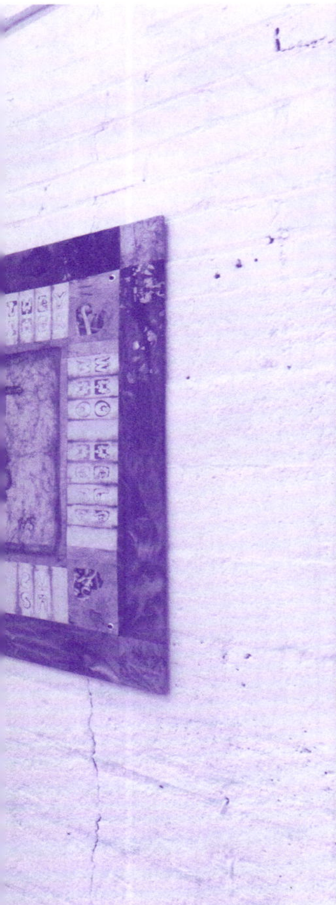

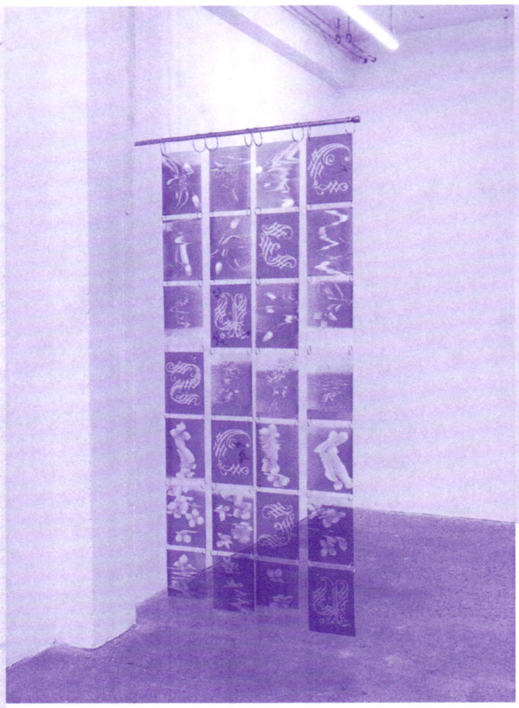

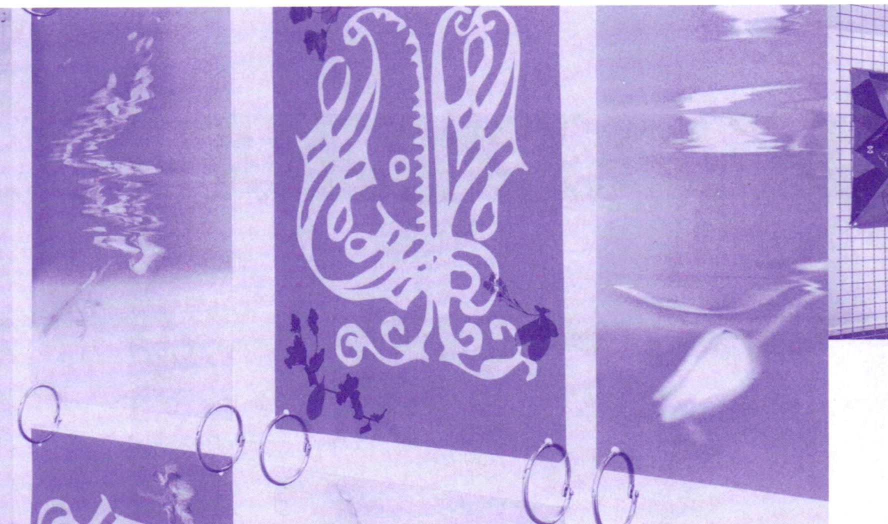

There's many a slip 'twixt the cup and the lip, 2020
Laminated plastic, steel rings
220 × 93 × 4.5 cm
Courtesy of the artist
and Franz Kaka, Toronto
Photo: LFdocumentation

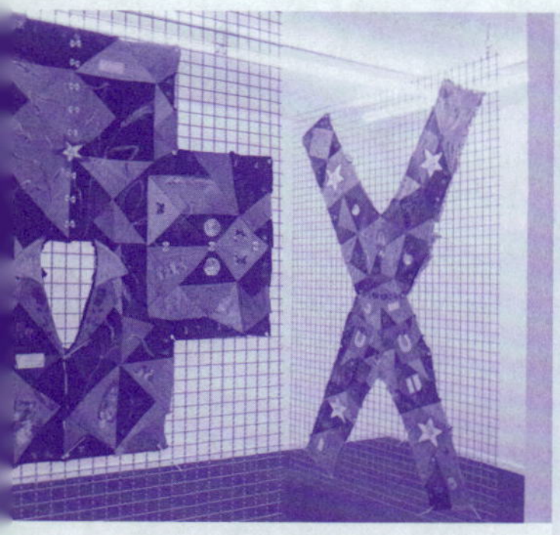

Installation view
Selfing
Mélange, Cologne, 2020
Courtesy of the artist
and Mélange, Cologne
Photo: Mélange

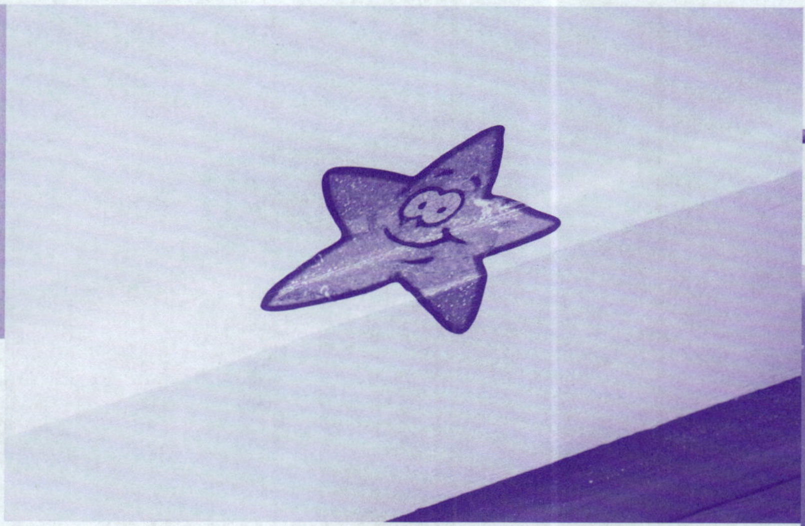

Untitled (mascot), 2020
Custom glitter sticker
10 × 10 cm
Courtesy of the artist
and The Tail, Brussels
Photo: graysc.de

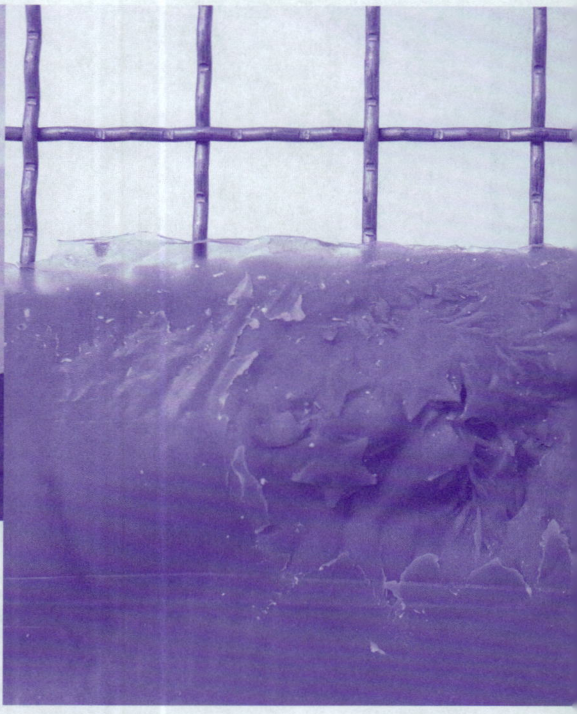

Selfing, 2020
Mixed media, denim
and silicon on steel
231 × 149 cm
Courtesy of the artist
and Mélange, Cologne
Photo: Mélange

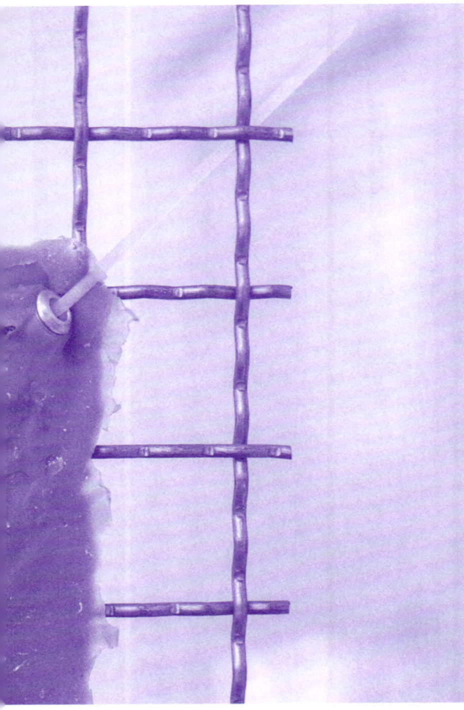

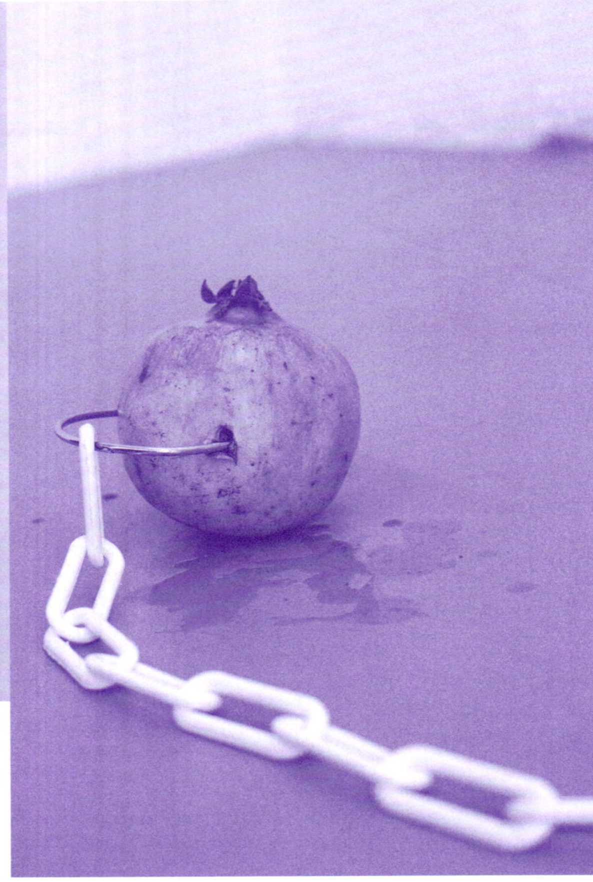

Installation view
No R.E.M.
Ashley, Berlin, 2017
Courtesy of the artist
and Ashley, Berlin
Photo: graysc.de

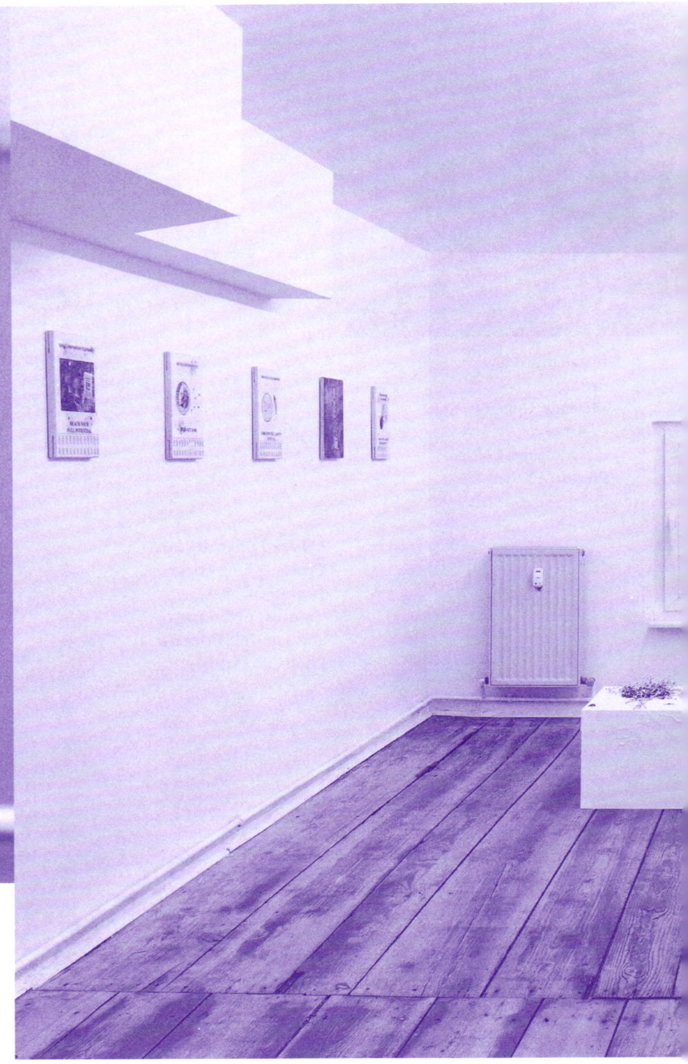

Installation view
What me worry
stadium, Berlin, 2019
Courtesy of the artist
and stadium, Berlin
Photo: groupshow.eu

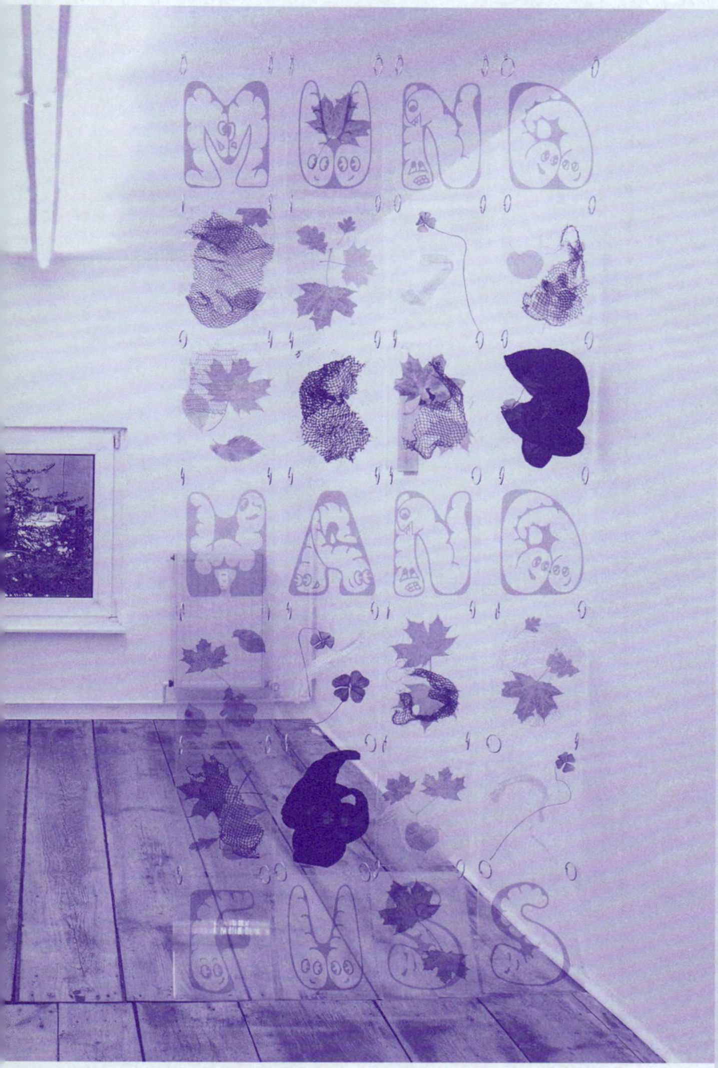

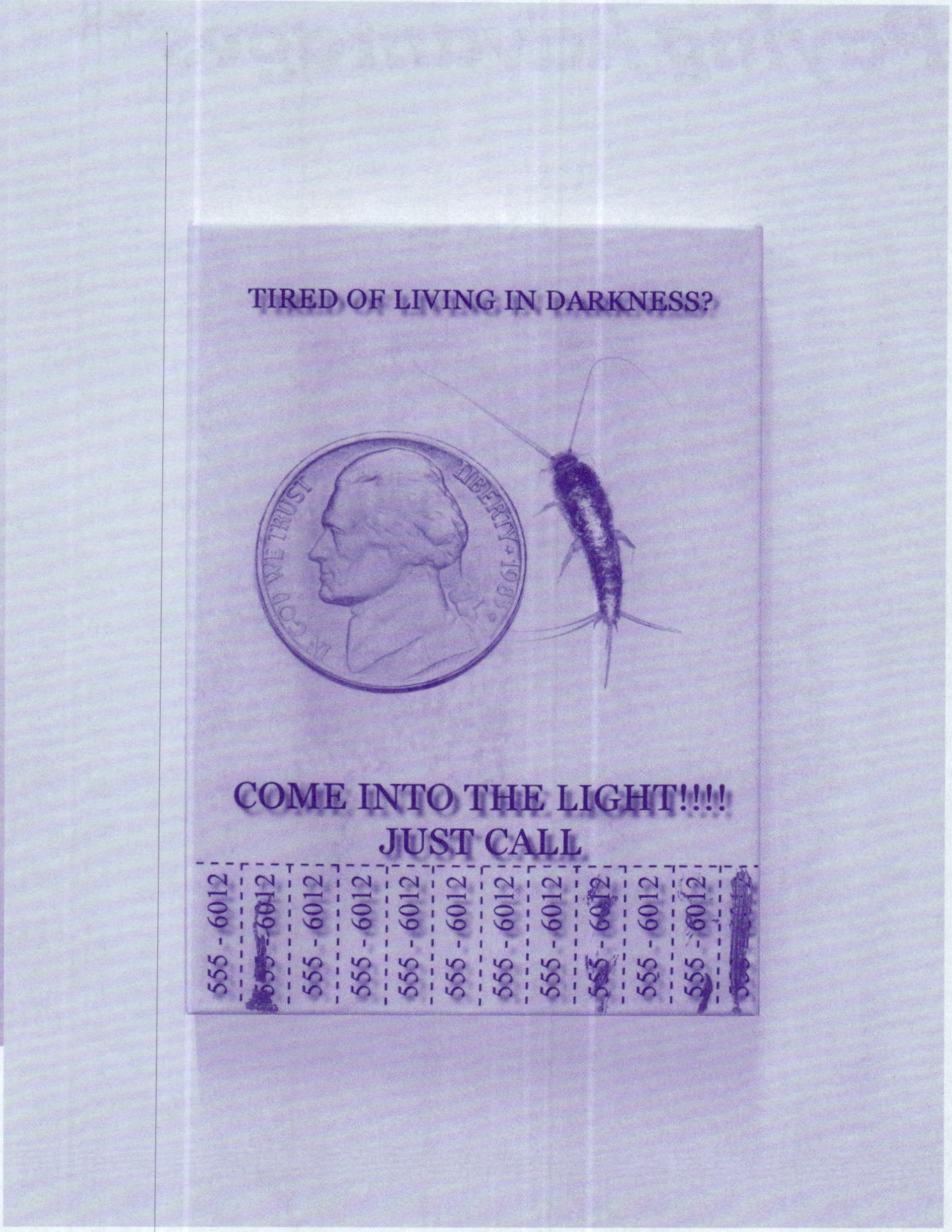

Come into the light, 2019
Inkjet transfer on silk, silver
30 × 21 cm
Courtesy of the artist

Paying Advantages**

Vera Palme

I.

It's always bittersweet making the rounds to the various Downtown casinos on the last day of your trip, knowing it'll be a while before you see them again.

It's sweet taking their money, though. We had three coupons for $25 matchplays at the D, and things had gone well on it, so that was our next stop. I like the fact that at the D (and the Gate) they give you chips for the matchplays. No screwing around with paper, ID, club cards, and so on at the table. The QuadQueen went off to play upstairs, and I went to play the matchplays on blackjack. I had a keno ticket to check, so I'd meet up with her after. I wandered along the Thump Thump pit at the D, looking for a ripe table to pillage. I found the perfect one, ready to deal, nobody on it. I don't like to interrupt the flow of a table just to dive in and out for a few matchplay hands. I also don't like anyone to see me screw up. I bought in for $100 and got to it. Green chip into betting the circle and a $25 matchplay on top. Won the hand. Won the second hand. Won the third hand. Nailed them all. Upstairs, I showed the QuadQueen my booty. I showed her the chips, too. We took the elevator downstairs, and I cashed in the chips. I checked for messages and there was one from BomberGal: "We're at the Golden Gate. Come down . . ." They couldn't be further away Downtown.

Our last stop was the El Cortez. We headed for the alcove, where our two favorite side-by-side dollar coin droppers are. The best of these is the 8/5 Bonus Poker machine that we've had a long, long relationship with. And there it was—gone. Just . . . gone. Replaced with something else. Shit. We hunted around but it was nowhere to be seen. This was incredibly sad. "There's no reason for me to come here, anymore," lamented the QuadQueen. I could see her point. It seems like bit by bit the fun and funky machines (and good paying ones) are being stripped from the El Cortez. Actually, it doesn't *seem* like that, it *is* like that. We did some kiosk stuff and a bit of freeplay couponing, and I bought my keno ticket for the road. Before heading out, I led the QuadQueen to one of the Double Deuces coin droppers, back by Subway. Maybe she could work some magic there. And I got a bright idea—I could grab a sub from Subway and take it back to the room for later. And that's what I did.

We arrived back at the Wynn ready to take on the casino one last final time for the trip. This would be before playing one last final time for the trip in the morning, and then playing one last final time for the trip at the airport. I had a good feeling about the row of newer IGT machines where I'd gotten the Pointies for $200. But I had unfinished business there, having been denied the kicker, yet again. Triple Double Bonus once again was my video elixir of choice. Because I am so crappy at getting kickers, I didn't bother to take a "before" picture. Suffice it to say that I was dealt three deuces and a 3 kicker. That old saw. We had a long discussion about what was the right thing to do. The QuadQueen leans toward keeping just the three deuces because getting four deuces would be great and you still might get a kicker. But drawing just one card, you'd have to get the one exact card. The cost in EV for this is maybe $2.50 over the long haul. I, on the other hand, like to play the right strategy. If I only held the deuces and got the fourth deuce and a non-kicker in place of the kicker I threw away—I'd be pissed. I'd feel like I lost $300. The best thing to do for these kinds of hands is to decide how you are going to play it always, and always play it that way. And that's what I did.

I pressed the draw button fully expecting to get the 8 of hearts or some other useless dog card. To my shock and amazement, the fourth deuce appeared! My mouth literally fell open and I turned to the QuadQueen and said, my eyes wide in wonder, "I . . . got it. I actually got it!!!" Four ducks. Got the kicker in all its kicker glory. A beautiful $500 hand to finish off my trip. Even though I'd nailed my unicorn hand at last, I still felt like I could get a keno hit one last time. We played for quite a while, but I perversed (sic), because I don't give up. I kept at it, too. I decided to keep it simple, a straight five spot play, 50 cents a pull. No hedging. Get it or nothing. Dammit if I didn't hit five out of five . . . Hmm, maybe I should have played a six spot corner. I took my pictures, played it down to $400, and cashed out.

"I'm done," I pronounced, with the air and seriousness of a spy gambler who is done.

"What do you mean, you're done?"

"I'm done. Done gambling for this trip. That's it. I'm not playing any more."

"What about tomorrow morning? What about the airport?"

"You know me. I say what I mean and I mean what I say, until I do something different."

Now the only thing left undone was paying BomberGal's bet off for the Grey Cup win. I still owe her a cocktail waitress tip. And with that, we packed up, and got ready to fly out of Vegas the next day, fortunately, at a reasonable hour.

I only lost $175 on the whole trip, including my El Cortez long playing keno ticket that added $20 to my wallet a day after we got home. The only room we paid for was at the Pearson Sheraton on the way back to Canada. That turned out to be a disaster that triggered a donation of 20,000 points to my Marriott account. We paid very little for food, maybe 80% of it being comped, including a side of beef's worth of meat at the steakhouses. Hard expenses including business class airfare, train fare, hotel, tips, food and liquor purchased, and bail money were about $3,150. Our comps almost balanced our costs, which to most people means a half-price trip, but to me, means a free trip, because . . . accounting spin!! And we won $53 to boot, so gambling cost was nil. You know how incredibly hard it is to do that over eleven days in Las Vegas. Yup! And, by the way, I didn't play any more after the final night. Shocking, but that's what I did.

Look, I've spent over sixty trips trying to solve Las Vegas. After the first three, losing all my bankroll every time, I thought there has to be a better way, an edge I can find, or some way I can lose less! Actually, some reading led me to learn that the return on slot machines is quite bad, and the return on blackjack, craps, and video poker can be much, much better. That's when I started to develop what I now call "Savvitude."

Savvitude is rooted in a general attitude that you are willing to make some effort in order to get a better deal, and that you are going to put yourself in the best position to win. I figured that if I am going to put my money at risk, I might as well try to reduce the amount I'm likely to lose. I've learned a little about odds and expected return, and picked up some strategies for my favorite games. I use slot clubs to my advantage, without being a slave to qualifying for tiers and racking up points, just to earn some tawdry casino swag, like a garter set, a shot glass, or a tin of Vermont's Original Bag Balm. I've introduced myself to a host or two at the properties I like to stay at. I ask for comps and sometimes get a free meal or some charges taken off my hotel bill. Basically, I have a positive attitude about the whole experience. I assume that I can win, that I am going to win, and do everything I can to ensure it happens. Read that again.

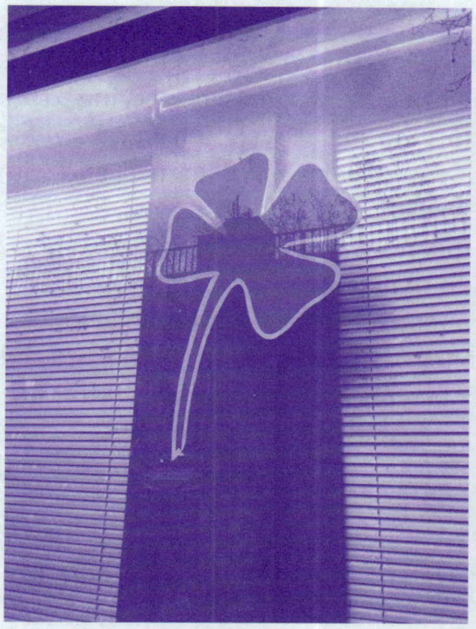

Prinzenstraße Casino, never open

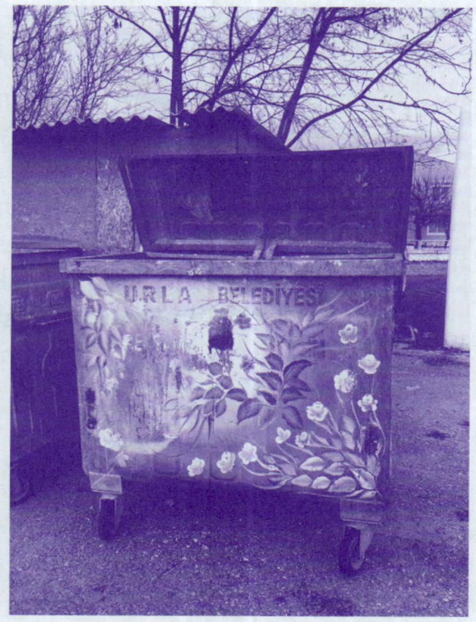

A municipality dumpster in Urla, Denizli prefecture

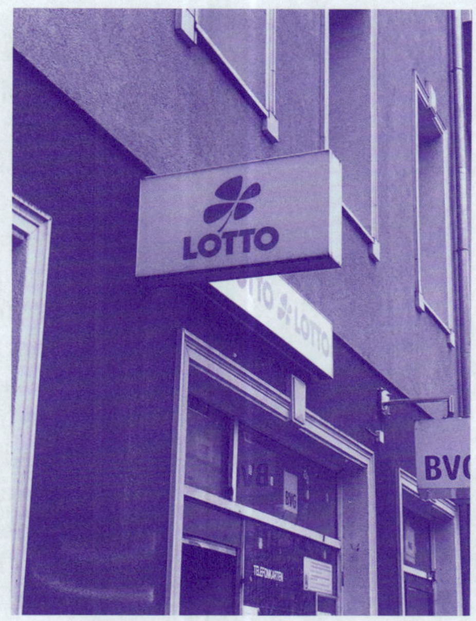

Lotto point, Britz

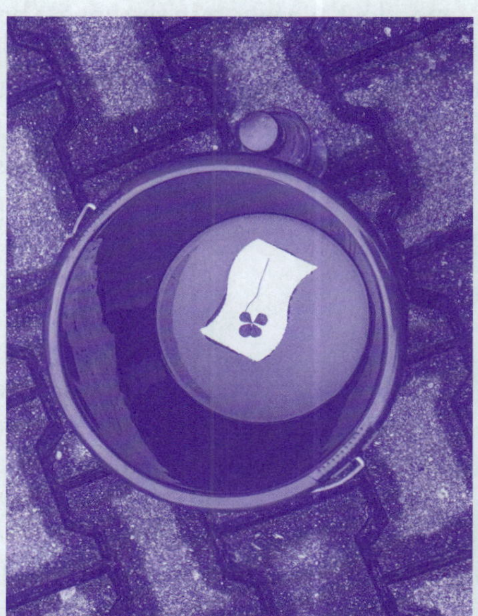

Lucky sponge in rakı

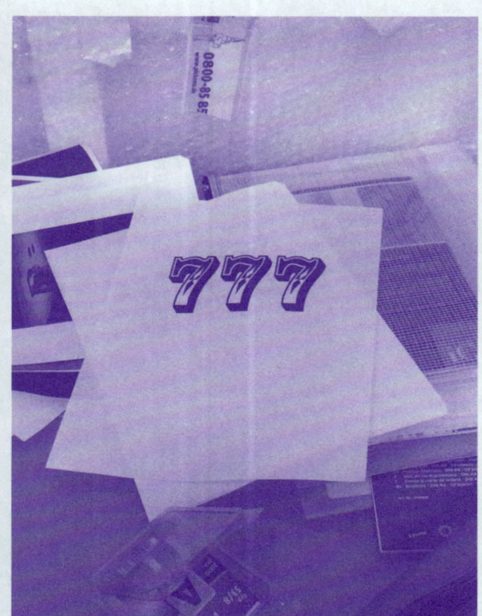

An omen

Now, nobody's perfect. *Occasionally* I have one too many pina coladas (sic), throw down a few huge cash bets on roulette, and end up puking in a potted plant while trying to take the elevator to my room—not knowing I'm in the wrong hotel. I am far from perfectly Savvitudinous. I drink while playing skill games, and sometimes I play the worst game in the house—keno. When I'm on a losing streak, I figure that keno actually saves me money because it costs maybe $20 an hour. I can easily lose hundreds in that same hour if things go badly. I don't plan to, but it happens. I play mostly video poker and blackjack, using strategies that return the most possible. I play craps too and sadly, I have a thing for Buffalo.

Having Savvitude means swinging the needle your way and shaving the house edge.

The potted plants will thank you.

II.

To paint small, if you must paint at all, *is a line of escape, yeah, but not a refuge,* to go as far as and with Gilles Deleuze and Félix Guattari on Kafka here, by all means no necessity, no, but it's enough to get to the point and that's what I have always said. And I need say no more. But since I am already here and renounce dibs on a substitute for a home, aka the idea of refuge, which is anyways as fugacious as the late night sub in Royal Flusher's victory lap, I will quote to you from the bonebook. However simple, the truth is a principle: sweep shit up like a barnacle. That's a spineless sessile parasite FYI. This resident drifter is a knapsack in and of itself, full of those transient desires that are made to cut through all layers of real cake. Short blades are more apt for short range action, domestic or not. Who cares if it's to feed from or in order to save them. Chips, coins, breadcrumbs. Something that doesn't need active letting go of since it was never ever had (I mean occupied) in the first place. And anyways only ever exists in the essence of dressing: for shit to go down swimmingly, sandwiched in between tempting sweet breads to suck up all of your good juice and not be spoiled, ever, or spilled. Nevermind exhaust. Get in while you can, it's to tank up, not to socialize. To go further in on the notion of homelessness here is as wrong as homeopathically far-fetched. And yet pushing similarities to become potent solutions for secure remedies is a practice that draws its strength from a deliberate lack of substantiality, a dynamised diluent packed with the remembrance of power. An abstract seed keeps afloat as a whole in the hostile brack waters of your groundbreaking ideas, escaping the larger riffraff's jam like a greased weasel. So yeah, in between Masters and the Royal Flusher sits the hard body of a coin that holds us. But like the fountain of abundance bends over eventually under its precious heftiness, that coin must melt.

III.

Masters is a man who lives by fire and dies by fire. He has this double thing of being an artist and a criminal, so naturally this feline sex appeal adds to the mystery that is his devillish allure. In his modernist villa/studio, showing off chic 1980s production design—White Leather, Venetian Blinds, Ikebana—Masters casts an unstretched canvas before him on the ground, kneels down and contemplates over it. Suddenly he rushes upstairs, staples the canvas to the outside wall and with a flick of his lighter sets it ablaze. The painting he burns looks kind of like him. He stares it down. Obviously Masters is used to burning a lot of things.

Yet finally, in a private warehouse somewhere in the desert at sunset, we do get a chance to witness magnificence. Wearing a short-sleeved, burgundy colored kimono, Masters demonstrates excellence in the minute art of counterfeiting money, shown to us in almost each meticulous detail under low, rather intimate lighting. Coined without irony, "the world's second oldest profession" includes a variety of artistic craftsmanship and in this (yes!) dreamy 1980s version of the deal it is slick, state of the art dry offset intaglio. The negative plates of four neat 20$ bills–hand-perfected by the wet tip of a brush's tongue that blackened out each tiny flaw— are brought to life by the artist's breath. His still vinyl-gloved hands mount the plates gently on the press. Oily black ink is applied thickly to rollers, swiftly followed by the creamy genesis of just the right kind of green which is an act off the cuff, but nevertheless a humble creation. While the machine is fed nonstop with virgin stacks of cotton paper it prints with uniform very high pressure. Masters' duplex ballet of tranquil accuracy continues, it deserves to bring all turns of expression to mind. Performed with the greatest of ease the gesture of simplicity is complete; a new order installed. Unperturbed, Masters crowns his unmatched olympian cool with the smile of appreciation that eludes the capitalist's chaos. At last those crisp cotton paper bills find their use in the laundry with a handful of multicolored rags and a bag's worth of gambling chips thrown in for good measure. A fun fact, the earliest known surviving examples of intaglio printmaking being undated designs for playing cards made in Germany, using drypoint technique, probably in the late 1430s.

Much later, squatting stark-naked in front of an open fire, Masters, the angry man, feeds this now hot paper to the flames. There go the spoils.

** Written with the utmost respect and appreciation for the works of Elif Saydam, royalflushervegas.com, and William fucking Friedkin.

Avanta Vermek**

Vera Palme

I.

Gezinin son günü bir süre buralara yolunun düşmeyeceğini bilerek merkezdeki kumarhaneleri son bir kez turlamak buruk bir keyif. Öte yandan dişime mangır değmesi de pek tatlı geliyor. D mekanında 25 papellik üç oyun için kuponumuz vardı. Önceden D'de işler iyi gitmişti, ondan sıradaki durağımız orasıydı. D'de ve Gemi'de oyunlar için jeton vermeleri hoşuma gidiyor. Masalarda öyle beldeyle, kafa kağıdıyla falan uğraşma derdi yok. DörtlüDilber oynamaya üst kata çıktı, ben de yirmi bire oturdum. Oynayacak bir sayısal fişim vardı, sonra buluşacaktık. İyice olgun, sağmaya hazır bir masa arayarak barbut güvertelerinin etrafında gezindim. Deliksiz bir tane buldum, dağıtmaya hazır, oynayan kimse yok, ortalık tın tın. Öyle birkaç oyun için bir masaya dalıp akışı bozmayı sevmem. Çuvallarsam da kimse görsün istemem. Yüz kağıda oyuna daldım ve başladım. Yeşil jetonla bahse girdim, üstüne de yirmi beş kağıtlık kuponum vardı. İlk eli ben kazandım, ikinciyi de öyle. Üstüne üçüncüyü de ben götürdüm. Hepsini bir güzel becerdim. Yukarıda DörtlüDilber'e ganimetimi ve jetonları gösterdim. Asansörle aşağı indik, jetonları bozdurdum. Mesajlarıma bakıverdim, ÇıtırBomba'dan bir mesaj vardı - Nuh'un Gemisi'ndeyiz, bu tarafa gelin. İyicene uzaktalardı.

Son durağımız Nazik'ti. Kameriye tarafına yöneldik, burada yan yana en sevdiğimiz iki makine dururdu. Bunların şahı ezelden beri dostumuz olan bir 8/5 bonus poker makinesiydi. Bir baktık ki ne görelim - parça yerinde yok. Yerine bir haltlar koymuşlar. Siktir. Bakındık ama bulamadık. Fena üzüldük. Bir daha da buraya gelmem diye nağme yapmaya başladı DörtlüDilber, pekala haklıydı. Görünen o ki tüm kıyak (ve sağlam kapik tutulan) makineler birer birer Nazik'ten gidiyordu. Görünen o ki demeye lüzum yok, bariz öyle işte. Gişelerde biraz oynadık, kupon falan yatırdık, bir de yolluk sayısal aldım. Çıkmadan DörtlüDilber'i dökme makinelerinden birine götürdüm, Büfenin yanındakine. Bir ihtimal orada sihrini konuşturabilirdi. Benim de kafamda bir ampul yandı - tost falan alıp odada karnımı doyurabilirdim, öyle de yaptım.

Bu gezinin son vurgununa hazır bir halde Wynn'e geri geldik. Tabi bundan sonra sabah da son bir oyun vardı, sonra da bir tur havaalanında uçağa binmeden döndürürdük. Buradaki yeni model havalı makinelerden umutluydum, daha önce 200 papel yatırıp okkalı bir miktar kaldırmıştım. Bir de burada kapanmamış defterlerim vardı - bir türlü cukkayı sağlama alamıyordum. Yine kendimi Üçlü Duble Bonus poker makinesinin sularında yüzerken buldum. O son kartı kapmakta pek becerikli olmadığımdan başlamadan fotoğraf bile çekmedim. Olan o ki, üç ikili geldiler, sonra da o yancı kart. Hep böyle derler zaten. Doğru hamlenin ne olacağı üzerine uzun uzun tartıştık. DörtlüDilber üç ikiliyi elimde tutmamdan yanaydı, bu şekilde belki dört ikili bulabilirdim, ya da halen işleri lehime çevirebilecek o yan kart gelebilirdi. Ama tek kart çekersem o seferde gereken kartı bulmak zorundaydım. Bunun beklenen değerden masrafı uzun vadede iki buçuk kağıt kadardı. Öte yandan ben doğru stratejiyle oynamayı severim. Eğer sadece ikileri elimde tutup dördüncüyü çeksem, ve attığım yancının yerine işe yaramaz bir kart gelse kafam atacaktı. Üç yüz kağıt kaybetmiş gibi hissederdim. Böyle ellerde en iyi hareket her seferinde nasıl oynayacağına karar verip hep öyle oynamaktır. Ben de öyle yaptım.

Kupa sekizi gibi çöp bir kart çekmeyi bekleyerek düğmeye bastım. Gelen kartı görünce feleğim şaştı - bir iki daha çekmiştim. Ağzım açık kaldı, DörtlüDilber'e döndüm, gözlerim faltaşı gibi, resmen uludum.. Yaptım!! Aldım! Çektim! Dört tane iki. O kıyak yan kart tüm güzelliğiyle karşımda. Bu turu beş yüz kağıtlık bir son dakika golüyle taçlandırmıştım.

Sonunda voleyi vurmuş olmama rağmen sayısaldan son bir cukka indirebileceğimi seziyordum. Epey bir süre oynadık, ama ben pes etmediğim için kırpılmaya başladım. Bastırmaya devam da ettim. Basit bir oyun taktiğim vardı, her seferinde elli kuruş yatırdığım beş sayılık fişler. Garanti yok, ya hep ya hiç. Beşte beş olacaktı, ya da halt etsindi. Düşününce, belki de altılı oynamalıydım. Çekeceğim fotoğrafları çektim, elimde dört yüz kağıt kalana kadar oynadım, sonra da fişlerimi bozdurdum.

Bitti, diye ilan ettim, hakikaten sona gelmiş bir hafiye kumarbaz edasıyla.

Ne demek bitti?
Bitti. Bu seferlik bitti. Daha fazla oynamayacağım.
E yarın sabah? Havaalanı?
Beni tanıyorsun. Sözümün eriyimdir, ta ki olmayana kadar.

Şimdi çözülmemiş tek mesele ÇıtırBomba'nın Gri Kupa zaferi için bahsini kapatmaktı. Kıza hala bir bahşiş borcum vardı. Onu da aradan çıkarınca pılımızı pırtımızı topladık, yarın Vegas'ı makul bir saatte terk etmek için hazırlandık.

Tüm gezide yalnız yüz yetmiş beş kağıt kaybetmişim, buna Nazik'te oynadığım, biz eve vardıktan sonra bana yirmi kağıt kazandıran sayısal fişi de dahil. Kalmak için para bayıldığımız tek oda dönüş yolundaki Sheraton oteldeydi. Burada öyle bir rezalet yaşadık ki, ödediğimizin neredeyse hepsini geri kopardık. Yiyip içtiğimizin çoğunu da beleşe getirmiş olduk, neredeyse bir bütün dana kadar et yemiş olsak bile. Birinci sınıf uçak bileti, tren biletleri, otel parası, bahşişler, yemek ve kafa çekmek gibi masraflar toplam üç bin yüz elli papel tuttu. Neredeyse bir o kadarını da bedavaya getirdik. Bu çoğu kişi için yarı fiyatına gezmek demektir, ama ben işin muhasebesini döndürmeyi iyi bildiğim için bana bedava demek. Üstüne üstlük 53 kağıt da kazandık, yani kumar masrafı sıfır. Bunu Kıbrıs'ta on bir gün geçirerek yapmanın ne kadar zor olduğunu bilirsiniz. Herhalde! Bu arada, son geceden sonra tekrar oynamadım. Hayret verici, ama hakikaten oynamadım.

Buraya tikel biraz, ben Kıbrıs'ı çözmek için sittin kez gidip geldim. İlk üç turda her seferinde sabunlandıktan sonra daha iyi bir yöntem olmalı diye düşündüm, daha az kaybetmek için bulabileceğim bir yol, yordam. Biraz mürekkep yaladıktan sonra makinelerde getirinin aslında çok düşük olduğunu, ama 21, barbut ve video pokerde çok daha fazla kazanılabildiğini öğrendim. İşte o zaman şimdi "İşbilirlik" dediğim olayı geliştirmeye başladım. '

İşbilirlik, daha iyi bir konumda olmak için biraz emek harcaman gerektiğini yansıtan bir tutumdan ve kendini kazanmak için en iyi konuma koymaya çalışma fikrinden beslenen bir kavram. Düşündüm ki, eğer paramı riske atacaksam en azından kaybetmem olası olan meblağı azaltmaya çalışayım. Biraz olasılık ve beklenen kazanç hakkında bilgi edindim ve en sevdiğim oyunlar için stratejiler oluşturdum. Slot makinelerinin olduğu kulüpleri avantajıma kullanıyorum, pazarlama oyunlarına gelmeden, puan biriktirmeye çalışmadan, sadece birkaç parça cafcaflı faça kapmaya çalışıyorum, jartiyer olur, shot bardağı olur, tabaka olur. Düzenli kaldığım mekanlarda kendimi tanıttım, bu şekilde indirimler, beleş yemek falan çözüyorum. Tüm olay hakkında kıyak bir hava benimsedim. Kazanabileceğimi varsayıyorum, hatta kazanacağımı, ve bunu sağlamak için elimden geleni ardıma koymuyorum. Tekrar bir oku bakalım.

Malumunuz, kimse mükemmel değildir. Ara sıra mazotu fazla kaçırıp rulet masasında okkalı bahisler oynayıp kendimi asansörle odama çıkmaya çalışırken bir saksı bitkisine kusarken bulduğum olur - yanlış otelde olduğumu bile fark etmeden. Harfi harfine İşbilir değilim asla. Beceri gerektiren oyunlar oynarken piyizlenirim, bazen de en berbat oyun olan sayısala düşerim. Eğer üst üste kaybediyorsam sayısal beni paklar, çünkü saatlik kaybedebileceğim miktar en fazla yirmi kağıt falandır. Başka bir oyunda saatte yüzlerce papel kaybedebilirim. Tabi plan bu değil, ama olmaz mı, olur. Genelde video poker ve 21 oynuyorum, en karlı olacak stratejileri uyguluyorum. Barbut da oynarım, maalesef Bufalo adlı slot oyununa zaafım var. İşbilirlik demek ibreyi kendi yolunuza çevirmek ve dükkanın kasasından kemirmektir.

Saksı bitkileri size teşekkür edecek.

II.

Ufak resimler yapmak, resim yapmak zorundaysanız eğer, *bir kaçış çizgisidir, evet, ancak bir sığınak değildir,* Kafka üzerine yazan Deleuze ve Guattari ile ve onların aldığı kadar yol almak gerekirse, hiçbir koşulda bir gereklilik değil, değil ki, ama konuya gelmek için kafi, ben de hep böyle dedim zaten. Dahasını da dememe gerek yok. Zaten ta buraya kadar gelmişken, bir ev muadili için yani bir sığınak fikri için kaleye mum dikmekten vazgeçmişken, ki o da Royal Flusher'ın zafer turundaki gece tostu kadar kaçamaktır, size kemikkitabından alıntı yapıvereyim. Ne kadar basit olursa olsun gerçek bir ilkedir: bir midye gibi bok toplayın. Midye omurgasız, yapışık bir asalaktır, bu arada. Bu yerleşik serseri kendi kendine bir sırt çantasıdır, gerçek bir pastanın tüm katlarını dişi kesemeyecek gelip geçici arzularla dolmuş. Kısa bıçaklar kısa menzilli harekatlara daha uygundur, yerli ya da yabancı. Beslenmek için mi kurtarmak için mi olduğu kimin umrunda ki zaten. Fişler, bozukluklar, kırıntılar. Hiçbir zaman sahiplenilmediği (yani işgal edilmediği) için kasten serbest bırakılmaya ihtiyaç duymayan bir şey. Zaten sadece garnitürün özünde var: her haltın tereyağından kıl çekercesine ilerlemesi adına, bozulmayan, dökülmeyen şugar suyunu emecek akıl çelen taptatlı ekmeklerin arasına kıstırılmış. Egzozu falan boşver şimdi. Hazır gelebiliyorken gel, depoyu doldurmaya çalışıyoruz, gullüm alıkmaya değil. Burada evsizlik fikrini daha da deşmek hem yanlış, hem de homeopatik olarak yersiz olacak. Öte yandan benzerlikleri okkalı dermanlar olacak kuvvetli çözümlere dönüşmeye zorlamak arkasını kasıtlı bir içi-boşluğa yaslar, gücün anımıyla tıka basa doldurulmuş, canlandırılmış bir seyreltici. Soyut bir tohum çığır açan fikirlerinin hasmane acı suyunda yekpare yüzüyor, alelade it kopuğun faslından yağlanmış bir sıçan gibi kaçıveriyor. Yani öyle işte, Masters'ın ve Royal Flusher'ın arasında bir jetonun bizi tutan sert vücudu yatar. Bolluk çeşmelerinin eninde sonunda kendi kıymetli ağırlıklarının altında eğilmesi gibi, o jeton erimelidir.

III.

Masters alevlerle yaşayıp alevlerle ölen bir adam. Hem sanatçı hem suçlu olduğundan kedimsi bir cilvesi var, bu da üzerindeki şeytan tüyünü iyice tutturuyor. Modernist villa/stüdyosunda 80'lerin şık üretim tasarımıyla caka satıyor, beyaz deri, jaluziler, ikebana. Masters yere gerilmemiş bir tuval seriyor, diz çöküp derin düşüncelere dalıyor. Birdenbire yukarı koşuyor, tuvali dış cepheye zımbalayıp çakmağının bir hamlesiyle ateşe veriyor. Yaktığı tablo biraz da kendini andırıyor. Tabloya gözlerini dikerek galip geliyor. Masters kesinlikle bir şeyler yakmaya pek alışık.

Yine de eninde sonunda çölde bir yerlerde özel bir depoda gün batarken ihtişama tanıklık edebileceğiz. Kısa kollu bordo bir kimono giyen Masters alengirli bir sanat olan kalpazanlıkta ustalığını sergiliyor, biz

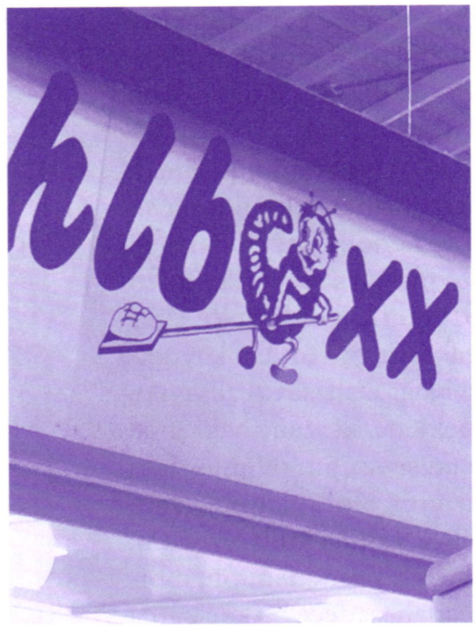

Mealworm at Arminiusmarkthalle

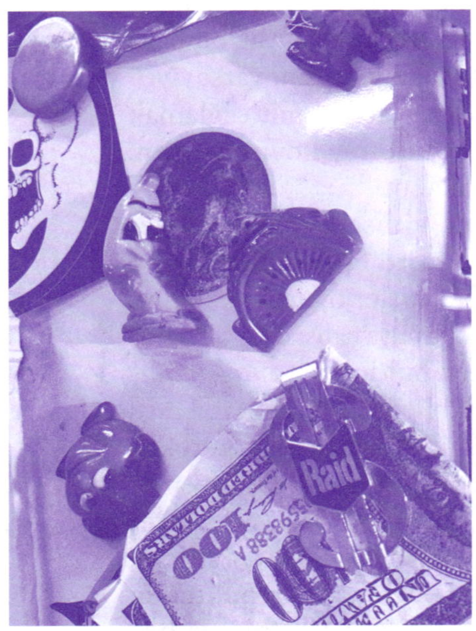

Magnet collection, VIDEO INN

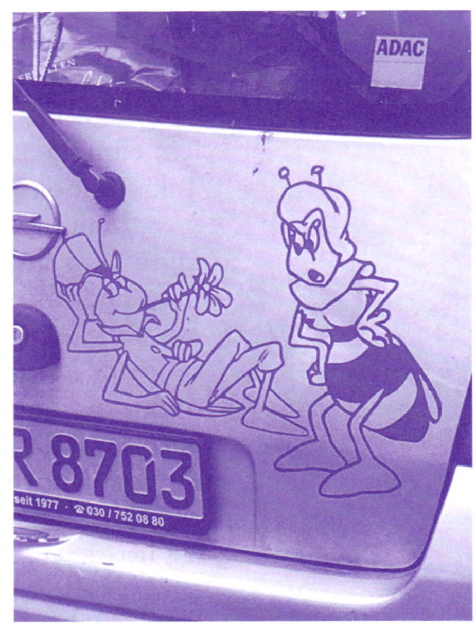

A vinyl scene on Sonnenallee

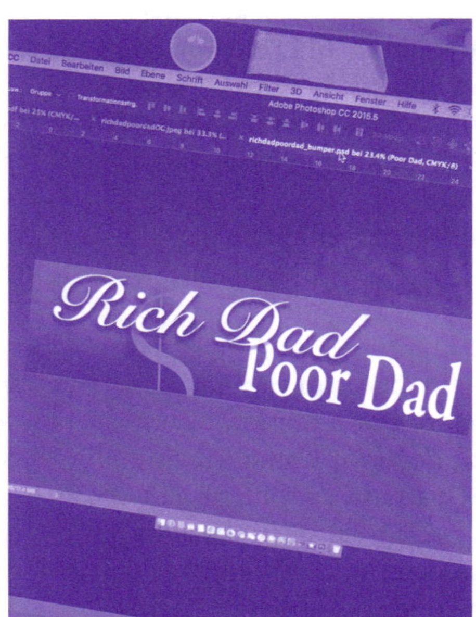

Rich Dad Poor Dad bumper stickers

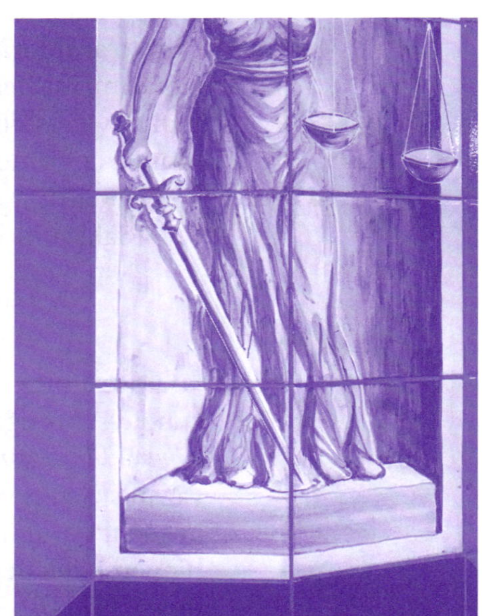

Justice at Turmstraße U-Bahn

de her minik detayı loş, neredeyse romantik bir ışıkta izliyoruz. Samimiyetle böyle tabir edilmiş "dünyanın ikinci en eski mesleği" bir dizi sanatçı zanaatkarlığı içeriyor ve olayın bu (bismillah!) rüyavari 80'ler versiyonunda konumuz alanının zirvesinde, son derece havalı kuru ofset oyma baskı. Ipıslak bir fırça darbesiyle mükemmelliğe ermiş dört adet yirmilik banknotun negatif levhaları sanatçının üflemesiyle doğuveriyor. Halen vinil eldivenle kaplı elleri levhaları nazikçe baskı makinesine diziyor. Yağlı siyah mürekkep silindirleri sarmalıyor, hemen ardından doğaçlama ancak mütevazı bir şekilde tam da gereken yeşillikte bir kaymak yaratılıyor. Makine mütemadiyen tomar tomar bakir pamuk kağıdıyla beslenirken tek tip yüksek baskı ile tabba devam ediyor. Masters'ın sakin ve hatasız çift sıra balesi, insanın aklına bin türlü mecaz getirerek sürüyor. Bu yalınlık ifadesi inanılmaz bir rahatlıkla icra edilip tamamlanıyor: yeni bir düzen çoktan oluştu. İstifini hiç bozmadan Masters rakipsiz, tanrısal rahatlığını bir de sermayedarın kaosundan kaçan kadirşinas bir gülümseme ile taçlandırıyor. Son aşamada o gıcır pamuk banknotlar çamaşır makinesinde rengarenk bezler ve işi sağlama almak için bir poşet jeton ile eskime fırsatı buluyor. Biliyor muydunuz ki, kabartma baskının günümüze dek gelebilmiş en eski örneklerinden biri muhtemelen 1430'lu yılların sonunda Almanya'da kuru kazı tekniği ile basılmış bazı zamansız iskambil kağıdı tasarımlarıymış.

Epey zaman sonra açıkta yanan bir ateşin önünde anadan doğma çıplaklıkta çömelmiş duran Masters, öfkeli adam, ısınan kağıtları alevlere yediriyor. İşte elden gidiyor ganimet.

** Elif Saydam'ın, royalflushervegas.com'un ve bela herif William Friedkin'in eserlerine içten saygı ve sevgi ile yazılmıştır.

Clueless, or There and Back Again

Adam Fearon

Thus hardy Theseus, with intrepid Feet,
Travers'd the dang'rous Labyrinth of Crete;
But still the wandring Passes forc'd his Stay,
Till Ariadne's Clue unwinds the Way
—John Gay, *Trivia*, 1716

Until the seventeenth century, the word "clue" referred to a ball of thread. "Clue," originally spelt *clew*, shares a root with "clay," *gleu*: "to gather into a mass." It is a Germanic word by origin, but the change in meaning from rolled-up string to a piece of evidence unraveling a mystery stems from a Greek myth: it is the thread Ariadne gave her lover Theseus so that he could find his way into her father's labyrinth to kill her half-brother, the Minotaur, the man with the head of a bull, and follow back out in order to elope with her.

Theseus did kill the Minotaur and found his way out again following the red thread, and he did take Ariadne away with him, but he abandoned her on a small, rocky island almost immediately. Not that this is the only version of the myth: in some, Ariadne is abandoned for her sister Phaedra; in some, she happily marries Bacchus (Dionysus); in others, she kills herself. As Roberto Calasso says in *The Marriage of Cadmus and Harmony* (1988): "No sooner have you grabbed hold of it than myth opens out into a fan of a thousand segments. Here the variant is the origin. Everything that happens, happens this way, or that way, or this other way. And in each of these diverging stories all the others are reflected, all brush by us like folds of the same cloth. If, out of some perversity of tradition, only one version of some mythical event has come down to us, it is like a body without a shadow, and we must do our best to trace out that invisible shadow in our minds."

It's fitting, then, that Ariadne and Theseus belong to the very early group of myths and heroes, the first generation of myths within the myths like that of Hercules, Achilles' hero, on top of which later tales, like *The Iliad*, were laid. Multiplicity is inherent in the idea of the maze. It contains a thousand possibilities at once. Ariadne's thread is like a record of each undertaking, each possible route tracing attempts at understanding, like language itself.

And for the hous is krynkeled to and fro
And hath so queynte weyes for to go—
For it is shapen as the mase is wrought—
Therto have I a remedye in my thought,
That, by a clewe of twyn, as he hath gon,
The same weye he may returne anon,
Folwynge alwey the thred as he hath come.[1]
—Chaucer, *The Legend of Good Women*, c. 1385

Ariadne hardly appears in medieval literature—the passing mentions she gets in Chaucer and Dante are exceptional—but, as interest in the classical past increased, there was a burst of plays, poems, operas, and popular songs focused on the myth. By the 17th century, the stories around Ariadne were fixed enough in the popular imagination to become the subject of satire and parody. And it's around then that the word "clue" shifts its meaning from the literal to the figurative.

1 "And as the house is crinkled to and fro
And has such complex ways to go—
For it is shaped as a maze is wrought—
I've a remedy for that in my thought,
That with a clew of twine the way he's gone
The same way he may return anon,
Following ever the thread till out he'll come."
Geoffrey Chaucer, *The Canterbury Tales*, translated by A.S. Kline. Poetry in Translation, 2008.

The first recorded use of the word in its modern sense is in *Logick: Or, The Right Use of Reason in the Enquiry after Truth* (1724), by the English hymnographer, theologian, and logician Isaac Watts (1674–1748): "When the Reader is passing over such a Treatise, he often finds a wide Vacancy, and makes an uneasy Stop, and knows not how to transport his Thoughts over to the next Particular, for Want of some Clue or connecting Idea to lay hold of." In this case, the *clew* is a line of thought. The maze is an idea, an abstraction the mind has to negotiate.

There are two types of mazes, "unicursal," meaning those with only one path that winds slowly towards the centre, and "multicursal," those with many possible routes and endings. And while latterly a sort of consensus has formed around the fact that "labyrinth" refers to the unicursal and "maze" to the multicursal, until recently the words were used interchangeably in English.

There is also—perhaps partly because of this attempt at clarification—an idea that unicursal labyrinths are ancient and that multicursal mazes, like the hedge maze at Hampton court, are more modern. This confusion is no doubt aided by the widespread habit, going back to ancient times, of illustrating texts with what became the symbol of the labyrinth, the unicursal spiral, regardless of which type of maze was being described. There's a contradiction from the start: if the Minotaur was to be trapped in an ingenious maze of Daedalus' invention, then, despite the ancient illustrations, surely it must be a multicursal one, or he'd just wander in and out of it.

The difference between the two words stems, in fact, purely from their separate etymologies. "Maze," like "amaze," comes from the Old English, *mæs*, meaning "delusion, bewilderment, confusion of thought," and is related to the Norwegian dialectal *mas* connoting "exhausting labor," and the Swedish *masa* which suggests being "slow or sluggish." It outlines the mental state that mazes induce rather than any physical manifestation of them so that in this way, the word is a kind of metonymy.

Therein lies an easy analogy to painting itself: it is slow and sluggish, an act of unexpectedly exhausting labor—especially oil painting. You can only do so much in one go: the layer stays wet, and if you keep going too long it just gets muddy and indistinct. Certain colors, depending on their pigmentation, take months to dry and cure. It's about layering and waiting and staring at "blind walls." You must sit on your hands and resist the temptation to fiddle in the meantime. The process is about getting lost and finding the way again many times before reaching an exit. It's also about constantly shifting perspectives. And, of course, it's about searching for, and leaving behind, clues.

Elif Saydam's works are crawling with clues: a rotating cast of characters, logos, and symbols. Their work is not figurative in any normal sense: there is no representation of reality, no use of illusionistic space, no straightforward figuration. Instead, a kind of lexicon of symbols builds up: padlocks, CLOSED signs, hearts, a frog or two, grapes, lemons, fresh fruit, rotten fruit, ladders, landlords, chromosomes, labels from honey jars, brain scans, chains, daisies, daisy chains, mosquitos, bees, bugs, smiley faces, a stomach, mood rings, bow-tie pasta, wilted roses, charged political slogans, ice tea, Antifa, 555-phone numbers, butterflies, a lucky star, bloodshot eyes, wheat, the hand of Fatima, four-leaf clovers, the iconic Blue Marble . . . and mazes.

These pictorial symbols float over a series of backgrounds that are themselves a series of interrelated layers and collaged images: scans of plastic bags and scraps of fabrics, black and white photographs, tie-dyed canvas, microscopic images of stomach cells, other detritus. These collaged images are printed onto cheap t-shirt transfers and melted onto a canvas, some of which are first dyed or manipulated to further set the stage—the ground of the painting—as confusing territory.

Saydam's paintings are linked firmly to the miniatures in the Ottoman and Persian

An example of a unicursal maze on the left, and a multicursal one on the right

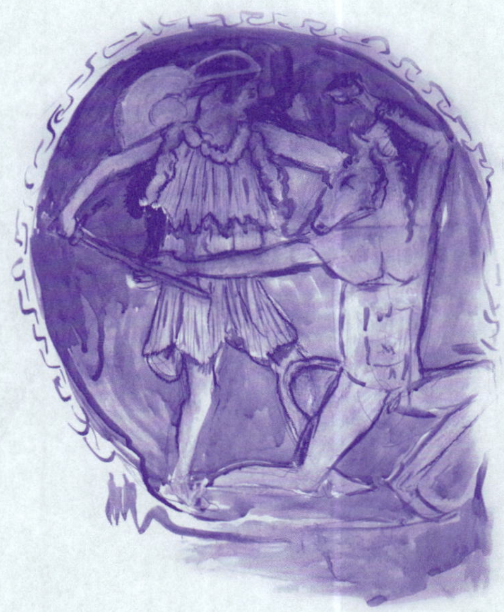

Theseus slays the Minotaur

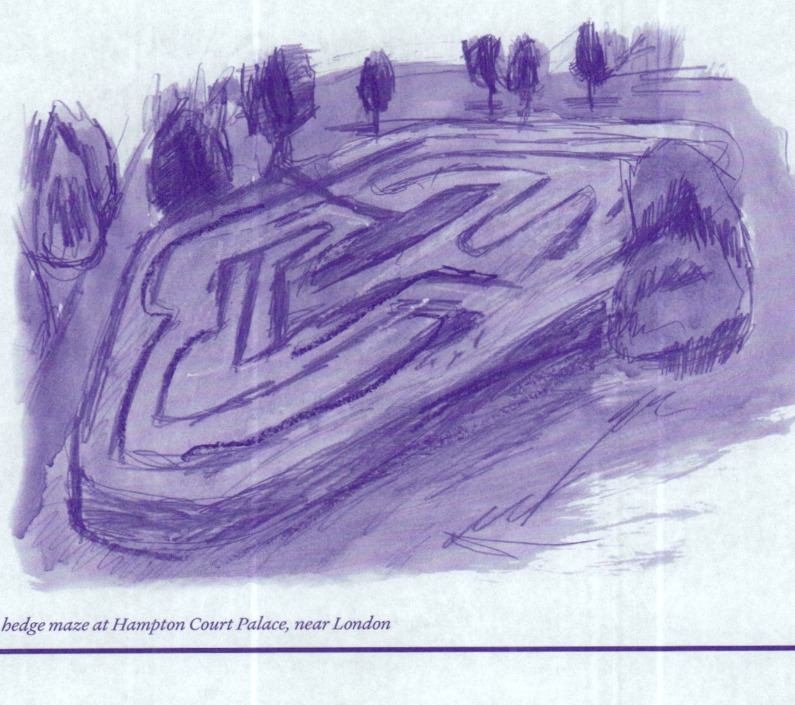

The hedge maze at Hampton Court Palace, near London

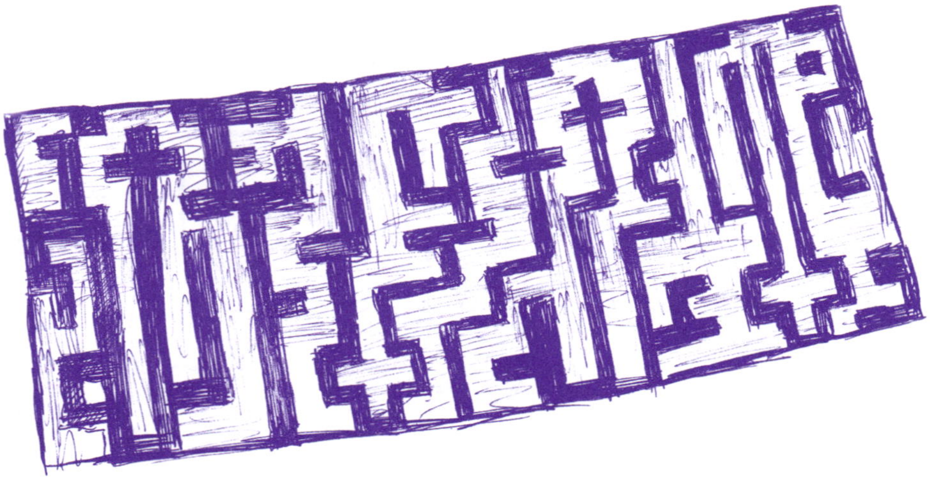

Mosaic from the facade of the Alhambra Palace in Granada

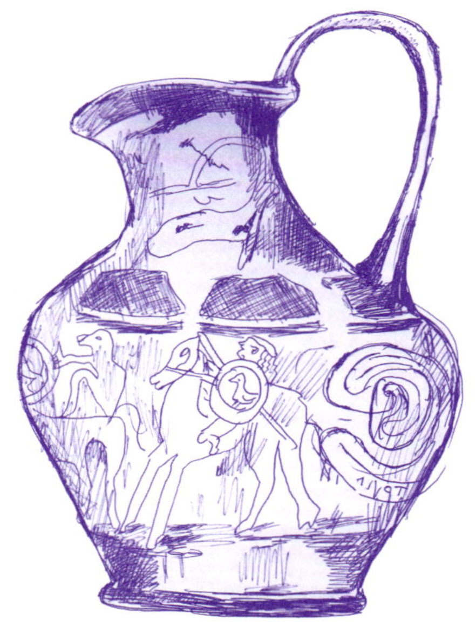

Drawing of Etruscan oinochoë *(wine-server), late seventh-century BC, from Tragliatella near Caere*

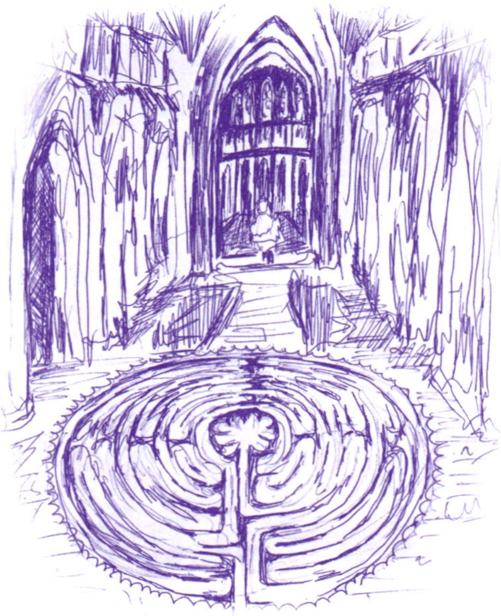

The labyrinth at Chartres Cathedra

tradition, where *mimesis* was rejected in favour of a heightened abstraction of figures and form and in which multiple perspectives and time-frames could be incorporated into the same painting. The idea of the fixed, singular perspective that developed in the Renaissance, and the world view this development implies, is antithetical to the multiplicities and possibilities embedded in these simultaneous overviews.

In many of Saydam's paintings, hovering between the background and the layers of symbolism, fragments of mazes are present, as though floating in a layer of interstitial fluid. There are unicursal mazes and multicursal ones, often in gold or silver leaf, sometimes painted inside the outline of a stomach, or sometimes framing a doorway, as well as mazes that are not mazes at all, but in fact the tracings of a particular, very geometric form of Arabic calligraphy, known as Square Kufic.

Calligraphy in the Islamic and Arabic traditions evolved and developed in ways that were infinitely more complex and refined than any script in Western Europe. There are many reasons for this. Scholars have cited, for example, the fact that the cursive nature of Arabic made it much less adaptable to early printing presses, and therefore the scribal traditions continued on, especially for religious texts. More pertinent perhaps is that, although it is not explicitly prohibited in the Qu'ran, Islamic tradition has favoured an injunction against the production of representative images, allowing for the sophisticated development of aesthetics in proximity to abstraction.

Kufic is the oldest form of Arabic calligraphy, named after the city of Kufah in modern Iraq where it is said to have originated. The earliest copies of the Qu'ran are written in Kufic, though its popularity eventually faded, and around 1,000 years ago, it was superseded by other types, related to the more cursive Naskhi form. Square Kufic, however, maintained longevity as a graphic adaptation of the script for mosaic: its sharp geometry a translation of the flowing Arabic script into bricks and tiles.

In the most complex examples, both the positive and negative spaces of the Square Kufic form spell out words. For example, in the Sultan Qalawun complex in Cairo built in 1284 AD, a wall panel incorporates the name "Muhammad" rotated four times, where the white space between these names forms the name "Ali." The same device is used in a rather more complicated building in Seville, Spain, which brought together, uneasily, the Christian and Islamic traditions.

In 1364, after the reconquest of Seville from the Almohad Caliphate, Pedro I, King of Castile and León (1334–1369), set about expanding the existing palace complex. He chose to do so using a mix of architectural traditions in a style which became known as 'Mudejar' and brought Muslim craftsmen from Granada, still then under the rule of the Nasrid Caliphate.

At the top of the facade of the building's entrance is a blue and white geometric mosaic. At first, it appears to simply be an abstract pattern repeating around Christian crosses. However, the craftsman—perhaps surreptitiously—incorporated the slogan of the rival Nasrid rulers of Granada at the time, "There is no victor but God," in Square Kufic script.

Saydam's source for the Square Kufic pattern used in their painting is specifically Ottoman, but the sleight of hand performed follows the same logic of their craftsman predecessors in Seville. What appears as abstract to one audience is interpolated completely differently for another. A ball of thread has two ends to pull from, after all.

It's said that the first labyrinths weren't mazes but dances. In *The Iliad* and in Virgil's *Aeneid*,[2] there are references framing the first labyrinths as "patterned

2 "As of old in high Crete 'tis said the Labyrinth held a path woven with blind walls, and a bewildering [double] work of craft with a thousand ways, where the tokens of the course were confused by the indiscoverable and irretraceable maze: even in such a course do the Trojan children entangle their steps . . ." From Penelope Reed Doob, *The Idea of the Labyrinth from Classical Antiquity through the Middle Ages,* Cornell University Press, 1990, p. 27.

places for dancing."[3] There are also ancient references to dances carried out in celebration of the end of Athenian tribute to Crete. The Romans later staged an elaborate horse ballet, known as *lusus Troiae*, or the Trojan Games, that also traced the labyrinth pattern. An Etruscan vase from the sixth or seventh century BC shows two horses and a maze pattern that the scholar Penelope Reed speculates suggests even more ancient connections between these movement rituals and the labyrinth.

It certainly makes sense to align the labyrinth with dancing, with the marks of movement left behind after the dust has settled. And after all, mazes do nothing if not control how we move.

The symbol of the maze, and its association with ritual and dancing, continue into the Christian tradition. There was a church built in Algeria during the fourth century, c. 324 CE, just after the Edict of Constantinople that made the practice of Christianity legal: St. Reparata in El Asnam, which has a geometric labyrinth pattern mosaic floor. It is almost identical to the popular Roman motif of a labyrinth maze with Theseus and the Minotaur at the centre, except the mythical figures are replaced by a palindrome formed from the words *Sancta Ecclesia* (Holy Church). Connections between the maze and Theseus and Christ would continue to be made, however, and there are medieval texts that explicitly draw analogies between the figures, likening Theseus' journey into the labyrinth with the "Harrowing" of Christ.

The original designer of the first maze, Daedalus, was occasionally associated with the Christian God's design for the universe, and it has been suggested the labyrinth was a way of explaining the gap between the difficulty and confusion of living, and the notion of an all-knowing God with a master plan; the schism between what is experienced and what is held to be conceptually true, a materialist/idealist dilemma. The labyrinths suggest that the difference between chaos and order is one of perspective, as though the confusion and difficulty of the experience of life would fade away if only we possessed, as a God would have, an overview of the plan.

There are accounts of clerics in Auxerre, France, performing ritual dances in church labyrinths on Easter Mondays: throwing a leather ball called a *pilota* at each other as they worked rhythmically, in a "garland-like" dance through the geometry. Scholars speculate that the ball might represent Christ as the sun, or indeed the *clew* that Ariadne gave Theseus, and in this instance, the thread represents wisdom, or divinity and guiding light.

Labyrinths were built in the majority of Gothic cathedrals in France and Italy, as well in several other locations across Europe, but most were removed in the late Middle Ages for reasons that are not well documented, but which clearly relate to their pagan connotations and the shift towards affiliating mazes with sites of pleasure, transgression, and sin.

> The quaint mazes in the wanton green, for lack of tread are undistinguishable.
> —Titania in *A Midsummer Night's Dream,* Act II Sc 1

Meanwhile, in parallel to the development of ecclesiastical labyrinths, there were separate, secular traditions of building mazes, including a peasant tradition of treading down the grass to create turf mazes outside villages in England which seem to date back to before the Roman invasion. The aristocratic tradition of building elaborate hedge mazes, documented throughout

3 "And on it the famed crook-legged god made a patterned place for dancing. Like that which once in broad knossos Daedalus created for Ariadne of the lovely hair." Homer, *The Iliad,* Book 18, Lines 586–590, translated by Caroline Alexander, Vintage Classics, 2017, p. 410.

the Middle Ages in England and France, stems as much from these traditions as from classical inspiration.

It is said that in the twelfth century, at Woodstock Palace in England, Henry II built a maze to shield his mistress, Rosamund Clifford, from his wife, Eleanor of Aquitaine. According to legend, Eleanor discovers her way through the maze to Rosamund, bearing a cup of poison in one hand and a dagger in the other, and offers Rosamund her choice of death. As in the Minotaur legend, the complex structure is built to fold in shame, and now, sin.

Although there is no evidence for any such structure at the site, which is where Blenheim Palace now stands, garden labyrinths were popular amongst the nobility of the time; there are log books recording the payments that Charles V (1364–1380) made to workers to maintain a "Maison Daedalus" in his gardens at the Hôtel Saint-Pol in Paris, and there are records of similar structures at the castle of Hesdin, the Hôtel des Tournelles, and many other properties during the Middle Ages, although details of what they might have looked like are lost to us.

In eighteenth-century London, those aristocratic gardens and mazes were the blueprint for the new public and commercial phenomenon of "pleasure gardens" where, for a fee, Londoners could enter neatly landscaped gardens with regular operas, masquerades, dinners, fireworks, and other entertainments. These gardens were also among the first places where artists such as William Hogarth showed their work publicly. They were at the centre of nightlife and the beginnings of modern commercial entertainment. Although expensive and designed to be "respectable," the pleasure gardens were also places for slippage between the strictly defined classes and—as constantly alluded to in the press at the time—spaces rife with transgression and sexual potential. In Paris, the Jardins des Tuileries was the first royal garden to be open to the general population in 1667. As with the pleasure gardens in London, these precisely laid out spaces were designed for promenading and display, bringing architecture and behaviour once strictly reserved for the aristocracy towards a broader public, and in so doing defined what "public" meant at the emergence of the modern, urban, consumer subject.

There are police records of men cruising each other in the Tuileries as early as the 1750s. Contemporary written reports by undercover police give us a sharp insight into life at that time. For example, Charles Gentil, who was subsequently arrested, accosted a man listening to music emanating from the Tuileries Palace by noting that "there are some fine instruments in this ensemble" and adding, "there are others that do not make so much noise but give more pleasure . . ."[4]

Contemporary cruising grounds are often a type of maze. Like the pleasure gardens of the eighteenth century, they are structures made to slow down time, a series of intersections by which one crosses and recrosses the same person over and over again. Like a shrunken city, it forces upon its dwellers all the direct interactions and eye contact with strangers that living in a city teaches us to avoid. The cruising ground compresses the streets of the metropolis and stages confrontations. Crucially though, there is no language: one doesn't speak. Silence is a thick and necessary part of the tension of desire, and chatter breaks it.

When you get lost in a maze, turning and turning again, perhaps the thrill of it is that you lose the thread of yourself. Michael Fried once wrote that entering the imaginative space of the painting means an erasure of the viewer's sense of self: the sense of self necessarily being tied to narrative

4 Jeffrey Merrick, "The Paris Cruising Scene in 1750," *The Gay & Lesbian Review Worldwide*, Vol. 26, No. 4 (July–August, 2019), p. 27.

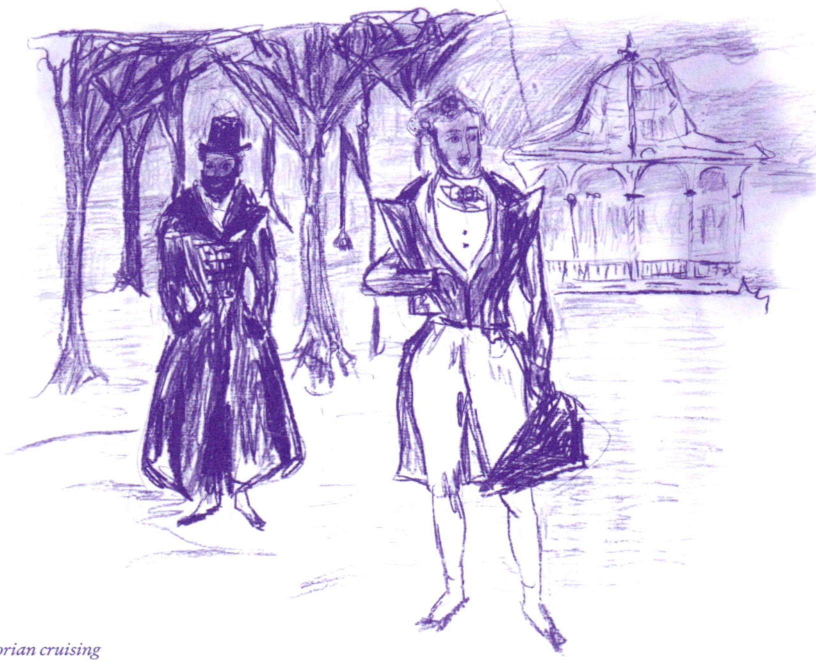

Victorian cruising

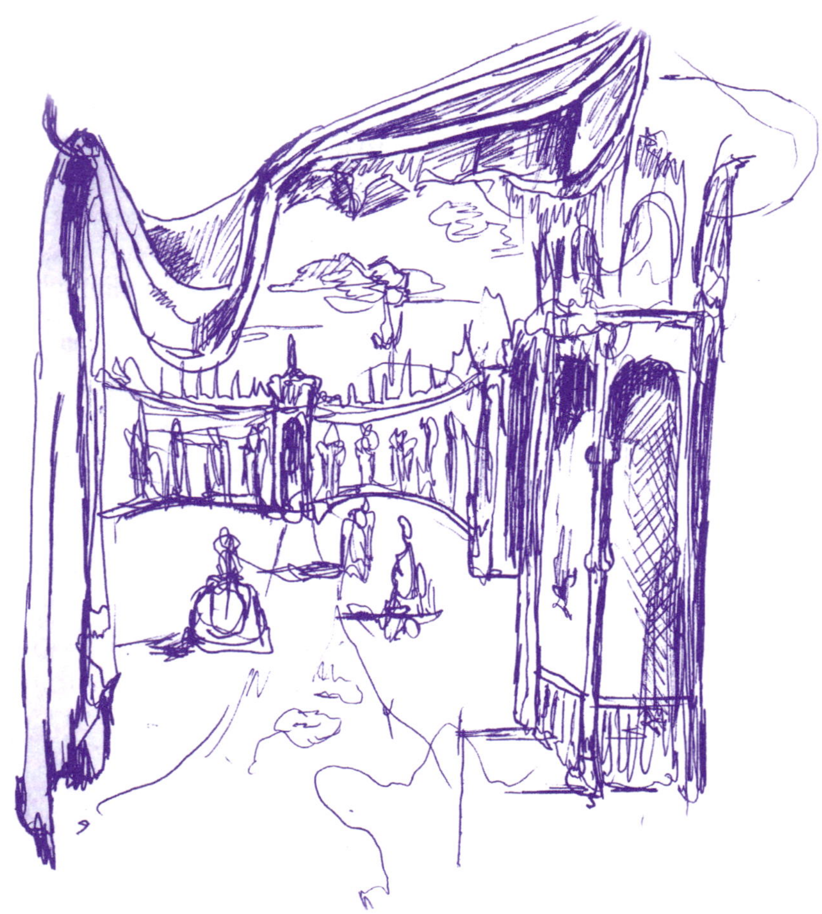

An English pleasure garden

and language.[5] But what of an overabundance of narrative, of too many clues, threads to follow, false promises of escape? Turning and turning again, there is a sameness to the blind walls. Painting, spending time with painting, the slow process of producing, the slow process of really looking, it is all unequivocally disorientating. A coherent sense of beginning and end is corrupted. Things start knotting together. Boundaries become unclear. There are no neat sentences.

5 Michael Fried, *Absorption and Theatricality: Painting and Beholder in the Age of Diderot*, University of California Press, 1980, p. 131.

Ahnungslos, oder hin und wieder zurück

Adam Fearon

Thus hardy Theseus, with intrepid Feet,
Travers'd the dangr'ous Labyrinth of Crete;
But still the wandring Passes forc'd his Stay
Till Ariadne's Clue unwinds the Way.[1]
—John Gay, *Trivia*, 1716

1 Der wackere Theseus mit beherztem Tritt
Das üble Kret'sche Labyrinth durchschritt;
Doch wandernde Gänge hemmten zunächst seinen Lauf
Bis Ariadnes Faden schließt den Weg ihm auf.
Nachdichtung, NGS. (2022)

Bis ins 17. Jahrhundert bezog sich das englische Wort „clue" auf ein Garnknäuel. „Clue", ursprünglich „clew", hat dieselbe Wurzel wie „clay", *gleu*, was so viel bedeutet wie: „sich zu einer Masse zusammenballen". Seiner Herkunft nach ist das Wort germanisch. Der Bedeutungswandel von einem aufgerollten Faden zu einem Anhaltspunkt[2], der bei der Enträtselung eines Geheimnisses hilft, geht jedoch auf einen griechischen Mythos zurück: auf den Faden, den Ariadne ihrem Geliebten Theseus gab, damit dieser den Weg in das Labyrinth ihres Vaters finden könne, um dort ihren Halbbruder, den Minotauros, den Mann mit dem Stierhaupt, zu töten, und dann dem Faden wieder nach draußen zu folgen und sich mit ihr davonzumachen.

2 Clue hat im heutigen Englisch ein breites Bedeutungsspektrum. Es kann je nach Kontext Indiz, Spur (im kriminalistischen Kontext), Tipp (Hinweis), Ahnung (Idee), Anhaltspunkt, Richt- oder Leitlinie und im übertragenen Sinne auch Faden oder Schlüssel bedeuten. (A.d.Ü.)

Und so geschah es auch: Theseus tötete den Minotauros und fand mit Hilfe des roten Fadens wieder heraus, und er nahm Ariadne auch mit sich, doch nur kurze Zeit später ließ er sie auf einer kleinen felsigen Insel zurück. Nicht dass dies die einzige Fassung des Mythos wäre: In einigen wird Ariadne für ihre Schwester Phädra sitzengelassen, in einigen geht sie eine glückliche Ehe mit Bacchus (Dionysos) ein, in anderen nimmt sie sich das Leben. Roberto Calasso schreibt in *Die Hochzeit von Kadmos und Harmonia* (1988):
„Will man den Mythos ergreifen, fächert er sich in viele Varianten auf. Die Variante ist hier der Ursprung. Jede Tat ereignet sich auf diese oder eine andere oder noch eine andere Weise. Und in jeder dieser divergierenden Geschichten reflektieren sich die anderen, jede streift uns wie der Saum desselben Stoffes. Wenn uns aufgrund einer Laune der Überlieferung nur eine Version von einer mythischen Begebenheit erhalten geblieben ist, so ist sie ein Körper ohne Schatten, und wir müssen versuchen, ihren unsichtbaren Schatten im Geiste nachzuzeichnen."[3]

3 Roberto Calasso, *Die Hochzeit von Kadmos und Harmonia,* aus dem Italienischen von Moshe Kahn, Berlin 2016 [1990], S. 160.

Dass Ariadne und Theseus zu den sehr frühen Mythen und Helden gehören, ist passend. Wie die Geschichte von Herkules, dem Helden Achilles' gehören sie zur ersten Generation der Mythen in den Mythen, die von späteren Erzählungen wie der *Ilias* überlagert werden. Mannigfaltigkeit ist der Idee des Labyrinths (*maze*) angeboren. Sie enthält tausend Möglichkeiten gleichzeitig. Der Ariadnefaden ist wie eine Aufzeichnung jedes Unterfangens, jeder möglichen Route, er zeichnet jeden Verständnisversuch nach, so wie die Sprache selbst.

And for the hous is krynkeled to and fro
And hath so queynte Weyes for to go –
For it is shapen as the mase is wrought –
Therto have I a remedye in my thought.
That, by a clewe of twyne, as he hath gon,
The same weye he may returne anon,
Folwynge alwey the thred as he hath come.[4]
—Chaucer, *The Legend of Good Women*, um 1385

4 Und weil das Haus total verschachtelt ist
Und klare Wege man vermisst –
Denn wie ein Labyrinth ist es gemacht
Hab ich mir eine Lösung ausgedacht:
Mit einem Knäuel Garn in Händen,
Könnt er dem Faden folgend an den Wänden,
Den Weg hinein auch raus verwenden.
Nachdichtung, N.G.S. (2022)

Ariadne kommt in der mittelalterlichen Literatur kaum vor (Chaucer und Dante, die sie flüchtig erwähnen, sind Ausnahmen), doch als das Interesse an der klassischen Vergangenheit zunahm, gab es plötzlich eine Fülle von Theaterstücken, Gedichten, Opern und volkstümlichen Liedern, in deren Mittelpunkt dieser Mythos stand. Im 17. Jahrhundert waren die Geschichten, die sich um Ariadne rankten, in der allgemeinen Vorstellungskraft so fest verankert, dass sie zum Gegenstand von Satiren und Parodien wurden. Und um diese Zeit herum, verändert das Wort „clue" seine Bedeutung von der buchstäblichen zur übertragenen.

Den ersten dokumentierten Gebrauch des Wortes in seiner modernen Bedeutung macht der englische Hymnograph, Theologe und Logiker Isaac Watts (1647–1748) in seiner *Logick: Or, The Right Use of Reason in the Enquiry of Truth* [Logik oder vom rechten Gebrauch der Vernunft bei der Suche nach Wahrheit] (1724): „Wenn der Leser ein solches Traktat durchschreitet, findet er häufig große Leerräume, und hält beunruhigt inne, und weiß nicht, wie er seine Gedanken zur nächsten Einzelheit befördern soll, weil er keines Hinweises *(Clue)* und keiner verbindenden Idee habhaft werden kann."

In diesem Fall ist der *clew* ein Gedankengang. Das Labyrinth (*maze*) ist eine Idee, eine Abstraktion, mit der der Kopf zurande kommen muss.

Es gibt zwei Arten von Labyrinthen, „unikursale", sprich diejenigen mit nur einem Weg, der sich langsam zum Mittelpunkt hinwindet, und „multikursale", diejenigen mit vielen möglichen Routen und Enden. Und auch wenn sich in letzter Zeit eine Art Konsens darüber herausgebildet hat, dass sich im Englischen „labyrinth" auf das unikursale, „maze" hingegen auf das multikursale Labyrinth bezieht, wurden beide Wörter bis vor Kurzem wie Synonyme benutzt.

Es gibt aber auch, vielleicht dank diesem Klärungsversuch, die Vorstellung, dass unikursale Labyrinthe antik und multikursale, wie der aus Hecken bestehende Irrgarten im Park von Hampton Court, eher neuzeitliche Phänomene sind. Zu dieser Verwirrung trägt zweifellos die weitverbreitete, bis in die Antike zurückreichende Praxis bei, Texte mit der unikursalen Spirale als dem späteren Sinnbild des Labyrinths zu illustrieren, unabhängig davon welcher Typus in diesen Texten beschrieben wurde. Es gibt hier von Anfang an einen Widerspruch: Wenn der Minotauros in einem genialen, von Daedalus ersonnenen Labyrinth gefangen gehalten wird, muss es sich, ungeachtet der antiken Illustrationen, um ein multikursales Labyrinth handeln, da der Minotauros ja andernfalls einfach hinein- und herausspazieren würde.

Tatsächlich hat der Unterschied zwischen den beiden Wörtern ausschließlich mit ihren unterschiedlichen Etymologien zu tun. „Maze" geht, wie „amaze", auf das altenglische Wort *mæs* zurück, das „Täuschung, Fassungslosigkeit, gedankliche Verwirrung" bedeutet und mit dem norwegischen mundartlichen *mas* „anstrengende Arbeit" und dem schwedischen *masa* „langsam oder schwerfällig sein" verwandt ist. Das Wort umreißt eher den mentalen Zustand, den Labyrinthe (*mazes*) herbeiführen, als deren physische Erscheinungsformen, sodass es sich um eine Art Metonymie handelt.

Hierin besteht eine naheliegende Analogie zur Malerei selbst: Sie ist langsam und schwerfällig, ein Akt unerwartet anstrengender Arbeit – vor allem die Ölmalerei. In einem Zug kann man nur so und so viel machen; die Farbschicht bleibt feucht, und wenn man zu lange weiter macht, wird sie schlammig und undeutlich. Je nach Pigmentierung benötigen bestimmte Farben mehrere Monate, um zu trocknen und zu härten. Es dreht sich darum, Schichten aufzutragen und zu warten und auf „blinde Wände" zu starren. Man muss auf den Händen sitzen und der Versuchung widerstehen, in der Zwischenzeit daran herumzufriemeln. Bei diesem Prozess geht es darum, häufig in die Irre zu gehen und den Weg wiederzufinden, bevor man zum Ausgang gelangt. Und es geht dabei um einen ständigen Perspektivenwechsel. Und natürlich geht es darum, nach Anhaltspunkten (*clues*) zu suchen und selbst welche zu hinterlassen.

In Elif Saydams Werken wimmelt es von *clues*: ein rotierendes Ensemble von Charakteren, Logos und Symbolen. Die Arbeit ist nicht figurativ in irgendeinem normalen Sinne: es gibt keine Darstellung der Realität, keine Verwendung illusionistischen Raums, keine unumwundene Figuration. Stattdessen ergibt sie eine Art Lexikon der Symbole: Vorhängeschlösser, *CLOSED* [GESCHLOSSEN]-Schilder, Herzen, ein Frosch oder zwei, Trauben, Zitronen, frische Früchte, verfaulte Früchte, Leitern, Vermieter, Chromosome, Etiketten von Honiggläsern, Gehirnscans, Ketten, Gänseblümchen, Gänseblümchenketten, Mücken, Bienen, Käfer, Smileys, ein Magen, Stimmungsringe, Farfalle, verwelkte Rosen, aufgeladene politische Parolen, Eistee, Antifa, 555-Telefonnummern[5],

5 Mit 555 beginnen fiktionale Telefonnummern in amerikanischen Spielfilmen, um mögliche Überschneidungen mit realen Telefonnummern zu vermeiden.

Schmetterlinge, ein Glücksstern, blutunterlaufene Augen, Weizen, die Hand Fatimas, vierblättrige Kleeblätter, die ikonische „Blaue Murmel“ ... und Labyrinthe (*mazes*).

Diese Bildsymbole schweben über einer Reihe von Hintergründen, die selbst eine Reihe zusammenhängender Schichten und collagierter Bilder sind: Scans von Plastiktüten und Stofffetzen, Schwarz-Weiß-Fotografien, gebatikte Leinwände, mikroskopische Bilder von Magenzellen, sonstige Überreste. Diese collagierten Bilder sind auf billige T-Shirt-Transferfolien gedruckt und auf Leinwände aufgebügelt, von denen einige zunächst gefärbt oder manipuliert wurden, um aus der Bühne, sprich dem Malgrund, ein möglichst verwirrendes Gelände zu machen.

Saydams Gemälde sind eng mit den Miniaturen der osmanischen und persischen Tradition verknüpft, wo die *Mimesis* zugunsten einer gesteigerten Abstraktion von Figuren und Form abgelehnt wurde und bei denen unterschiedliche Perspektiven und Zeitrahmen in dasselbe Gemälde einbezogen werden konnten. Die Idee einer festen, singulären Perspektive, die in der Renaissance entstand, und die Weltsicht, die mit dieser Entwicklung einhergeht, stehen im Gegensatz zu den in diesen simultanen Überblicksdarstellungen eingebetteten Mannigfaltigkeiten und Möglichkeiten.

In vielen von Saydams Bildern finden sich, zwischen dem Hintergrund und symbolistischen Schichten schwebend, Fragmente von Labyrinthen, die anmuten, als würden sie in einer den Zwischenraum ausfüllenden fluiden Schicht schweben. Häufig in Form von Blattgold oder -silber, manchmal im Inneren der Umrisslinien eines Magens gemalt und manchmal einen Durchgang umrahmend, finden sich sowohl unikursale als auch multikursale Labyrinthe, aber auch solche, die eigentlich gar keine sind, sondern Nachzeichnungen einer besonderen, sehr geometrischen, als Quadratkufi bekannten Form arabischer Kalligrafie.

In der islamischen und der arabischen Tradition entwickelte sich die Kalligrafie auf unendlich viel komplexere und raffiniertere Weise als irgendeine Schrift in Westeuropa. Hierfür gibt es zahlreiche Gründe. Forscher*innen haben etwa darauf hingewiesen, dass der kursive Charakter des Arabischen sich kaum für die frühen Druckerpressen eignete und daher die Tradition der Schreiber, vor allem für religiöse Texte, fortbestand. Relevanter ist aber vielleicht die Tatsache, dass die islamische Tradition der Herstellung gegenständlicher Bilder, trotz des Fehlens eines ausdrücklichen Verbots derselben im Koran, eher ablehnend gegenüberstand, was die Entwicklung einer anspruchsvollen, in der Nähe zur Abstraktion angesiedelten Ästhetik beförderte. Kufi ist die älteste Form der arabischen Kalligrafie und nach der Stadt Kufah im modernen Irak benannt, aus der sie ursprünglich stammen soll. Die frühesten Ausgaben des Koran sind in kufischer Schrift verfasst, auch wenn deren Beliebtheit allmählich nachließ, sodass vor etwa 1000 Jahren andere Schrifttypen an ihre Stelle traten, die mit der kursiveren Gestalt der Naschi-Schrift zusammenhingen. Als grafische Adaption für Mosaik-Schriften überdauerte die quadratische Kufischrift jedoch, da ihre scharfe Geometrie eine Übertragung der fließenden arabischen Schrift auf Ziegel und Kacheln ermöglicht.

In ihren komplexesten Ausführungen ergeben die positiven wie die negativen Räume der quadratischen Kufiform Wörter. So enthält etwa eine Wandtafel im 1284 errichteten Grabkomplex des Sultans al-Mansur Qalawun in Kairo den vier Mal gedrehten Namen „Muhammad“, während der weiße Zwischenraum den Namen „Ali“ ergibt. Derselbe Kunstgriff kommt in einem noch komplexeren Gebäude im spanischen Sevilla zum Einsatz, das auf komplizierte Weise christliche und islamische Traditionen miteinander verband.

1364, nach der Rückeroberung Sevillas vom Almohaden-Kalifat begann Pedro I., König von Kastilien und León (1334–1369), den vorhandenen Palastkomplex auszubauen. Dabei kombinierte er in einem später als „Mudéjar“ bekannten Stil verschiedene Architekturtraditionen miteinander und beschäftigte auch muslimische Kunsthandwerker aus Granada, das damals noch unter der Herrschaft der Nasriden stand.

An der Fassade über dem Eingang des Gebäudes befindet sich ein blauweißes geometrisches Mosaik. Auf den ersten Blick scheint es sich lediglich um ein abstraktes Muster zu handeln, das sich um christliche Kreuze herum wiederholt. Doch die Kunsthandwerker fügten, möglicherweise heimlich, die Losung der damals gegnerischen nasridischen Herrscher von Granada („Es gibt keinen Sieger außer Gott“) mit quadratkufischen Schriftzügen in das Mosaik ein.

Die Quelle für das quadratkufische Muster in Saydams Malerei ist spezifisch osmanisch, der angewandte Taschenspielertrick aber folgt der Logik von Saydams kunsthandwerklichen Ahnen in Sevilla. Das, was dem einen Publikum abstrakt erscheint, stellt sich einem anderen völlig anders dar. Schließlich hat ein Garnknäul ja zwei Enden, an denen man ziehen kann ...

Es heißt, bei den ersten Labyrinthen habe es sich nicht um Irrgärten (*mazes*) gehandelt, sondern um Tänze. Sowohl in der *Ilias* als auch in Vergils *Aeneis*[6] gibt es derartige Hinweise,

6 „Wie denn das Labyrinth auf dem hohen Kreta vor Zeiten
Manch geheimen Weg in dunklen Wänden und tausend
Trügrische Gänge enthielt, ein unentwirrbares Irrsal,
Ohne Rückweg, verhindert, den leitenden Spuren zu folgen
Also verflechten in kreuzendem Lauf die Söhne der Teukrer
Immer die Spur und verschlingen im Spiele Angriff und Rückzug."
Vergil, *Aeneis, Epos in zwölf Gesängen*, unter Verwendung der Übertragung Ludwig Neuffers übersetzt und herausgegeben von Wilhelm Plankl unter Mitwirkung von Karl Vretska, Ditzingen 1989, S. 129 (Fünfter Gesang, Verse 388–393).

und die ersten Labyrinthe werden als „gemusterte Tanzplätze"[7] beschrieben. Außerdem

7 „Einen Reigen auch schlang der hinkende Feuerbeherrscher,
Jenem gleich, wie vordem in der weitbewohnten
Knossos Dädalos künstlich ersann der lockigen Ariadne."
Homer, *Ilias*, Buch 18, V. 590–592, übersetzt von Johann Heinrich Voß, Frankfurt am Main 1990, S. 370.

gibt es antike Hinweise auf Tänze, die zur Feier des Endes des athenischen Tributs an Kreta veranstaltet wurden. Die Römer führten später ein aufwändiges, als *Iusus Troiae* oder Trojanische Spiele bekanntes Pferdeballett auf, das ebenfalls das Labyrinthmuster nachzeichnete. Es gibt eine etruskische Vase aus dem 6. oder 7. Jahrhundert v. Chr., welche zwei Pferde und das Muster eines Labyrinths zeigt und, wie die Wissenschaftlerin Penelope Reed mutmaßt, auf noch ältere Verbindungen zwischen diesen Bewegungsritualen und dem Labyrinth hindeutet.

Sicherlich ist es sinnvoll, das Labyrinth mit dem Tanz in Verbindung zu bringen, mit den Spuren der Bewegung, die übrigbleiben, nachdem sich der Staub gelegt hat. Schließlich machen Labyrinthe nichts anderes als zu kontrollieren, wie wir uns bewegen.

Das Symbol des Labyrinths und seine Verbindung mit Ritual und Tanz finden auch in der christlichen Tradition eine Fortsetzung. In Algerien gibt es eine Kirche, die im vierten Jahrhundert, um 324 n. Chr., errichtet wurde, kurz nach dem Edikt von Konstantinopel, das die Ausübung des Christentums legalisierte: St. Reparata in El Asnam, die einen Mosaikboden mit geometrischem Labyrinthmuster hat. Es entspricht fast dem populären römischen Motiv eines labyrinthischen Irrgartens mit Theseus und dem Minotauros in der Mitte, außer dass die mythischen Figuren durch ein Palindrom der Wörter *Sancta Ecclesia* (Heilige Kirche) ersetzt sind. Die Verbindung zwischen dem Labyrinth und Theseus und Christus blieb jedoch erhalten, und es gibt mittelalterliche Texte, die explizit einen Zusammenhang zwischen den Figuren herstellen und Theseus Weg in das Labyrinth mit dem Abstieg Christi in die Unterwelt in Verbindung bringen.

Dädalus, der Gestalter und Baumeister des ersten Labyrinths, wurde mitunter mit der Erschaffung des Universums durch den christlichen Gott in Verbindung gebracht und das Labyrinth als eine Möglichkeit gedeutet, die Kluft zwischen den Nöten und dem Durcheinander des Lebens und der Vorstellung eines allwissenden Gottes mit einem Masterplan zu erklären: die Spaltung zwischen dem Erlebten und dem, was man für begrifflich wahr hält ein materialistisch/idealistisches Dilemma. Die Labyrinthe legen nahe, dass der Unterschied zwischen Chaos und Ordnung einer der Sichtweise ist, als würden das Durcheinander und die Nöte des gelebten Lebens schwinden, hätten wir nur einen Überblick über den Plan, wie das bei Gott der Fall wäre.

Es gibt Berichte über Geistliche in Auxerres, Frankreich, die am Ostermontag rituelle Tänze in Labyrinthen von Kirchen vollführten, bei denen sie einander in einem „girlandenartigen" Tanz einen als *pilota* bezeichneten Lederball zuwarfen und sich dabei rhythmisch durch die Geometrie bewegten. Wissenschaftler*innen spekulieren, dass der Ball Christus als Sonne oder in der Tat das Garnknäuel repräsentieren könnte, das Ariadne Theseus gab, und dass der Faden in diesem Fall Weisheit oder das Göttliche und das Leitbild repräsentiert.

Labyrinthe wurden in den meisten gotischen Kathedralen in Frankreich und Italien ebenso wie an mehreren anderen Orten in ganz Europa errichtet, doch die meisten wurden im Spätmittelalter aus Gründen entfernt, über die wir nichts Genaues wissen, die aber offenkundig etwas mit ihren heidnischen Konnotationen und einer veränderten Haltung zu tun haben, welche Labyrinthe mit Orten des Vergnügens, der Verfehlung und der Sünde in Verbindung brachte.

Unkennbar sind die art'gen Labyrinthe /
Im muntern Grün, weil niemand sie betritt.[8]
—Titania in *Ein Sommernachtstraum*, Zweiter Aufzug, Erste Szene

8 In der Übersetzung von August Wilhelm Schlegel und Ludwig Tieck, „Ein Sommernachtstraum," in: Shakespeare, *Sämtliche Werke*, St. Gallen 2002, S. 99.

Indessen gab es parallel zur Errichtung kirchlicher Labyrinthe entsprechende säkulare Traditionen, die bis auf die Zeit der römischen Invasion zurückzugehen scheinen, darunter auch eine bäuerliche in England, bei der man außerhalb der Dörfer das Gras festtrat, um Rasenlabyrinthe anzulegen. Die aristokratische Tradition der Errichtung von Heckenlabyrinthen, die sich in England und Frankreich für das gesamte Mittelalter nachweisen lässt, geht ebenso sehr auf diese Traditionen zurück, wie sie durch die Antike inspiriert ist. Es heißt, dass Heinrich II. im 12. Jahrhundert ein Labyrinth errichten ließ, um seine Mätresse Rosamund Clifford vor den Blicken seiner Frau Eleanor von Aquitanien zu schützen. Doch Eleanor, in der einen Hand eine Tasse Gift, in der anderen einen Dolch, findet der Legende nach den Weg durch den Irrgarten zu Rosamund und überlässt dieser die Wahl, auf welche Weise sie sich das Leben nehmen will. Wie in der Legende vom Minotauros erfüllt das komplexe Gebilde den Zweck, darin die Schande und nun die Sünde zu verbergen.

Obwohl es am heutigen Standort des Blenheim Palace keine Belege für die historische Existenz einer solche Anlage gibt, waren Gartenlabyrinthe in jener Zeit beim Adel sehr beliebt. So gibt es Rechnungsbücher von Charles V. (1364–1380), in denen Zahlungen an Arbeiter für die Pflege eines „Maison Daedalus“ in seinen Gärten des Hôtel Saint Pol in Paris vermerkt sind, sowie Aufzeichnungen über ähnliche Gebilde in der Burg von Hesdin, dem Hôtel des Tournelles und vielen anderen Anwesen im Mittelalter. Details über ihr Aussehen allerdings sind uns nicht überliefert.

Solche Gärten und Labyrinthe der Aristokratie lieferten im London des 18. Jahrhunderts die Vorlage für das neue öffentliche und kommerzielle Phänomen der Lustgärten, wo die Londoner gegen eine Eintrittsgebühr harmonisch gestaltete Landschaftsgärten mit regelmäßig stattfindenden Opern, Maskeraden, Abendessen, Feuerwerken sowie andere Annehmlichkeiten genießen konnten. Diese Gärten gehörten auch zu den ersten Orten, wo Künstler wie William Hogarth ihre Werke öffentlich ausstellten. Sie standen im Mittelpunkt des Nachtlebens und markierten den Beginn des modernen kommerziellen Entertainments. Obwohl sie kostspielig waren und „anständig“ sein wollten, waren diese „Pleasure Gardens“ auch Orte der gleitenden Übergänge zwischen den ansonsten streng getrennten Klassen und, wie die zeitgenössische Presse immer wieder andeutete, ein Raum mit einem erheblichen transgressiven und sexuellen Potenzial.

In Paris waren die Jardins des Tuileries der erste königliche Garten, der 1667 für die Allgemeinheit geöffnet wurde. Wie bei den Londoner Lustgärten dienten diese präzise gestalteten Räume dazu, sich im Freien zu ergehen und zur Schau zu stellen, und brachten Architekturen und Verhaltensweisen, die bis dahin ausschließlich dem Adel vorbehalten waren, einer breiteren Öffentlichkeit nahe und definierten damit, was „Öffentlichkeit“ in der Entstehungszeit der modernen, städtischen Konsument*innen bedeutete.

Schon seit den 1750ern gibt es polizeiliche Aufzeichnungen über Männer, die in den Tuilerien miteinander „verkehrten“. Zeitgenössische schriftliche Spitzelberichte vermitteln uns einen genauen Einblick in das Leben jener Zeit. So näherte sich etwa ein gewisser Charles Gentil, der anschließend festgenommen wurde, einem Mann, der Musik lauschte, die aus dem Tuilerien-Palast kam, mit den Worten „in diesem Ensemble gibt es einige schöne Instrumente“, um dann hinzuzufügen, „und es gibt andere, die nicht so laut sind, doch mehr Vergnügen bereiten . . .“[9]

9 Jeffrey Merrick, „The Paris Cruising Scene in 1750“, in: *The Gay & Lesbian Review Worldwide*, Vol. 26, No. 4, July–August 2019, S. 27.

Heutige „Cruising Grounds“ haben häufig etwas Labyrinthartiges. Wie die Pleasure Gardens des 18. Jahrhunderts handelt es sich um Anlagen, die der Verlangsamung der Zeit dienen, eine Serie von Kreuzungen, die einem Gelegenheit geben, derselben Person immer wieder über den Weg zu laufen. Als wäre die Stadt geschrumpft, drängen sie einem all die direkten Interaktionen und den Blickkontakt mit Fremden auf, welche das Leben in der Stadt uns zu vermeiden lehrt. Der Cruising Ground staucht die Straßen der Stadt und setzt Konfrontationen in Szene. Entscheidend aber ist, dass es dort keine Sprache gibt: Man spricht nicht miteinander. Das Schweigen ist ein mächtiger und notwendiger Teil der Spannung des Begehrens, und Geplapper macht sie zunichte.

Wenn man sich in einem Labyrinth verliert und immer wieder umdrehen muss, besteht der Reiz womöglich darin, dass man den eigenen Faden verliert. Michael Fried hat einmal geschrieben, das Betreten des imaginären Raums des Gemäldes bedeute eine Auslöschung des Selbstempfindens der Betrachter*innen, da das Selbstempfinden zwangsläufig mit einem Narrativ und mit Sprache verknüpft ist.[10] Aber wie steht es um eine Überfülle von Narrativen, zu vielen Anhaltspunkten (*clues*) und zu verfolgenden Fäden, falschen Verheißungen eines Auswegs? Wenn man sich immer wieder umdreht, beginnen die blinden Wände alle gleich auszusehen. Malen, Zeit mit Malen Verbringen, der langsame Prozess des Herstellens, der langsame Prozess des Wirklich-Hinsehens, das alles ist zweifellos verwirrend. Ein stimmiges Gefühl von Anfang und Ende wird zerstört. Dinge beginnen zu klumpen. Grenzen sind unklar. Es gibt keine sauberen Sätze.

10 Michael Fried, *Absorption and Theatricality: Painting and Beholder in the Age of Diderot*, Berkley 1980, S. 131.

List of works

p. 25
Lucky star, 2020
Copper, inkjet transfer, custom stickers and oil on dyed canvas
30 × 21 cm
Courtesy of the artist and Tanya Leighton, Berlin. Photo: Gunter Lepkowski

p. 26
Day Fool, 2019
23k gold, lavender oil, hair and oil on canvas
30 × 21 cm
Courtesy of the artist and Galerie Rüdiger Schöttle, Munich. Photo: Wilfried Petzi

p. 27
Fall Fool, 2020
23k gold, lavender oil and oil on canvas
30 × 21 cm
Courtesy of the artist and Galerie Rüdiger Schöttle, Munich. Photo: Wilfried Petzi

p. 28
Spring Fool, 2019
23k gold, lavender oil and oil on canvas
30 × 21 cm
Courtesy of the artist and Galerie Rüdiger Schöttle, Munich. Photo: Wilfried Petzi

p. 29
Zu spät (III), 2021
23k gold, inkjet transfer and oil on canvas
30 × 21 cm
Courtesy of the artist and Tanya Leighton, Berlin. Photo: Gunter Lepkowski

p. 30
Zu spät (I), 2021
23k gold, pure silver, copper, inkjet transfer and oil on canvas
30 × 21 cm
Courtesy of the artist and Tanya Leighton, Berlin. Photo: Gunter Lepkowski

p. 31
Some fool's shopping basket, 2019
23k gold, lavender oil, inkjet transfer and oil on dyed canvas
30 × 21 cm
Courtesy of the artist and Galerie Rüdiger Schöttle, Munich. Photo: Wilfried Petzi

p. 32
Zu spät (II), 2021
23k gold, inkjet transfer and oil on canvas
30 × 21 cm
Courtesy of the artist and Tanya Leighton, Berlin. Photo: Gunter Lepkowski

p. 33
World, 2022
23k gold, custom sticker, inkjet transfer and oil on canvas
30 × 21 cm
Courtesy of the artist and Tanya Leighton, Berlin. Photo: Gunter Lepkowski

p. 34
Artists (ripe), 2020
23k gold, inkjet transfer and oil on canvas
30 × 21 cm
Courtesy of the artist and Tanya Leighton, Berlin. Photo: Gunter Lepkowski

p. 35
Free Market, 2020
23k gold, inkjet transfer and oil on canvas
30 × 21 cm
Courtesy of the artist and Tanya Leighton, Berlin. Photo: Gunter Lepkowski

p. 36
Austerity, 2021
23k gold, inkjet transfer and oil on canvas
30 × 21 cm
Courtesy of the artist and Tanya Leighton, Berlin. Photo: Gunter Lepkowski

p. 37
Landlords, 2021
23k gold, inkjet transfer and oil on canvas
30 × 21 cm
Courtesy of the artist and Tanya Leighton, Berlin. Photo: Gunter Lepkowski

p. 39
Fancy Fool, 2019
23k gold, lavender oil, inkjet print and oil on dyed canvas
30 × 21 cm
Courtesy of the artist and Galerie Rüdiger Schöttle, Munich. Photo: Wilfried Petzi

p. 41
Artists (Kotti), 2020
23k gold, inkjet transfer and oil on canvas
30 × 21 cm
Courtesy of the artist and Tanya Leighton, Berlin. Photo: Gunter Lepkowski

p. 42
Mobility ;), 2021
23k gold, inkjet transfer and oil on canvas
30 × 21 cm
Courtesy of the artist and Tanya Leighton, Berlin. Photo: Gunter Lepkowski

p. 43
Making lemonade, 2021
23k gold, inkjet transfer and oil on dyed canvas
59 × 41.5 cm
Courtesy of the artist and Tanya Leighton, Berlin. Photo: Gunter Lepkowski

p. 45
Zu spät (V), 2022
23k gold, inkjet transfer and oil on canvas
30 × 21 cm
Courtesy of the artist and Tanya Leighton, Berlin. Photo: Gunter Lepkowski

p. 46
Bad apples, 2022
23k gold, inkjet transfer and oil on canvas
30 × 21 cm
Courtesy of the artist and Tanya Leighton, Berlin. Photo: Gunter Lepkowski

p. 47
Fantasy, 2021
23k gold, inkjet transfer and oil on canvas
30 × 21 cm
Courtesy of the artist and Tanya Leighton, Berlin. Photo: Gunter Lepkowski

p. 49
Zu spät (IV), 2021
23k gold, inkjet transfer and oil on canvas
30 × 21 cm
Courtesy of the artist and Tanya Leighton, Berlin. Photo: Gunter Lepkowski

p. 50
Artists (lucky), 2020
23k gold, ballpoint pen inkjet transfer and oil on canvas
30 × 21 cm
Courtesy of the artist and Tanya Leighton, Berlin. Photo: Gunter Lepkowski

p. 51
Artists (gossip), 2020
23k gold, inkjet transfer and oil on canvas
30 × 21 cm
Courtesy of the artist and Tanya Leighton, Berlin. Photo: Gunter Lepkowski

p. 53
Artists (rotten), 2020
23k gold, silver, inkjet transfer and oil on canvas
30 × 21 cm
Courtesy of the artist and Tanya Leighton, Berlin. Photo: Gunter Lepkowski

p. 54
Mood maze, 2020
Copper, squid ink, inkjet transfer and oil on canvas
30 × 21 cm
Courtesy of the artist and Tanya Leighton, Berlin. Photo: Gunter Lepkowski

p. 55
Testosterone, 2020
Copper, stickers, inkjet transfer and oil on canvas
30 × 21 cm
Courtesy of the artist and Tanya Leighton, Berlin. Photo: Gunter Lepkowski

p. 56
Decisions, 2020
Copper, inkjet transfer and oil on dyed canvas
30 × 21 cm
Courtesy of the artist and Tanya Leighton, Berlin. Photo: Gunter Lepkowski

p. 57
Trouble, 2020
Copper, squid ink, inkjet transfer and oil on dyed canvas
30 × 21 cm
Courtesy of the artist and Tanya Leighton, Berlin. Photo: Gunter Lepkowski

p. 59
Misrecognition, 2022
23k gold, inkjet transfer and oil on canvas
30 × 21 cm
Courtesy of the artist and Tanya Leighton, Berlin. Photo: Gunter Lepkowski

p. 61
Right to be lazy, 2022
23k gold, squid ink, inkjet transfer and oil on canvas
30 × 21 cm
Courtesy of the artist and Tanya Leighton, Berlin. Photo: Gunter Lepkowski

p. 62
Fatima in the wheatfields, 2020
Squid ink, inkjet transfer and oil on canvas
30 × 21 cm
Courtesy of the artist and Tanya Leighton, Berlin. Photo: Gunter Lepkowski

p. 63
Fatima . . . help!, 2019
23k gold, lavender oil, inkjet transfer and oil on dyed canvas
30 × 21 cm
Courtesy of the artist and Galerie Rüdiger Schöttle, Munich. Photo: Wilfried Petzi

p. 64–65
Digestion, 2022
32 canvases; 23k gold, inkjet transfer and oil on dyed canvas
110 × 190 cm
Courtesy of the artist and Tanya Leighton, Berlin. Photo: Gunter Lepkowski

Diese Publikation erscheint im Rahmen der Ausstellung / This publication is released on occasion of the exhibition

Elif Saydam *...schläft sich durch*
Kunstverein Harburger Bahnhof
10.4.–20.6.2021

Kunstverein Harburger Bahnhof

Team Kunstverein Harburger Bahnhof

Annette Hans
Kuratorin der Ausstellung / Curator of the exhibition

Tobias Peper
Künstlerische Leitung / Artistic director

Marie Kuhn
Kuratorische Assistenz / Curatorial assistant

Johanna Glover, Sophie Hamann
Praktikantinnen / Interns

Tim Ehrich, Paul Glaw, Nikita Kotliar, Merlin Reichart
Aufbau / Installation

Cordula Ditz, Lorenz von Geyso, Ursula Herbst, Dr. Lutz Hoffmann, Julia Sökeland
Vorstand / Board

Klaus T. Edelmann, Petra Hagedorn, Martin Köttering, Prof. Dr.-Ing. Jürgen Pietsch, Thomas Sello, Prof. Dr. Rainer-Maria Weiss
Kuratorium / Advisory Board

Das Programm des Kunstverein Harburger Bahnhof wird ermöglicht von / The program of Kunstverein Harburger Bahnhof is made possible by

Hamburg | Behörde für Kultur und Medien

LIEBELT STIFTUNG HAMBURG

PUBLIKATION / PUBLICATION

Herausgegeben von / Edited by:
Annette Hans, Elif Saydam

Konzept / Concept: Elif Saydam

Leiterin der Publikationsabteilung / Publishing Editor:
Ilaria Bombelli (Mousse)

Texte / Texts: Adam Fearon, Vera Palme, Asa Seresin, Maxi Wallenhorst

Übersetzungen / Translations:
Leyla Çolpan, Good & Cheap Art Translators, Nikolaus G. Schneider, Alaz Ada Yener

Lektorat / Copy editing: Rosa Aiello, Annette Hans, Elif Saydam, Stacy Skolnik, Agnese Cantelmi (Mousse)

Grafische Gestaltung / Graphic Design
Massimiliano Pace (Mousse)

Fotografie / Photography:
Fred Dott, LFdocumentation, graysc.de, groupshow.eu, Gunter Lepkowski, Wilfried Petzi, Elif Saydam

Die Ausstellung und der Katalog wurden unterstützt durch die Alfried Krupp von Bohlen und Halbach-Stiftung im Rahmen des Förderpreises „Kataloge für junge Künstler".
The exhibition and publication were supported by the Alfried Krupp von Bohlen und Halbach-Stiftung under its support prize "Catalogues for Young Artists."

Alfried Krupp von Bohlen und Halbach-Stiftung

NEU START KULTUR

Wir bedanken uns für die Unterstützung durch den Canada Council for the Arts.
We acknowledge the support of the Canada Council for the Arts.

Canada Council for the Arts | Conseil des arts du Canada

Die Ausstellung war Teil von Kanadas Kulturprogramm als Ehrengast der Frankfurter Buchmesse 2021 und wurde unterstützt durch die Botschaft von Kanada.
The exhibition was part of Canada's culture program as Guest of Honour presentation at the Frankfurt Book Fair in 2021. We acknowledge the support of the Embassy of Canada.

Singular Plurality | Singulier Pluriel
CANADA Guest of Honour Frankfurt Book Fair 2020/2021 | CANADA Invité d'honneur Foire du livre de Francfort 2020/2021 | KANADA Ehrengast Frankfurter Buchmesse 2020/2021

Botschaft von Kanada

Thank you to Gerüstbau Bartels for exhibition support, and to Tanya Leighton Gallery, Franz Kaka, and Galerie Rüdiger Schöttle for assistance in realizing this publication; extended gratitude to all the contributors, translators, copy editors and photographers involved in its orbit. Special thanks to Beth Collar.

For teenagers, for grandmothers, and for Faggots and Their Friends Between Revolutions. For others, once strangers, now lovers. But most of all for Hülya.

Published and distributed by:

Mousse Publishing
Contrappunto s.r.l.
via Pier Candido Decembrio 28,
20137, Milan–Italy

Available through:

Mousse Publishing, Milan
moussemagazine.it
DAP | Distributed Art Publishers, New York
artbook.com
Les presses du réel, Dijon
lespressesdureel.com
Antenne Books, London
antennebooks.com
Idea Books, Amsterdam
ideabooks.nl

First edition: 2022
Printed in Italy
by Artigiana Grafica

ISBN 978-88-6749-510-8
€ 25 / $ 29.95